THE
SHAAR
PRESS

THE JUDAICA IMPRINT
FOR THOUGHTFUL PEOPLE

Rebbetzin Tziporah Heller

Battle

How to Fight
the Yetzer Hara

A
SHAAR
PRESS
PUBLICATION

Sara Yoheved Rigler

Plans

According to
Maharal, Ramchal,
Chassidic and
Mussar Masters

Published by **SHAAR PRESS**
Distributed by MESORAH PUBLICATIONS, LTD.
4401 Second Avenue / Brooklyn, N.Y 11232 / (718) 921-9000 / www.artscroll.com

Distributed in Israel by SIFRIATI / A. GITLER
6 Hayarkon Street / Bnei Brak 51127

Distributed in Europe by LEHMANNS
Unit E, Viking Business Park, Rolling Mill Road / Jarrow, Tyne and Wear, NE32 3DP/ England

Distributed in Australia and New Zealand by GOLDS WORLD OF JUDAICA
3-13 William Street / Balaclava, Melbourne 3183 / Victoria Australia

Distributed in South Africa by KOLLEL BOOKSHOP
Ivy Common, 105 William Road / Norwood 2192, Johannesburg, South Africa

ISBN 10: 1-4226-0896-4
ISBN 13: 978-1-42260-896-8

Printed in the United States of America by Noble Book Press
Custom bound by Sefercraft, Inc. / 4401 Second Avenue / Brooklyn N.Y. 11232

To my beloved teacher,

Rebbetzin Chaya Korf

who followed the ways of Hashem,
who made something out of nothing,
by starting me on my path.

Rebbetzin Tziporah Heller

To my father

Irving (Israel) Levinsky

ישראל בן יוסף יהודה ז"ל

*A paragon of hands-on chesed, generosity,
selflessness, filial devotion, ahavat Yisrael,
and taking responsibility for the
welfare of everyone he knew.*

*In a lifetime of striving, I have attained
a mere fraction of his level.*

And to my father-in-law

Donald Rigler

דוד בן אברהם פראנק הלוי ז"ל

*A paragon of patience, integrity,
humility, and devotion to family.*

*Every day I benefit from the sterling
character traits that he, through heredity
and example, bequeathed to my husband.*

Sara Yoheved Rigler

Rabbi Simcha Bunim Cohen
Rav, K'hal Ateres Yeshaya
Lakewood, New Jersey

שמחה בונם קאהן
רב ד'קהל עטרת ישעיה
ליקוואוד, נוא דזערזי

יום א' פרשת ויקרא
שנת תשס"ט

Chazal teach us: אמר רבי יצחק יצרו של אדם מתחדש עליו
בכל יום — The evil inclination is constantly coming up with
new ideas to draw us toward sin. We are always working
or keeping vigil, and being on guard from our enemy who
seeks our utter destruction.

The *sefer* "Battle Plans" was written by Rebbetzin T.
Heller and S.Y. Rigler, two great מזיכי הרבים, who bring
boundless amounts of חיזוק and inspiration to countless of
our Jewish brethren through their writings and speeches.

In this *sefer*, the authors compiled a broad spectrum
of ideas from *mussar* and *Chassidus*, from classic works of
gedolim of the past generation to contemporary *gedolim*.
The *sefer* conveys a message: There is danger that lurks and
a battle to be fought, and with a plan one can ultimately win
it. This *sefer* is truly a masterpiece! Praiseworthy is your lot
for authoring such a beautiful work. May Hashem give you
both strength to inspire the holy Jewish nation for many
happy and healthy years.

Simcha Bunim Cohen

Table of Contents

Authors' Note

We are two authors with many personal stories. To clarify which of us is telling a story, we have adopted the following usage: I [TH] *is Tziporah Heller speaking.* I [SR] *is Sara Rigler speaking.*

Throughout this book, all references to "depression" and "feeling depressed" refer not to clinical depression, but rather to a circumstantial mood of sadness and dejection. People who suffer from clinical depression should consult a health care professional.

Acknowledgments

of Rebbetzin Tziporah Heller:

MY THANKS TO:

The great scholars whose wisdom cannot be measured by contemporary standards and who lived their teachings with a level of consistency that we have never seen deserve to be acknowledged not only by me, but also by everyone who reads even one chapter of this book. No one started out as Maharal, who we can only see through a distant mirror, or as Rav Dessler, who walked on the same streets that we do when we visit Bnei Brak. They saw reality through a different and far more honest lens than we do.

My teachers, who introduced me to learning, and my students, who demand that I give them far more than I have, are responsible for this book more than anyone else is.

Neve Yerushalaim and Naaleh.com have touched countless lives by making learning possible to virtually any woman who sincerely wishes to know. It is a great privilege to be associated with them. Most of the book comes from classes that took place in their programs. **Ruth Pepperman** transcribed the classes efficiently and cheerfully.

Sara Rigler is my dear and inspiring friend for more than 20 years. She has made the book readable and enjoyable. Knowing her and working with her is part of Hashem's ongoing kindness.

The entire staff at ArtScroll has been more than helpful.

My husband's patience, dedication, and commitment, coupled with my children's willingness to carry some of the burden of running a busy household, have made writing this book possible.

Acknowledgments
of Sara Yoheved Rigler:

MY DEEPEST THANKS TO:

HaKadosh Baruch Hu, Who gives me all the words.

The revered *Rebbe of Amshinov*, *shlita*, whose guidance keeps me straight.

Rebbetzin Chaya Nechama Milikovski of Amshinov, whose gentle wisdom and unwavering encouragement so enhance my life.

Rebbetzin Tziporah Heller, who for me has been the conduit of Toras Moshe. I met Rebbetzin Heller the first night I came to Israel, 23 years ago. Without her broad vision and profound teaching, who knows if I would have stayed? At Neve Yerushalayim, I became a "Rebbetzin Heller groupie," following her around from class to class. (Don't tell Rav Chakowski!) She answered all my questions, solved all my issues, and resolved all my doubts, because her answers were always deeper than my questions. In addition to being my mentor, she is my personal example of chesed and commitment to spiritual growth. This book chronicles many of the battles that Rebbetzin Heller and I have fought against the yetzer hara, she as the general, and me as the buck private following her brave lead.

Rav Leib Kelemen, for his Mussar teachings, which fill Chapter 15 and crop up throughout the book. His influence on my life is inestimable.

Rabbi Meir Fund, Rabbi Yosef Polak, and *Rabbi Dovid Din, a"h,* who got me started on the wondrous path of Torah, and *Rav Dovid Refson* for creating Neve Yerushalayim, who gave me a place to land and learn.

Pamela and Aba Claman, who allowed me to write in the wondrous atmosphere of their mitzvah house, overlooking Har Habayit.

Ruth Shlossman, who lovingly transcribed many of Rebbetzin Heller's classes that were given in my house.

Uriela Sagiv, whose expert literary advice is indispensible in every book I write.

Ruth Pepperman, who transcribed all the other classes and gallantly responded to my last-minute call to transcribe five lectures in one week.

Rabbi Asher Stern, my cousin, for picking out for me the perfect laptop to finish this book.

The ArtScroll team: *Rabbi Nosson Scherman,* who granted my specific requests about this book; *Shmuel Blitz,* whose faith in and enthusiasm for this book spurred me to keep writing; *Judi Dick,* my adept editor, who is a pleasure to work with; *Faygie Weinbaum,* who proofread diligently; *Mendy Herzberg,* who skillfully coordinated the project; *Eli Kroen,* for the striking and creative cover; *Aviva Whiteman,* for the clear, inviting page design; *Sury Englard,* who patiently entered the many editorial revisions.

Leah Lintz Levinsky, a"h, my mother, who bequeathed to me writing talent and who provided a luminous example of someone who was truly victorious over the yetzer hara.

Evelyn Rigler, my mother-in-law, for all of her love, encouragement, and great example of flexibility, loyalty, and forgiveness.

Leib Yaacov Rigler, my husband, who encouraged me to write this book, gave constructive criticism of some of the chapters, proofread, and made Shabbos during the last hectic month before the deadline.

In my battle against my yetzer hara, he is my adviser, restrainer, consultant, and example of self-control, calmness, and sensitivity.

Pliyah Esther Rigler, my daughter, whose help making and serving Shabbos was indispensible while working on this book. Her sweetness, helpfulness, and competence are a blessing in my life.

Yisrael Rohn Rigler, my yeshivah-bachur son, whose great middos (which he has been working on since he was a child) and devotion to *limud*-Torah fill my life with joy.

Introduction

Two Tuesdays a month, the Israel Defense Forces conducts induction ceremonies in the Kosel Plaza. The novice soldiers, outfitted in their spanking new uniforms, stand in formation as their proud parents look on. Each one is issued a *Tanach* and a gun.

Being born into this world is actually an induction as a soldier. As the Ramchal states in his classic *Mesillas Yesharim*: "In truth a person is put into the middle of a raging war." The uniform is the human body, the *Tanach* is the wisdom of Torah, and the gun is the inner weapons needed to fight this war.

Some of us are born warriors; others prefer to pursue peace. Whatever our disposition, however, we must recognize that life in this world is an ongoing battle, and the enemy is the yetzer hara, the force of darkness, negativity, and evil. Our battle assignment is to scale the mountain of lofty thoughts, words, and actions. The yetzer hara's job, assigned by Hashem, is to pull us down into the abyss of depressed thoughts, condemning words, and depraved actions. The very name "Yisrael" was conferred on our forefather Yaakov by the angel of darkness after a night-long battle. That struggle against evil is the prototype of the life of every Jew. In this world, our choice is not between war and peace, but only between victory and defeat.

Our cherished hope is that this book of battle plans based on the teachings of our sages will help every reader to achieve victory.

Section One

Inspired by
the Writings of
the Maharal of Prague,
Rabbi Yehudah Loewe

The Yetzer Hara's Secret Code

1

DEFEATING THE ENEMY REQUIRES MORE THAN superior strength and strategy. For example, everyone knows the military strategy by which Israel won the Six Day War. Israeli fighter jets, flying below the tracking altitude of Egyptian radar, attacked and destroyed Egypt's entire air force on the ground in the first hour of the war. Few people know that Egypt could have totally avoided defeat had one bungling sergeant known how to decode an incoming message.

That morning Egyptian intelligence at a radar station in northern Jordan did indeed pick up the scrambling Israeli aircraft. They sent a red alert message to the bunker of the Egyptian Supreme Command in Cairo. At that point, Egypt would have had enough time to get its planes off the ground and into the air and thus save them, but the sergeant on duty in the decoding room attempted to decipher the red alert using the previous day's code. His failure to properly decode the message led to catastrophe for his country.

Army intelligence is as important to the Israel Defense Forces as its elite combat units. Intelligence includes, among other things, intercepting the enemy's communications and then properly decoding them. The most crack combat unit in the world cannot win a battle if intelligence fails to appraise it of the enemy's plans and strategies.

In the same way, we cannot hope to defeat the yetzer hara without intelligence: becoming aware of the enemy's strategy and properly decoding its messages. The Maharal starts his treatise on "The Power of the Yetzer Hara" by breaking the code of the yetzer hara's messages to us.

He begins with a quotation from *Proverbs*: "If your enemy is hungry give him bread, and if he is thirsty pour out water for him to drink, because you'll be pouring hot coals on his head, and Hashem will repay you." "The enemy," according to the Maharal, is the yetzer hara. This enemy is always characterized by hunger and thirst, that is, by lack. It is the voice inside each of us that carps on lack.

The message of the yetzer hara is always: "You don't have what you need." This encoded message has a thousand different versions:

◆ I don't have a spouse, so of course I'm depressed.

◆ I have a husband, but he's not emotionally sensitive to me.

◆ I have a wife, but she doesn't keep the house neat enough.

◆ I don't have children, so I can't get on with my life.

◆ I have children, but they have learning disabilities.

◆ My son won't be accepted to a good yeshivah or college.

◆ My daughter desperately needs a shidduch.

◆ I don't have enough money to buy a house.

◆ I have a house, but it's too small.

◆ The house is big enough, but I desperately need a new kitchen.

◆ The house is too big for me to clean by myself; I need household help.

◆ I don't have a job that pays enough.

◆ I have a lucrative job, but I don't have the kind of boss I need.

The Maharal reveals the secret that statements of lack are a code and the dispatcher is always the yetzer hara.

Battle Plan #1:
Identify The Voice Of The Yetzer Hara

Whenever you hear your inner voice complaining about what you lack, go on high alert and assume battle position. You are under the attack of the yetzer hara.

This does not mean that you can't have legitimate wants: to get married, to have children, to own a home, to work at a good job. In fact, most of the blessings of Shemoneh Esrei are requests: for healing, livelihood, redemption, etc. These blessings must be accompanied by genuine yearning.

*You cross the line and start working for the enemy, however, when you heed the yetzer's commands instead of Hashem's. For example, if you find yourself complaining about or leveling hurtful criticisms at your spouse, or speaking **lashon hara** about your children, boss, or coworkers, you have fallen into the hands of the enemy. The feeling, "I don't have what I need," leads to many sins, as the yetzer hara offers you more and more blandishments to satisfy your needs by means that violate halachah.*

Once you have cracked the code, and you are aware that your laments about what you lack are messages sent by the yetzer hara, you switch from intelligence to combat. You take out of your arsenal two effective weapons developed especially to liquidate this form of the yetzer hara.

Battle Plan #2:
"Everything I Need I Have"

The best armor to protect yourself from the yetzer's attack is the attitude, "Everything I need I have (because Hashem provided everything)." Indeed, this is the meaning of the blessing we say every morning, "she'asah li kal tzarki," thanking Hashem "Who provided me my every need." At the time you recite this blessing and throughout the day, you should feel that, at this moment, you have everything you need. This does not preclude wanting things in the future, but a bedrock belief in Hashem's goodness and kindness to you at this very moment is the best battle stance against the yetzer hara.

You achieve this attitude by shifting your focus from what you don't have to what you do have. We are familiar with the automatic rifle carried at all times by Israeli soldiers: the M16. To fight the yetzer hara of lack we must carry one of two weapons: the G(Gratitude)16 and the G17. To use the G16, stop obsessing on what you don't have and refocus your thoughts on the details of what you do have:

◆ *You may not yet be married, but you do have many of the components necessary to live a life of meaning, such as good friends and an interesting job. Take time to think about and be grateful for each one of your friends and the specific pluses of your job.*

◆ *You may need knee-replacement surgery, but your eyes and ears work just fine. Take time to think about and be grateful for all the complex gifts of vision and hearing, which allow you to achieve the most significant goals that you have set for yourself.*

◆ *You may not have a large-enough house for all your children, but you are blessed with children. Take time to think about and be grateful for the special qualities of each one of your children. Each one is an entire universe.*

◆ *You may not have a pleasant job with amiable coworkers and a reasonable boss, but you do get a paycheck every week. Take time to think about and to be grateful for everything your paycheck pays for, and how your job and your paycheck enable you to be a giver, as Hashem is a giver.*

The weapon G17 works like the precision missiles the Israeli air force uses to target particular terrorist leaders in the Gaza Strip. It can destroy a third-floor apartment without damaging anything on the fourth and second floors. The G17 is a very sophisticated weapon. While the G16 involves shifting your focus from what you don't have to what you do have, the G17 ferrets out the blessing hidden within the lack itself.

◆ *You may not have a spouse, but your single status allows you its own unique avenues for your spiritual expression. In fact, because you are not yet married, you have the time to nurture yourself and others spiritually and materially in ways you won't have time to do later when you have a family. One wonders whether Sarah Schenirer would have founded the Bais Yaakov movement, and thus changed the Torah world, if she had lived the life she no doubt wanted, taking care of a husband and children.*

◆ *You may not be healthy, but your illness may engender what you most want: a closer relationship with Hashem and with the people you love the most. Illness can bring about positive changes in your character and spiritual growth. Dr. Rahamim Melamed-Cohen avers that the years since he was*

> stricken with Lou Gehrig's Disease and became
> completely paralyzed have been the best years of
> his life from the standpoint of inner growth.
>
> ◆ You may not have children, but you do have a
> spouse and the time to devote yourself to your mar-
> riage and to that area that may in fact be your true
> mission in life. Witness the accomplishments of R'
> Yaakov Moshe and Chaya Sara Kramer as described
> in **Holy Woman**.

Focusing on what you have rather than what you don't have
is a foolproof weapon against the yetzer hara. Utter the formula,
"Everything I need I have (because Hashem provided everything),"
feel joy and gratitude to Hashem, and you've won the battle.

Uncovering the Disguises of the Yetzer Hara

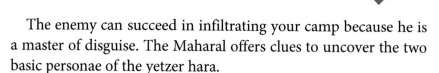

The enemy can succeed in infiltrating your camp because he is
a master of disguise. The Maharal offers clues to uncover the two
basic personae of the yetzer hara.

The first form is called *yitzra d'ervah,* the yetzer hara of lust.
Of course, if this yetzer hara came sauntering into your camp
undisguised, wearing the bright red apparel of the base drive for
illicit relations, you would immediately vanquish him. The *yitzra
d'ervah,* however, has a much more subtle identity, which the
Maharal reveals. This yetzer hara seduces you into using the pleasure of physical reality to fill the empty space within you.

Remember that the yetzer hara thrives on a sense of lack. The
truth is that many of us feel a spiritual void in our lives. While
this chapter will offer concrete ideas for filling that void, many

people are habituated to filling that void with physical things: food, designer clothes, a magnificent house, a fancy car, the latest hi-tech gadget, or other material objects. Using anything physical to fill the void is succumbing to the *yitzra d'ervah*.

This does not mean that a Jew must reject or avoid the physical world. According to Judaism, the physical world is purposeful and good. Take, for example, food. Food is terrific; it's nutritious and life sustaining, and it tastes good. Food, however, is not meant to fill the empty space within you. Food is dangerous when used as a solution for the "no one loves me" problem. Food is dangerous as a solution to the "I'm so bored" syndrome. Food is actually lethal when used to prove that you're in control, which is what eating disorders are all about. There is nothing wrong with food per se, but using food to fill the void is *yitzra d'ervah*. Similarly, exploiting any material object as an answer to the message, "I lack," is falling into the hands of the *yitzra d'ervah*.

The second persona of the yetzer hara is called *yitzra d'avodah zarah*. Again, in its extreme form, the actual worship of idols, it would be decimated the moment it paraded into our camp. So it disguises itself. The Maharal reveals that *avodah zarah* is another ploy to fill the void created by lack. We could fill that void either by making ourselves bigger, which requires a lot of inner work, or by attempting to make God smaller and more immediate in our eyes, to the convenient point where we have no need to uplift ourselves because we have made God small enough to reach from where we are.

A common disguise of the *yitzra d'avodah zarah* is the worship of nature. It's easier to worship the creation instead of the Creator because the creation is more accessible, yet it still has a spiritual charge. Another way of attempting to make God small is the adoration of images, even images which do not purport to be God, such as a Christian saint or a meditative statue. These images reduce the Divine to a single quality, such as motherly nurture or tranquility. Anything which thus makes God small is *avodah zarah*.

When people worship idols they are taking some admirable aspect of themselves and worshiping that. Therefore, *yitzra d'avodah zarah*, in its deeper sense, means taking your yearning for meaning and connection, and degrading it by settling for something that is less than God, rather than stretching yourself toward the immensity and infinitude of Hashem. Therefore any act that glorifies and gives centrality to what is not God is the disguise of the *yitzra d'avodah zarah*.

No one reading this book is likely to worship a statue, but the worship of one's own ego is also *avodah zarah*. For example, speaking lashon hara is attaching importance to something less than Hashem, in this case your own ego. When you speak lashon hara, you elevate yourself as the judge over someone whom you portray as inferior to you. You also make yourself the center of attention, because you are the one "in the know" to whom everyone else is listening. Thus, every form of self-aggrandizement is a capitulation to the *yitzra d'avodah zarah* in its insidious disguise.

"Drag Him to the Beis HaMidrash"

Once you have identified the enemy, you must give it the bread of Torah and the water of spirituality. If you allow that space in you to remain empty, you are making yourself easy prey for the yetzer hara.

The Maharal quotes the Gemara, "If you happen to find this despicable one [the yetzer hara], drag him to the Beis HaMidrash. If he is stone, grind him down, and if he is iron, blow him up."

How does learning Torah annihilate the yetzer hara? To explain how this mechanism operates, the Maharal divides mitzvos into positive and negative commandments.

Fulfilling a positive mitzvah entails getting up and doing something. Indeed, the void within can be filled relatively easily by getting up and doing something that's spiritually fulfilling, as we've all experienced. The part of us that resists doing positive mitzvos is like stone.

Children say things that adults think but would never say. I [TH] was once telling my children stories about Reb Aryeh Levin, about his selflessness, his *mesiras nefesh* to help other people, his zeal to serve Hashem. At the end, I asked them, "Wouldn't you like to be just like Reb Aryeh when you grow up?"

One of my children answered, "I don't want to be like Reb Aryeh. I want to have a friend like Reb Aryeh, who'll do anything for me."

This child was vocalizing what we all feel sometimes: "I don't want to take initiative and do; I want to sit back and let others do for me. I want to rest. I want to lie on the couch and eat potato chips." That's the state of feeling like a stone.

The Maharal explains that this propensity to be like a stone is the nature of the physical body. The body was created from the earth, and the earth doesn't move unless you move it. So the more we identify with our bodies, the more our yetzer hara will manifest as stone.

On a deeper level, the human inclination to despair renders us like stone. When we despair, we no longer believe in our own ability to move situations or events. This yetzer hara paralyzes us with fears and doubts about our inadequacies. We don't do what we should do, what deep down we *want* to do, because we have lost faith in ourselves. This is always a consequence of having lost faith in Hashem, Who made us as we are.

This form of yetzer hara can cripple children as young as 8 or 9. If they don't do well in school, are not adept athletes, often lose or break things, or have trouble making friends, they may despair of their ability to accomplish anything at all. These children will not even try. Their parents often accuse them of laziness, but the actual villain who has them by the throat is the yetzer hara of despair.

The yetzer hara of despair can be fought by "grinding it down." This means taking the positive action that seems so formidable and frightening, and breaking it down into small parts that are clearly within your capacity.

Many years ago, my [TH] son was volunteering for Yad Eliezer, an organization that distributes food to the needy. The organizer gathered a group of volunteers who were told to go to the North and ask farmers for donations of food. He told my son to bring back a few hundred cartons of eggs. My son was abashed. He protested, "How can I just go and knock on a farmer's door and ask him for free eggs? The farmers are not rich. They're producing eggs so they can sell the eggs, not give them away."

The organizer replied, "I'll tell you how to do it. Knock on the door. Say, 'I'm collecting for the needy in Jerusalem. Could you give me an egg?' See what happens next."

So my son went up North, knocked on the door of a farmer, and asked for an egg. The farmer said, "An egg? You want one egg?"

My son said, "Yes, an egg. Please give me one egg for the needy of Jerusalem. It's something." The farmer ended up giving him many cartons of eggs.

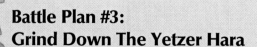

Battle Plan #3:
Grind Down The Yetzer Hara

The way to battle the yetzer hara that is like stone is to grind it down. This means taking small, even minute, steps to fulfill positive mitzvos in the same way you would grind glass, little by little. When you undertake such small steps, the yetzer hara is lulled into thinking that you have no possibility of victory, and will not even bother to mount a defense. Such small steps, however, gradually lead to the courage and the will to act.

Say, for example, you don't feel you have the energy and stamina to host Shabbos guests. You feel you should do this mitzvah, but your dread of cooking, serving, and cleaning up from a table full of guests makes you want to hide under the covers. The battle plan the Maharal is offering here is to start by inviting one guest. You know you can handle one guest. Then, when you see you have the ability to host one Shabbos guest, you start inviting two Shabbos guests. This is an effective strategy for grinding down the yetzer hara of stone.

A prime illustration of this is Rebbetzin Henny Machlis. In their modest Jerusalem apartment, Rabbi Mordechai Machlis, Rebbetzin Henny, and their 14 children host approximately 150 guests for every Friday-night seudah and for every Shabbos-day lunch, 51 weeks a year. (They go away for Pesach.) I [TH] once asked Rebbetzin Henny how they became involved in such a massive chesed project. She replied that she never intended to host 300 people every Shabbos. She and her husband just wanted to provide a Shabbos meal for these people this Shabbos. Gradually she realized she could do it every week. Instead of looking at the enormity of the task she was taking on, she looked at what was directly in front of her.

This is how to grind down the yetzer hara that doesn't want you to undertake positive actions.

The second form of yetzer hara is like iron, which is used in weapons of war. This facet relates to the negative mitzvos, the prohibitions that keep us from deeds that would destroy our relationship to Hashem and to people. When this yetzer hara grips us, we want to indulge in destructive actions.

Nietzsche, who provided the philosophical rationale for Nazism, said that destruction is as pleasurable as creation. We see this in children. They can spend an hour building a tower, and then with zestful glee, they knock it down. Adults too derive a sordid satisfaction from destruction, from their feeling of empowerment when they reduce someone to tears or break the limits of morality.

The Gemara states that this yetzer hara of iron, of destructive tendencies, can be exploded by dragging it to the Beis HaMidrash.

Learning Torah fills the empty space. The feelings of pleasure and empowerment that come from destruction can be replaced by the pleasure and empowerment that come from learning and incorporating Torah into one's life.

For example, imagine a person who was raised by extremely difficult parents, parents who were controlling and harsh. Now, as an adult, she is visiting her parents. Her father begins to yell at her and to berate her. She's about to counterattack, to let fly with accusations about what a failure he is as a father and as a human being. As a child, she was powerless to hurt him back, but now she is an eloquent adult, who could verbally beat her father to a pulp. The yetzer hara of iron, of destruction, is about to score a victory. But suddenly her Torah learning pops into her head. She remembers what she learned about the mitzvah of honoring parents, about the bottom-line level of gratitude to parents for bringing her into the world, about the mitzvah to honor parents being on the same side of the *luchos* as the mitzvos pertaining to Hashem. The very act of remembering what the Torah says puts her mind in control. Now she's thinking and considering what to do. *Why should I let my father determine who I am?* she ponders. *Do I really want to descend to his level and become a screaming, hurtful monster?* In this way, Torah learning vanquishes the yetzer hara of destruction.

The best way to blow up the yetzer hara of iron is to blow up the illusions it fosters. For example, your friend is sick and confined to bed for a couple of weeks. You decide that, even though she lives quite a long distance away, you will do the mitzvah of visiting the sick. As you're preparing to leave your home, you're trying to think of a present to bring, and music comes to mind. Music cheers the soul and a person in bed can easily listen to music. So you take the latest Chassidic pop-hit CD, and you copy it on your computer, and you bring your friend the copied CD. You consider yourself a real *tzaddik* because you're not only visiting the sick, but you're also bringing the perfect gift.

This, of course, is an illusion. You're not a *tzaddik*, you're a thief! Copying commercial CDs is a violation of halachah, as is printed on every album. In fact, the widespread *aveirah* of copying music CDs has all but ruined the Jewish music business, as no one but the superstars can now afford to release new albums without incurring financial loss.

My [SR] husband Leib Yaacov once had an experience that perfectly illustrates this method of "explode the yetzer hara." For years he played keyboard in a klezmer wedding band. On his way to work one night, he listened to a Torah tape about labeling actions for what they really are. The following night, he played at a lavish wedding. He noticed that the benchers were exceptionally nice. They had a painting on the front, each page was laminated, and the print was large enough to be visible even to guests who had forgotten their glasses. Rationalizing that the benchers were a free giveaway, he collected twelve benchers and put them in his backpack. Then he remembered the Torah tape he had recently heard on labeling actions for what they are. With horror, he realized, "This is stealing." By saying those words, he exploded the yetzer hara that had seduced him into transgressing the negative mitzvah against stealing. He hurriedly took the benchers out of his backpack, and went to look for the *baal simchah*. When he told him how much he liked the benchers and would like to have some for his own Shabbos table, the *baal simchah* graciously gave him a dozen.

Battle Plan #4:
Explode The Yetzer Hara

This battle plan requires exploding the illusions fostered by the yetzer hara by cutting through rationalizations and calling sins what they are. The way to explode such illusions is by learning Torah. For example, studying the halachos of "not moving the border marker" and of not stealing would

> *quickly eradicate the yetzer hara that prompts you to steal.*
> *The more halachah you learn, the more you will be able to*
> *slice through the yetzer's seductions with the sharp sword*
> *of true clarity. Thus:*
>
> ◆ *When you yell at your children, instead of calling it*
> *"discipline," call it what it really is: the sin of onaas*
> *devarim, hurting other people with words.*
>
> ◆ *When you complain about a neighbor, instead of*
> *calling it "constructive," call it what it really is: the sin*
> *of lashon hara.*
>
> ◆ *When you criticize someone harshly, making him or*
> *her hate you and everything you stand for, instead of*
> *calling it the mitzvah of rebuke, call it what it really is:*
> *the transgression that follows the mitzvah of rebuke:*
> *"Do not bear a sin because of him."*

How Learning Torah Works

Learning Torah is an indispensable weapon to vanquish the yetzer hara. By setting firm guidelines for action, the Torah prevents us from wallowing in our base nature. Even more, the wisdom of the Torah fills that empty space with what is holy and sublime, so that there's no room for the yetzer hara to infiltrate.

This is why even a few days of true Torah learning can completely turn a person around, as we see with weekend seminars and learning programs for the general population in Israel. People who were engrossed in torpid or destructive lifestyles are quickly moved by the beauty and depth of Torah.

The bread of Torah fills the empty places, satisfies the sense of lack, and thus defeats the yetzer hara.

I [SR] know a young woman whom I'll call Bonnie. Raised in England without a Torah education, at the age of 17 Bonnie and her friend Marna came to Israel to volunteer on a secular kibbutz. The girls' behavior was so wild that they were thrown off the kibbutz. They then spent a few months living on the beach in Eilat. At 18, Bonnie married an Israeli. They had a daughter. By the time she was 26, Bonnie was back in England, divorced and continuing to lead a vacuous lifestyle.

Meanwhile, her brother came to Jerusalem on the Aish HaTorah Fellowships Program. He was so moved by the classes in Judaism that he became religious and stayed at the yeshivah to learn Torah. When Bonnie became dejected because of the emptiness of her life, her mother convinced her to go to Jerusalem for one week to visit her brother. "And take out your nose ring and don't pack your jeans," her mother warned her.

Bonnie spent one week in Jerusalem's Old City. The example set by the religious Jews with whom she stayed and the impact of the Torah classes she attended totally transformed her. Today, she is observant, and married to a rabbi.

The Maharal continues by explaining how the Torah fills the empty space deep within us. When a person is actually learning Torah, at that moment he is comparable to an angel in terms of level of awareness and closeness to Hashem. At that moment his will is to do what Hashem wants of him, like an angel who exists only to fulfill its God-given mission. As the angels are described in the liturgy: "They are all beloved; they are all flawless; they are all mighty; they are all holy, and they all do the will of their Maker with dread and reverence." When a person is in that state, he is far, very far, above the place of lack, the breeding ground of the yetzer hara.

Learning Torah actually moves a person to the place of *sechel.* The *sechel* of Torah that the Maharal speaks about differs in essence from ordinary intellectual pursuits. Ordinary intellect is totally dependent on human observation. The process of attaining knowledge is observation, understanding, then drawing conclusions. Thus human knowledge is subjective because human observation is qualified by time, space, and the limitations of the observer. The truth is, we humans don't see all that much. Our lives are very short, our subjectivity is very great, and our devotion to truth is very limited.

Torah, on the other hand, takes us above human observation to a place that is absolutely pure and objective. When a person enters the *sechel* of the Torah, the infinitude of the Torah could fill any empty space.

This presupposes, of course, that a person is learning Torah for a pure motive, not as a means of accruing material gain or aggrandizing the ego. While it is true that learning Torah for ulterior motives often leads to learning Torah for its own sake, one has to have as his ultimate goal to learn Torah for pure motives. Then the Torah can eliminate the baseness in our character—the materialism and the egoism—and fill our empty space with that which is pure and real.

The Maharal explains this even more deeply. He says that the Torah is perfect, and nothing else that we have is complete.

Rabbi Avraham Czapnik of the Jewish Learning Exchange in Los Angeles told me [TH] this story: His brother Yossi went to the funeral of the previous Bobover Rebbe, Reb Shloime. He noticed an unusual mourner, a large, black man, who was weeping copiously, like a baby. Rabbi Czapnik's brother was intrigued, because this man was obviously not a convert, not a Jew, so what connection could he have had with the Bobover Rebbe? He went over and asked him.

The man, whom I'll call Jackson, told him his story. Twenty-five years before, when he first began his profession as a house painter, the Rebbe called him and engaged him to paint his house. When Jackson arrived the first morning, ready to begin filling in the cracks and the other preliminary work, the first thing the Rebbe asked him was, "Did you eat breakfast?"

Jackson replied, "No." He thought the Rebbe would say, *There's a diner across the street. Why don't you go and eat breakfast and then come back?* But that's not what happened.

The Rebbe began taking out of the fridge all sorts of food that he would serve someone for breakfast. Of course, Jackson, coming from a different ethnic background, wasn't so thrilled with *chalav Yisroel* cottage cheese and all of the other goodies that the Rebbe thought constituted a nice breakfast. But he ate it. And he did his work.

The next day he came back ready to begin the painting. The Rebbe said to him, "I want to tell you something before you start."

Jackson thought he was going to hear, *You'd better do a good job, because I'm paying you top dollar.* That's not what he heard. Instead the Rebbe said, "It doesn't have to be perfect."

Jackson was surprised. "What do you mean it doesn't have to be perfect? I'm a very good painter. Why shouldn't it be perfect?"

The Rebbe gazed at him and said, "In this world, nothing is perfect."

"Nothing is perfect?" Jackson faltered.

The Rebbe explained, "We Jews once had a Temple in Jerusalem that was perfect. But since then, nothing is perfect."

Jackson absorbed what the Rebbe said. He painted the house, and finished the job. Months later he was hired by another rabbi to paint his house. Jackson thought he knew the routine. Better eat first, otherwise you have to eat cottage cheese. He arrived and no one offered him breakfast. The first day he did the preliminary work. The second day when Jackson arrived, the rabbi said, "There's something I want to tell you before you start."

Jackson thought, *I know what he's going to say.* But instead the rabbi said, "I want a perfect job. I don't want to see any mess. I don't want to see imperfect corners. I don't want to see any paint on the ceiling. I don't want to see anything on the floor where your drop cloth didn't quite make it. I want a perfect job."

Jackson responded: "Rabbi, in this world, nothing is perfect. You Jews once had a Temple in Jerusalem and that was perfect. But since it was destroyed, nothing in this world is perfect."

At the Rebbe's funeral, Jackson turned to Rabbi Czapnik's brother and said, "That Rebbe, he's my man." He opened his wallet and showed a picture of the Rebbe, one of those card-collection pictures of *tzaddikim* that children trade.

Hashem is perfect. The perfection of the Beis HaMikdash was real because it brought Hashem's Presence into the world. The way

Hashem communicates His perfection to us is through the Torah, therefore the Torah is perfect. In the end everything else leaves a void, a place of emptiness.

Historically, when masses of Jews have abandoned Torah, we have felt the pain of the empty space, and we have sought to fill it with other things. Those things seemed to work for a while, but in the end they left nothing but disillusionment. For example, many of the early Communists were Jews. They were enamored of the prospect of social justice for all. The secular Zionists, too, clung to the ideology of building up the land, Jewish labor, etc. as a way to fill that empty space. But the act of draining swamps and building roads can't ultimately fill that empty space. That's why the same Zionists who built the land are now in the process of destroying it.

The Maharal asserts that the only way to successfully fill the empty space is with Torah, because only Torah is perfect.

Battle Plan #5: Learn Torah

"Dragging the yetzer hara to the Beis HaMidrash" for men means literally going to the Beis HaMidrash and learning Torah, surrounded by the voices of other men likewise engaged in learning. Since we are all influenced by our environment, the environment of the Beis HaMidrash itself is like fighting the yetzer hara from inside a tank. Even if a man's learning is on a beginner's level, he would do well to find a class taught by a rabbi in a yeshivah setting, rather than learning on his own.

For women, a similar principle applies. If her beginning stage takes place as an adult, a woman should surround herself by a Torah-learning environment, such as attending one of the many seminaries in Jerusalem. Throughout her life, she should attend classes to the extent her family's needs allow. While men have a mitzvah to learn Torah every day, women are required to learn all the Torah they need to know in order to properly fulfill the mitzvos. This would include classes on halachah as well as hashkafah [Torah outlook]. Since women, like men, are obligated in the Six Constant Mitzvos, which include loving and fearing Hashem, trusting Hashem, and knowing that no other power holds sway in life, every woman has quite a lot of Torah that is incumbent upon her to learn.

Even if a woman was raised in an observant home and received a thorough Torah education, she needs to be honest about her present level of inspiration. She may discover that her love and fear of Hashem have remained at the level she was at when she graduated Bais Yaakov, and they are no longer adequate now that she is an adult. When this is the case, listening to CDs, attending a shiur, learning on her own, or (possibly best of all) becoming a "partner in Torah" so that she must prepare a mini class to give over on the phone to another adult woman enables her to sharpen her hashkafos and deepen her own inner life.

Throughout her life, a woman can bring the "Beis HaMidrash" into her home by recalling what she learned and consciously living it. When faced with a decision, she should ask herself, "What is the Torah's position on this issue?" This is using Torah to defeat the yetzer hara.

Learning Torah protects against both chronic and acute attacks of the yetzer hara. By incorporating Torah learning into your life regularly, whether it's going to a class or learning with a friend chavrusa-style in person or on the phone, you are building a staunch defense against the yetzer hara. Acute attacks of the yetzer hara are those situations that hit you out of the blue, when you least expect it, like your child breaking a valued object or someone denting your new car. At such times, if you can bring to mind even one sentence you have learned, it can save you from losing the battle.

Filling Yourself with Good

2

HISTORICAL ACCOUNTS OF GERMANY'S DESCENT INTO Nazism always begin with the Versailles Treaty. The Allied nations, who had lost millions of lives and most of their wealth during World War I, decided that Germany should pay for the war it had started. The Versailles Treaty imposed such severe financial penalties on Germany that the country's economy was virtually ruined. Runaway inflation ensued. It took a wheelbarrow full of German marks to buy a loaf of bread. Nazism—which was evil incarnate— then stepped in to fill the national lack.

In the wake of World War II, the Allies, having learned from bitter experience, took the opposite tack. The Marshall Plan was developed to rebuild Germany and other European nations by an influx of American dollars. The Allies understood that lack is the breeding ground for evil.

An important principle in the Maharal's teaching about the yetzer hara is: If a person feels lacking, the yetzer hara will rush in to fill the void. Therefore the best defense against the yetzer hara is to fill yourself with good. A cup that is filled to the brim with milk will have no room for poison.

In the previous chapter, the Maharal advocated filling that empty space with Torah. Now he quotes the Gemara: "Happy are you, O Israel, at the time you are busy with Torah and acts of kindness." The Maharal asserts that the yetzer hara is silenced by the combined force of Torah and *gemilas chassadim* [acts of loving-kindness].

Evil as Egocentricity

What exactly is evil? The Maharal quotes the Torah that a person's inclination is evil from the day of his birth. This is a strange concept. On the contrary, we usually think of babies as being totally pure and innocent. Imagine visiting your friend in the hospital the day after she's given birth. You wish her, "Mazel tov," and she leads you to the nursery, where you view her baby. Can you imagine saying, "He looks evil"? Of course not.

The Vilna Gaon explains that evil is synonymous with egocentricity. This certainly would describe babies, who, because of their innate dependency, are total takers, their adorableness notwithstanding. Imagine a mother saying to her 18-month-old. "Sweetheart, relationships should be reciprocal. I gave you a lot of my time last night, so tonight I expect you to reciprocate by giving me an uninterrupted night's sleep." This isn't going to work with a baby.

By the time a child is 5 years old, however, he is capable of giving, as indicated by the sweet handmade birthday cards that 5-year-olds present to their parents. Of course, the 5-year-old's birthday card is not perfect altruism as much as it is his own self-expression.

Spiritual development is a process of becoming less egocentric and more giving. When my [SR] son Yisrael Rohn was 10 years old, he learned to give *maaser* [a tithe of his income]. My mother-in-law arrived in Jerusalem for a visit. As she was unpacking, she handed Yisrael a gift from his Uncle Jamie: $100 in cash. Yisrael was ecstatic to receive such a large sum of money. Then I explained to him that a Jew gives *maaser*, which meant relinquishing $10 of his precious gift. He resisted, but I explained that when you give *maaser*, Hashem pays you back. Reluctantly, he coughed up $10 for *tzeddakah*. An hour later, as his grandmother continued to unpack, she handed Yisrael an envelope from her good friends the Freemans. Inside was a $10 bill. Yisrael saw that Hashem really does pay back, so he immediately took $1 and gave it to *tzeddakah*. A few hours later, his grandmother gave him a dollar. So at this age, he was happily giving *tzeddakah*, but only from a place of knowing he wouldn't lose out.

When people reach Bar Mitzvah or Bas Mitzvah, the grip of ego-centricity weakens to the point that they can empathize with the plight of other people. When Yisrael Rohn became Bar Mitzvah, he was already committed to giving *maaser*. He chose to give 10 percent of the gifts of money he had received for his Bar Mitzvah to Yad Eliezer. When his father and I accompanied Yisrael to the Yad Eliezer office, the coordinator told us about a boy soon to become Bar Mitzvah, one of seven children, whose father had been permanently wounded as a soldier in the Israeli army. The army had awarded the father sufficient funds to buy an apartment, but since the father couldn't work, the family didn't have enough money to buy tefillin for their son. Yisrael was moved by this boy's plight, and gladly donated several hundred dollars to buy tefillin. That act of *chesed* was not coming from a place of "I know I'll get it back." Yisrael at 13 was spiritually mature enough to empathize with the other boy's situation.

It takes all the way until age 20 for the voice of the soul and the voice of the ego to be heard equally loudly. That's why people are judged by Hashem only from the age of 20. Thus, while Yisrael gladly donated 10 percent of his Bar Mitzvah money to an under-privileged boy, he had not worked for that money and did not identify with it. A 20-year-old, however, has the capacity to give even his hard-earned money to someone less fortunate.

How much a person continues to mature spiritually after the age of 20 is a choice he or she makes. "Spiritual maturity" in this sense means moving away from the tyranny of egotism.

Chesed is the opposite of egotism. *Chesed* requires putting another's needs above one's own. Since evil is synonymous with egocentricity, a prime battle plan for vanquishing the yetzer hara is to do *chesed*.

How *Chesed* Works

The Maharal advocates filling the empty space with Torah and with acts of kindness. How do these vanquish the yetzer hara?

The Torah offers you goodness. People are mistaken when they think that learning Torah is a matter of acquiring information, like learning chemistry or medieval history. Rather, learning Torah is a process of actually acquiring goodness.

Learning Torah changes the way you think. You get a picture of how Hashem wants the world to look: without gossip or dishonesty in business, without grudges or stealing, a world filled with holiness and kindness, a world in which the creation is not separated from the Creator. Even learning that which seems to have nothing to do with your actual life, such as the sacrificial offerings in the Holy Temple, shows you how Hashem wants the physical world elevated through human actions. Therefore learning Torah gives your mind a relationship to goodness.

Doing acts of kindness similarly gives your soul, your *nefesh*, a relationship to goodness. *Nefesh* is the spiritual self manifested through the walls of the body. The more your soul is involved in your acts of kindness, the more the good you do becomes you.

The key here is to involve your *nefesh* in your acts of kindness.

Chesed can be done in two different ways. One way is when you get an appeal in the mail, and you lose the accompanying brochure so you are not even sure what cause you're donating to, and you write a check, put it into an envelope, and mail it. You could even make the process easier by just calling the toll-free number and donating by credit card. This is definitely *tzeddakah,* but it's not the kind of *chesed* that fills you with good.

Here's an illustration of a second way to do *chesed*: An *avreich* named Hershel Puretz moved from Brooklyn to Jerusalem to learn Torah. He lives in the neighborhood of Mattersdorf. He's 29 years old and married, with two children. Four winters ago, he heard about families living in unheated apartments who couldn't afford to buy heaters. Instead of just shaking his head at this unfortunate situation, Hershel collected money and bought 40 heaters at cost and distributed them to needy families. He thought he had finished with this *chesed,* but then he began receiving phone calls from indigent people who had heard that he was giving away free heaters. He collected more money and gave away a total of 100 heaters. When he heard that some of the heaters were still in their boxes because the recipients couldn't afford to pay for electricity to run the heaters, Hershel went to the Israel Electric Corporation and asked them to let him pay for part of the electric bills, equivalent to the average heating cost, for families who could not afford heat. The electric company refused, because their computers were not set up to take partial payments. Hershel persisted, and finally the Israel Electric Corporation revamped their computer system to accommodate Hershel's requirements. To date, Hershel Puretz has helped 2,000 poor families throughout Israel by giving them heaters and/or paying their heating bills. He continues to learn Torah full time and does this *chesed* only in his "spare time," during *bein hasedarim* yeshivah lunchtime break in the afternoon and until 2 a.m. every night.

This second way of giving, with hands-on, personal involvement, actually transforms the doer of the *chesed.* The more such *chesed* you do, the more the good you do becomes you.

When the empty space is thus filled with good, there's no room for the yetzer hara. Several years ago the social workers of the Municipality of Jerusalem decided that they had to provide a summer program for teenagers from dysfunctional homes lest they turn to drugs or other destructive pastimes. A certain budget was allocated to provide activities for these teenagers. Then someone (perhaps a student of the Maharal?) had a brainstorm. Instead of using the money to take the teenagers to a swimming pool or the beach, the municipality inaugurated a program where the teenagers would spend their mornings in the Yad Eliezer warehouse packing food cartons for the needy. The municipality paid the teenagers' bus fare, as well as a token hourly wage. The teenagers loved their work. In addition to the camaraderie and fun atmosphere in the warehouse, they felt that they were contributing something significant. Their *chesed* work filled the empty space, leaving no room for yetzer hara pastimes. The program was so successful that it has been repeated every summer since.

Battle Plan #6: Do *Chesed*

Doing chesed, which involves putting the needs of another above your own, leaves no room for the yetzer hara, which is synonymous with egotism.

In formulating a chesed battle plan, keep this principle in mind: Chesed, like giving charity, must begin with your own relatives. Doing the shopping for your parent, running an errand for your husband, helping your wife wash the Shabbos dishes, and helping your children with their homework are all acts of chesed.

Many women would like to do chesed, but they feel "burned out." If you have young children and/or work outside the home, do not feel discouraged that you have no time for other forms of chesed. Taking care of your family is chesed.

If, after taking care of your family, you still have time for more chesed, consider inviting Shabbos guests, especially single people who might otherwise be alone or Jews who would otherwise never experience Shabbos. Hosting Shabbos guests involves giving both on the physical level of a delicious meal and on the spiritual level of a warm, welcoming ambience. Other forms of chesed that can be done without leaving your own home are:

◆ *Making phone calls to facilitate a shidduch*

◆ *Phoning your friends to sell tickets or otherwise raise money for tzeddakah*

◆ *Phoning a widowed or elderly acquaintance or a friend who is undergoing a difficult period.*

◆ *Trying to match someone looking for a job with one of your friends who employs people in that field.*

Depending on your stage of life, you may find that your path of doing chesed takes you out of the home. When choosing a chesed, pick an avenue that resonates with your personality and utilizes your talents. If you prefer children to the elderly, don't visit nursing homes, but do volunteer at schools for disabled children. If you can't stomach illness, the hospital is not the place for you, but setting up a tape library may be. If you can play a musical instrument, you can cheer up patients in rehab centers and nursing homes. If you are trained in bookkeeping, a few hours of your time each week could put an incipient tzeddakah organization on its feet.

I [TH] visited a friend in the hospital last week. Boys from the yeshivah in Mitzpeh Yericho came to her ward. They not only sang and played guitar for the patients, they also asked their names and said a perek of Tehillim, mentioning each patient individually. When they left, they handed out little cards wishing everyone a good Shabbos from "your brothers." These boys are a virtual commando unit that obliterates the yetzer hara.

Redefining Pleasure

Imagine doing a *chesed* such as visiting the sick. Let's say you live in Brooklyn or Queens and your gravely ill friend is in a hospital in Manhattan. First, you have to free up the time for this visit, which will take several hours total. Then you may want to bring her something, so you go to the store and spend money for a gift. Then you have the "delight" of the subway ride into Manhattan. Next, you enter the hospital building, which some people find frightening. Then, you actually find her room and her bed. Some people find it stressful to visit a gravely ill person because it means confronting their own vulnerability or mortality. But then you hand her the present, and she feels happy you came, and she smiles and feels cared for. And how do you feel? You experience pleasure, real pleasure, in this mitzvah.

Now this is a major advance against the yetzer hara's territory, because you have moved from the realm of associating pleasure with physical sensation, the *yitzra d'ervah,* to associating pleasure with doing a mitzvah. In fact, the subway ride into Manhattan was not at all physically pleasurable, nor was walking through the hospital, smelling the disinfectant, seeing the really sick patients, or hearing an occasional groan. But there you are, feeling pleasure, the pleasure of helping another person. Your *chesed* has redefined the concept of pleasure for you. You have moved into the transcendental world, the world that is not limited by physical things.

What about when you do a *chesed* and you don't feel that spiritual pleasure? What if the *chesed* is so difficult that it overwhelms you or repels you?

So much of what you derive from performing *chesed* has to do with your expectations, as is evident from the following true story.

There's a fatherless family in Jerusalem with many young children, and the mother is simply not capable of coping. The woman who is in charge of *chesed* projects at a certain school wanted to help, so she sent some girls there to do *chesed*. Instead of coming back inspired and uplifted by the *chesed* they had done, the girls came back disgusted and disheartened. They complained that the apartment was such a mess it was impossible to clean it up. There were nine started ketchup bottles. There was no system of organization in the apartment. Even if they had washed, dried, and sorted the laundry, there were no specific drawers for any particular child. The kids were dirty and impudent. Of course, these *chesed* volunteers did not want to go again.

Then another teacher in the same school appealed to a different class. She said, "Who wants to go to a *chesed* family where there will be no return? You will not solve their problems. When you come back the second week, it will look like you were never there the first week. This is *chesed lishmah,* for its own sake. This is doing *chesed* in the fast track."

The second teacher got more volunteers than the first teacher did, and those volunteers were willing to go back week after week. They felt a sense of elation. Not a sense of accomplishment, which is what the first group expected, but a sense of elation, because they were pouring out *chesed* to people who desperately needed it.

Expectation is what also accounts for our not feeling pleasure in the *chesed* we do for our own family. If you expect gratitude for folding the laundry, your laundry folding will be mechanical and, even worse, resentful. But if you concentrate on the act of giving itself, you will feel joy in even the most mundane *chesed*.

Sometimes we're afraid to take pleasure in a mitzvah, because we worry that the pleasure we derive takes away from the mitzvah or from the merit we earn by performing the mitzvah. It's a myth that the more you don't enjoy a mitzvah, the holier you are. In fact the Torah itself states that tremendous suffering will come upon us because we don't serve Hashem with *simchah*. The Rambam even says that a mitzvah performed without joy is not properly performed.

The source of this fallacy—that the more you suffer when you do a mitzvah, the greater your reward—is the misunderstood Gemara, "*lefum tzara agra*," which means, "according to the difficulty is the reward." Here's what this Gemara doesn't mean: It doesn't mean that you get *kvetch* points. It doesn't mean that if you convince yourself that the elderly person you're visiting is boring and has nothing in common with you, you'll get a greater reward than if you see her as someone you can learn from, and feel something of her warmth and humanity, and actually enjoy the visit.

"*Lefum tzara agra*" means that in order to get the reward of a mitzvah, you have to make trade-offs. However, the more you value what you're getting, the less painful those trade-offs will be. The more you value what you're getting, the happier you'll be to do the difficult mitzvah.

For example, if you were asked, "Is $50,000 a lot of money?" you would say, "Yes." However, if you were told you could buy a five-room apartment in Jerusalem with a large balcony and a garden for $50,000, you would say, "$50,000? That's nothing!!" If you think that you're getting something worth far more than you're spending, you'll be filled with joy. If, on the other hand, you think that what you're getting is worth less than what you're spending, you'll feel cheated.

The same is true with doing *chesed*. If you spend a lot of time, energy, or money doing a certain *chesed*, your joy level will be commensurate with how much you value the mitzvah. And "what you get" from doing a *chesed* is mostly your own self-transformation into becoming the person you always wanted to be. If you were told that you'd have to spend $60,000 and four years of hard work to become a clinical psychologist, you wouldn't balk at the cost if that's what you want to become. The more *chesed* you do, the more the good you do becomes you. How much is it worth to you to become your better self?

Hanoch Teller wrote a story that beautifully illustrates this concept. A man in Israel was very ill. He came to the United States to be treated, but the treatments didn't help. He was dying. He wanted to return to his family in Israel, but by that time he was so sick that the airlines refused to take him. A representative of the Bikur Cholim Society, a distinguished, well-dressed woman, took the sick man to the airport. Reb Hanoch was standing near the check-in counter and witnessed this scene. The airline clerk behind the counter, who had the authority to decide whether or not to allow this man to fly, was refusing to accept him as a passenger. The woman from the Bikur Cholim Society subtly took off her pearl necklace, put it on the counter, and slid it toward the clerk. The clerk silently took the pearls and gave the man a seat.

This woman was motivated to give up her pearls because *chesed* was worth more to her than the pearls. Obviously she valued the pearls, or she would not have bought them. But she valued the mitzvah of *chesed* more. She did not leave the airport feeling resentful over the loss of her pearls. She left feeling ennobled, feeling joyous. She had succeeded in getting this dying man a seat on the plane. She won more than she lost, and she knew it. Her reward was huge, because she left the airport a greater person than when she walked in.

Battle Plan #7:
Undertake A Heroic *Chesed*

Big acts of chesed fill the empty space so completely that the yetzer hara never finds a foothold. Here are some heroic acts of chesed undertaken by real people:

◆ *Several 12-year-old American girls relinquished lavish Bas Mitzvah parties, and instead gave the money that their parents would have spent to organizations that feed the poor in Israel.*

◆ *Lori Palatnik donated one of her kidneys to a woman she didn't know, the mother of seven children, who suffered from a fatal kidney disease.*

◆ *R.S. drives a neighbor, a divorced mother she did not know well, to chemotherapy treatments. She stays with the woman for the duration of the treatment, and distributes her own homemade muffins to all the patients receiving chemotherapy, telling jokes and cheering up all those present. The woman suffering from cancer told me that she has such a good time with R.S. that she actually looks forward to her chemo treatments.*

◆ *T.A.I. heard of a poor girl in Israel who suffered from a serious disease and who wanted to get married but lacked the needed funds. He undertook to raise the entire cost of the wedding, some $11,000.*

◆ *M.B., the mother of eight children, stays up late Thursday nights cooking for Shabbos so that she has time every Friday morning to visit the cancer ward of Hadassah Hospital. She distributes snacks to the patients, chats with them, and forms bonds with many of them.*

◆ *D.M. became a "big brother" to a boy whose father had abandoned the family. He took the boy out to play, helped him with his homework, and modeled for him the example of a caring, conscientious father figure.*

When Hashem Chooses for Us

In choosing a *chesed*, sometimes it's difficult to find the balance between one that is big enough to be significant yet not so big that it overwhelms you, robbing you of the pleasure. In general the Maharal says that in choosing an optional *chesed*, go where your potential will be fully utilized but where you won't be pushed beyond your capacity.

This applies to those acts of *chesed* that we choose. Sometimes, however, Hashem chooses for us. Sometimes we find ourselves facing a huge *chesed* that seems, and really is, beyond our present capacity. For example, your parent develops Alzheimer's Disease, or a severely handicapped child is born to you, or your spouse suffers an accident that leaves him or her disabled. At such times, you have to know that Hashem thinks it's time for you to graduate to the next level of *chesed*. You have to know that if you accept the huge challenge Hashem is putting before you, you will become the person who is capable of performing such heroic *chesed*, even though now that level seems totally beyond you.

My [TH] daughter works at a kindergarten called Gan Harmony that caters to healthy children and children with various disabilities. One day some of the parents had arrived early to pick up their children, so they were sitting outside on the stoop conversing. One of the mothers, a petite and lively Yemenite woman, had a child in the kindergarten who was stricken with a very debilitating syndrome. This woman was visibly expectant. Another woman had the chutzpah to say to her, "Aren't you afraid that this baby also may have the same syndrome?" My daughter, who witnessed the scene, was flabbergasted. But the Yemenite woman, without missing a beat, replied, "I don't make babies. Hashem makes babies. I want whatever baby He gives me."

This doesn't mean not to pray for a healthy baby. It does mean that if you are confronted with a situation where you have to be doing *chesed* 24/7 for years on end, then that's the altitude at which Hashem knows you're capable of flying. Embrace it with the knowledge that this is your ticket to spiritual greatness. Remember, the secret of joy in mitzvos is to know that what you get is worth much more than what you give.

Does this mean that everyone put in a situation of having to do 24/7 *chesed* becomes a great *tzaddik*? Observably not. Does it mean that the battle plan we've been discussing in this chapter, filling the empty space with *chesed* so that the yetzer hara cannot get in, applies also when the *chesed* is not self-chosen, when the *chesed* is "assigned" to you?

It depends on where you want to go. There's a principle that applies here. The Gemara asserts: "In the way that a person wants to go, in that way he is led." Human beings have free choice. Some people "assigned" to perform 24/7 *chesed* become embittered and resentful. Others do become self-transcendent. It depends in which direction you choose to go. The general rule is: In spiritual things, you get what you want. In physical things, you get what Hashem considers good for you.

Battle Plan #8: Aim For Spiritual Greatness

A soldier could be allocated a state-of-the-art weapon, but if he doesn't know how to properly aim it, he won't hit the target.

Repeatedly ask yourself: "What is my target?" Just as you have personal goals and professional goals, make sure you have a spiritual goal. Your professional goal is specific. By the time you're in fourth year of medical school, you're not saying, "I want to be a doctor." You're saying, "I want to be a neonatologist." Similarly, your spiritual goal should be specific. Not "I want to grow spiritually," but "I want to learn all of Shas." "I want to do tremendous chesed with the handicapped." "I want to become so self-controlled that nothing can make me lose it." This opens up the possibility of then asking yourself honestly how you can go about attaining the goal. Only when your goal is clear can you really do something to make it happen.

The entire multibillion-dollar advertising industry has only one purpose: to create wants. You may not want or need a new car, but a skilled advertisement can succeed in creating a desire within you, so that now you really want that new model SUV with 27 new features. How do you advertise spiritual growth so that you lead yourself to want it? Read stories of tzaddikim or of ordinary people who passed big tests, so you'll desire to be like them. Spend time with the founder of a chesed organization so that you'll covet being like he or she is. Hang out with friends who are one step above you spiritually because, as every advertising executive knows, the more you are exposed to something, the more you want it.

Cultivate in yourself the desire to do chesed and to let the chesed you do become you.

Hadassah Weisel relates that when she was a young bride, she used to go to the Kosel almost every day after work and beg Hashem to let her do mitzvos. She felt, "If a person earns money, he always wants to earn more. Why in spiritual acquisitions should a person be satisfied? Mitzvos are the diamonds most precious in the world." She was just 24 years old when her husband Rabbi Yaakov Weisel asked her, "What do you want to do in your life?" Hadassah replied, "I want not only to raise children, but also to do something worthwhile." She had neither the skills nor the resources to start a chesed organization, but ten years later she and her husband found themselves the unlikely founders of Yad Eliezer, which has become Israel's largest food provider to the needy.

Practice aiming high.

The Seven Names
of the Yetzer Hara

3

MANY OF OUR TORAH LEADERS HAVE CONCLUDED that the biggest problem of our generation is that we no longer despise sin. Sin should be revolting and abhorrent to us, but most often we view it as mildly harmful and even neutral. We feel, *I can live with it,* so that's exactly what we do: We live with sin.

It's as if you have a darkened patch of skin on your upper arm. No one sees it and it doesn't hurt, so you say, "I can live with it." Then it turns out that the sore is a melanoma: malignant cancer! Only then do you realize that you can't live with it. You literally cannot live with it. This is the nature of sin. Only when we identify it for what it is in all its horrific danger, do we take firm steps to eradicate it from our lives.

Imagine sin as a serial murderer at loose in your neighborhood. You would shudder in fear and repugnance, lock your door, then fasten the deadbolt.

But what if, somehow, that serial murderer, in his daytime persona, gained legitimate entrance into your home, perhaps as the plumber you hired to fix a leak? The longer he's in your home, the more comfortable you become with him. Now he's good ole Mr. MacKenzie, and you offer him a cup of coffee. You notice he has a pleasant demeanor and he's a skillful plumber who cleans up after himself, so you even start to like him.

The next day, the newspaper headline blares: SERIAL MURDERER IAN MACKENZIE ARRESTED. Now it's hard to despise and detest him, because he is familiar to you and you can't help but remember how nicely he cleaned up after himself. Good ole MacKenzie.

In our generation, sin has become familiar, and even acceptable to us. This is the result of living in a society where the ultimate value is tolerance. This tolerance extends to terrorists, perverts, and all kinds of miscreants. In modern society, the act of distinguishing between good and evil has become a relic of an outdated past, as outmoded as ostrich-feather hats and bow ties.

This is glaringly obvious in popular culture, where the media refuses to label anyone as "evil." Terrorists who murder children in cold blood are labeled "freedom fighters," as if they are driven by high ideals rather than bloodthirsty hatred.

The zeitgeist demands: "Tolerate! Embrace!" Defeating the yetzer hara, however, demands: "Distance yourself! Reject!"

A good example of this is the Internet. When the Internet first appeared, many of us happily invited it into our homes. We appreciated its instant access to information, where, with a few clicks, you could find anything from today's news to the most effective cure for hives or the best soufflé recipe. Good ole Internet.

When the leading rabbis of our generation vociferously condemned the Internet because of its easy access to depraved sights, some people thought the rabbis were overreacting. Because these people were already familiar with the Internet, because they appreciated its benefits, they could not see its vileness, and even dismissed the option of buying "kosher" Internet filters (which are approved by most rabbis). Such people were oblivious to the danger posed by the Internet, and thus could easily fall prey to its power to corrupt young people, break up marriages, and destroy lives. In many cases, familiarity does not breed contempt; familiarity breeds acceptance.

The Seven Names of the Yetzer Hara

The Maharal in the first chapter of *Nesiv HaYetzer*, quoting the Gemara, teaches that the yetzer hara has seven names. As we analyze these seven identities, we will see that the yetzer hara becomes progressively more familiar and therefore more acceptable and ultimately more difficult to defeat, because we don't even recognize it as an enemy.

A name is important because a name defines what this thing is to you. Drawing from *pesukim*, the Gemara enumerates the seven names given to the yetzer hara by Hashem through Moshe, Dovid, and then by various prophets:

> Hashem – *ra* [evil]
>
> Moshe – *areil* [uncircumcised]
>
> Dovid – *tamei* [impure]
>
> Shlomo – *oyeiv* [the enemy]
>
> Yeshayahu – *michshol* [stumbling block]
>
> Yechezkel – *ehven* [stone]
>
> Yoel - *tzif'oni* [viper]

Evil as the Absence of Hashem

Hashem Himself called the yetzer hara "*ra*" [evil]. The Maharal explains what good and evil really are. Hashem is the Source of all goodness, all light, all creativity, all giving. All of the lofty and noble qualities are manifestations of Hashem's goodness. Evil is everything that is opposite. Evil is everything that conceals Hashem's goodness.

According to the Maharal, goodness is absolute and real, because it is a manifestation of Hashem, Who is Ultimate Reality. Everything that Hashem created is a manifestation of Him, the same way a building is a manifestation of the will and wisdom of the architect. Therefore, when we look at Hashem's creation, we see His goodness. That's why, in the Torah's account of creation, Hashem proclaims that what He created that day is good. When the Torah says "*ki tov* — it was good," it means that that particular creation bears testimony to the Creator's reality and goodness.

If good is that which reveals the Creator, then evil is that which conceals Hashem, that which makes God seem to be absent.

How does evil do that? It is implicit in the creation itself. In the Maharal's essay on Chanukah, called *Ner Mitzvah,* he asserts that the four empires — Babylonia, Persia, Greece, and Rome — under whom the Jewish people were exiled are hinted at during the very creation of the world. The second verse of the Torah reads: "And the world was formless and chaotic, darkness on the face of the depths." The Maharal shows how these four phrases — formless, chaotic, darkness, the depths — refer to the four empires. These empires were evil according to our definition; they concealed Hashem in different ways.

That evil is alluded to in the very beginning of the creation account means that evil is an inherent part of creation. In fact, evil is a result of the world being a creation, because of the inherent distance between the Creator and the creation. Before the creation, there was only Hashem. As soon as Hashem began the process of creation, there was something other than Hashem: the created world. This otherness allowed the possibility of evil, which, as we said, is the sense that Hashem is absent. The yetzer hara is the force of Divine absence.

In truth, evil is an illusion, because Divine absence is an illusion. In the ultimate sense, evil does not exist. In this world of apparent duality, however, it is easy to be blind to Hashem's all-encompassing Oneness. Thus, Hashem's own definition of evil is the absence of good, the apparent absence of Hashem.

Battle Plan #9:
Put Hashem Into The Picture

Since the yetzer hara operates by making Hashem appear to be absent, the yetzer hara can be defeated simply by experiencing Hashem's presence, by putting Hashem into the picture.

This means that whenever you are about to succumb to the yetzer hara, remind yourself that Hashem is present (which is, in fact, the truth!).

Conjure up a sense of the presence of Hashem. Yosef used a version of this method when he was tempted by Potiphar's wife. He visualized the face of his father Yaakov before him. In the presence of his father, he simply could not descend to the low level of adultery.

Imagine that you are a 19-year-old seminary girl boarding a Jerusalem bus, and you're about to lie to the bus driver about your age so you can buy a youth ticket and thus save half the fare. Suddenly you notice that the man standing behind you in line is Rabbi W., the dean of the seminary. In Rabbi W.'s presence, will you lie or tell the truth? And if Rabbi W.'s presence can so effectively catapult you to a higher level of behavior, what about Hashem's presence? If, on the edge of sin, you can simply say to yourself these four words: "Hashem is here now," and make that truth real to yourself, the battle is over and you are the victor.

The Descending Order of Disgust

With the remaining six names of the yetzer hara, the Maharal points out that as the generations descend, the yetzer hara seems less loathsome. Thus people become less committed to do battle against it.

He starts with Moshe Rabbeinu. Moshe called the yetzer hara *areil* [uncircumcised]. A person who is *areil* is a different creation than a person who is circumcised. The act of circumcision was a physical manifestation of the covenant Hashem made with Avraham. The covenant sealed by *bris milah* means that Hashem indeed changed his relationship to Avraham and his descendants. This relationship is marked by the ability to have such a strong spiritual connection that even physical reality can be uplifted. This makes the circumcised Jew entirely different than the person who is not part of this covenant.

For Moshe, the *areil* (and thus the yetzer hara) was entirely other. He had no commonality with it at all.

As we will see, in later generations the yetzer hara assumed a fluid identity, sometimes appearing as part of us, sometimes not. For Moshe, however, the circumcised person was entirely other than the uncircumcised, the *areil*. The circumcised person can never become uncircumcised. So, the Maharal tells us, Moshe was on such a high level that the yetzer hara no longer had any connection to him. The yetzer hara was despicable to him. Moshe was *nivdal*, transcendent. The yetzer hara was forever in the category of other.

Dovid called the yetzer hara "*tamei* — impure." According to the Torah, a person who is *tamei* has to leave the camp. For example a person with *tzara'as,* as he walked from the camp, had to call out "*Tamei, tamei!*" to warn others not to touch him.

A *tamei* person was repulsed; others instinctively kept their distance from him. Thus, Dovid's definition of the yetzer hara as repulsive was loftier than the definitions of those who succeeded him. But compared to Moshe's definition, Dovid brought the yetzer hara one step closer to acceptability. After all, an impure person is still a person like you and me. He's not another sort of being. He's *tamei*, I'm *tahor*. He's out of the camp, I'm in the camp. But we're both people.

In other words, Dovid saw the yetzer hara as being an aspect of humanity. Of course, it's the part that we reject, the part that we battle against, but it's part of us.

Moshe, by contrast, was so transcendental that he saw the yetzer hara as totally separate from him. To illustrate Moshe's level: There are sins we would never do. None of us, for instance, are tempted to perform human sacrifice. It's not a sin we struggle against; it's totally out there, not part of us at all. For Moshe, every sin was out there. He was on the level of *nimol* [circumcised], and sin was *areil,* entirely other.

Dovid was closer to our level. He could define the yetzer hara as something like himself: not him, but *like* him. It's not what he wanted, but he could relate to it. The difference between Dovid and us is that he was able to label the yetzer hara as something disgusting that he rejects. The yetzer hara for Dovid was as loathsome as a person who is *tamei*. He wanted no connection with it.

Shlomo regarded the yetzer hara as an "*oyeiv* — an enemy." An enemy is also separate from the person. An enemy has an adversarial relationship with the person; one has to do battle with an enemy.

An enemy, however, doesn't defile you by touch. Dovid saw the yetzer hara as *tamei;* it defiled you if you merely touched it for a moment. You could even be defiled if you merely touched someone who touched a *tamei* object or person. You had to keep a real distance.

Shlomo regarded the yetzer hara as an enemy. But he wasn't afraid to touch it. We see this in Shlomo's life. One area of challenge involved the numerous women he married. His intent was lofty: to take whatever holiness lay hidden in the societies from which these women came and to elevate it. This is a process known to the mystics as bringing the *klipat noga* [the translucent shell, which refers to life choices that are neither holy nor evil, but can be moved in either direction] up to *kedushah.* And for a significant portion of his life, Shlomo succeeded in this mission. But according to the Maharal it was a sin, because Hashem forbade it, which meant that ultimately it was not *klipat noga.* For Dovid, doing something that Hashem forbade would have been repulsive. For Shlomo the yetzer hara was an adversary, but an adversary can be quite respectable, even attractive.

There is a well-known painting depicting the surrender of General Robert E. Lee, the commander of the Confederate forces, at the end of the American Civil War. The war was bitter, and General Lee was certainly the enemy of the Union. In the painting, however, he appears like a distinguished elderly gentleman with his white goatee. He looks gallant, even noble (which, according to the history books, he was). So it's possible for an enemy to be respectable rather than repulsive.

In fact, if you look at American war propaganda from World War II, you see that a lot of effort went into making the enemy — both the Germans and the Japanese — look monstrous. Those who produced these posters understood that if they wanted to mobilize support for the war effort, they had to make the enemy look vile and contemptible. Today, in the War against Terror, a salient cause of the American public's ambivalent attitude is that many in the media insist on giving the terrorists "a human face." An enemy who looks respectable and relatable is almost impossible to defeat.

In the Maharal's descending list of definitions, Shlomo was thus the first to make the yetzer hara something other than repulsive.

Next on the list is Yeshayahu, who called the yetzer hara a "*michshol* — stumbling block." Notice that there is nothing intrinsically bad about a stumbling block. You don't hate a stumbling block; you merely pick it up and move it out of your way. It is not even an adversary, but just an inconvenience.

Yechezkel saw the yetzer hara as stone, as it says: "And I will remove the heart of stone from your flesh." We all experience periods when we feel like our hearts are hearts of stone. During these periods, our prayers are mechanical and unfeeling; our love for our fellow person is forced at best and non-existent at worst. During these periods, we don't feel that the stone is our enemy. We consider it normal. We make peace with it. It's not even a stumbling block that has to be removed. Instead, it feels like a part of our personality. The "heart of stone" resides inside us. No repulsion. No distance. No adversarial relationship. It's part of us. This is a much lower level of relating to the yetzer hara.

The last is the Prophet Yoel, who called the yetzer hara "*tzif'oni* — viper." The word "*tzafon*," is related to the word "*tzafun*," which means "concealed." According to this definition, the yetzer hara is hidden in my heart, and I don't even know it's there.

For example, you hear that strawberries this year are infested, and the only permissible way to eat them is to peel every strawberry. Since you are not someone who is going to take the time to peel every strawberry, you have two options: to not eat strawberries this year or to shrug your shoulders and say that it's just rumors spread by people who are nit-picking and overly *machmir*. Since you happen to love strawberries, you are not even aware that your temptation to ignore the infestation alert comes from your yetzer hara. Your yetzer hara to eat the infested strawberries, which is totally dominating your heart at this point, is hidden from you.

This last definition of the yetzer hara — *tzif'oni* — is the most difficult to battle because you don't even realize it's there. It's like bacteria. You can't see them, but they can kill you. Only when you do detect that the bacteria are present in your body (through a blood test, for example), do you take steps to fight them.

So how can we climb back up the ladder of the generations and regain a sense of repugnance to sin? Jewish tradition has long made use of visualization to make abstract feelings viscerally real. Thus, when reciting the first paragraph of the Shema, when we say, *'b'chal nafshecha,"* committing ourselves to love Hashem with all of our physical body, we should visualize ourselves being burned at the stake or otherwise giving up our life for love of God.

On the second morning of the ground invasion of the recent Gaza war, I [SR] was on my way home from the Kosel after davening Shacharis. I stopped at my friend Perel's house to discuss something with her, but first I wanted to know, "Have you heard any news? What's happening with the war?"

Perel looked pained. "It's terrible news. Three of our boys killed, and 24 wounded."

"Oh, no!" I exclaimed, as my tears started to flow.

Perel continued: "We did it to ourselves. Our own tank fired on a house where we thought Arabs were hiding, but our own soldiers had taken cover inside."

I gasped in horror at the thought that we had killed and wounded our own boys.

"We do it to ourselves all the time," Perel declared, her face stricken.

"What do you mean?" I asked, confused. "Incidents of friendly fire?"

"No," Perel said. "I mean we fire on each other all the time."

Suddenly I was gripped by the image of our critical, condemning words against other Jews becoming missiles that end up killing our own sons. "We fire on each other all the time." In my mind's eye, I saw every word of lashon hara issuing from my mouth transforming into a mortar shell that makes a circuitous journey through the air and ends up exploding on another Jew. I remembered the words of the Chafetz Chaim: "The speaker of lashon hara causes death and swords and killings in the world." I had thought that his statement was metaphorical, but at that moment, hearing the news of our attack on our own soldiers, I realized that his words are literally true.

In the last 23 years, I have attended many classes on *Shmiras HaLashon*. Numerous times I have gone to the giant *Shmiras HaLashon* conventions held in Jerusalem's largest auditorium. I have learned the entire book *Chafetz Chaim: A Lesson a Day* with a chavrusa on the telephone. Nevertheless, while I do not gossip about individuals, I often permitted myself to utter critical, condemning remarks about groups of Jews who differ from me religiously or politically. That day, standing in Perel's house envisioning every word of lashon hara as a missile that finds its target on my fellow Jews, I was so horrified that I went cold turkey on speaking lashon hara. Since that devastating morning, whenever I feel tempted to speak negatively about other Jews, I visualize a mortar shell issuing from my mouth, and I am so repulsed that I have no trouble keeping silent.

Battle Plan #10: Make Sin Repulsive

In this battle plan, we employ the technique of visualization to make aveiros [sins] repulsive to us.
Here are some possibilities:

◆ *When you are about to commit the sin of onaas devarim (hurting someone with words) by, for example, making a hurtful, critical comment to your teenage child, imagine a terrorist with a two-foot-long knife about to attack your child. As with all visualizations, the more detailed the scene, the more* powerful its impression on you. So, see the glint of the sharp knife, the crazed and hateful expression of the terrorist, the look of fear and impending disaster on your child's face. The truth, as attested to by psychologists, is that verbal abuse can be more damaging than physical abuse, so this scene is not an exaggeration of the harm we can do with words. Visualize your words as the sharp knife in this scene until you are totally horrified and repulsed at the prospect of committing the sin of onaas devarim.

◆ When you are tempted to eat a food without a proper hechsher or a fruit you have not checked for bugs, imagine that there are maggots inside the food.

◆ When you are about to steal time from your employer by, for example, making personal phone calls on company time, imagine yourself sticking your hand into a tzeddakah box and taking out $2 to buy yourself a diet Coke.

◆ If you're about to make a critical remark about a rabbi of a different group, imagine that you are standing at the funeral of the victims of the Mumbai massacre. Leaders from across the spectrum of Am Yisrael are present, as well as Jews of every stripe. The martyred, shroud-wrapped bodies of Rabbi Gavriel and Rivka Holtzberg, Hy"d, lie before you. Now imagine that this precious moment of unity is shattered by your critical words blaring over the loudspeaker. Feel the horror of your defiling the achdus that the holy martyrs of Mumbai bought with their lives. Imagine how you would feel if you were the culprit in that scene, and know that every time you speak ill of rabbis of any group, you are indeed that culprit.

Think of your most common weaknesses and make each of them equivalent to something that is repulsive to *you. Actually visualize the images in detail, using those above or creating your own. Make a list of such equivalencies. Spend your downtime (on your way to the car, bus, or train, driving, getting dressed) visualizing these equivalencies. The more specifically you can visualize the scene, the more real it will become for you. The more often you visualize it, the more likely it will pop into your head when you are actually confronting the sin.*

Satisfaction

The Maharal concludes this section by saying that the yetzer hara disguises itself as that which gives us satisfaction.

What is satisfaction? Satisfaction is not only physical. The proof is that we observe people who have everything materially and they are not satisfied with their lives. Nor is satisfaction only spiritual, because if a person doesn't have her basic needs met, she's not satisfied. True satisfaction is a way of taking the physical and giving it spiritual depth and meaning. For example, true satisfaction can result from giving money to buy a therapy room in a school for handicapped children. When you see photos of the donors visiting the room they donated and witnessing how much the children are being helped, you see real satisfaction on their faces.

When, however, this mechanism (of taking the physical and giving it spiritual meaning) is not operational, people's yearning for meaning takes them to wanting to satisfy the empty place within them, and they often turn to forbidden acts. The yetzer hara's sales slogan is: "This will give you satisfaction in your life."

Battle Plan #11: No Vacancies

When you feel a lack of satisfaction in your life, when you feel that empty space, be especially on guard, because the yetzer hara will definitely try to fill that empty space with acts that will bring you down.

It's as if a room in your house becomes vacant. So you put a sign in the window, "ROOM FOR RENT." Soon someone knocks on your door. He would like to occupy that room. He looks very honest and attractive: whatever is your idea of attractive, either distinguished or exotic or interesting or cool. The yetzer hara is a master of disguise. So how can you tell if the one who would like to fill the vacancy is the yetzer hara? After all, he looks perfectly fine.

The answer is that he is definitely the yetzer hara! Your mistake was in putting up the sign. Even before that, your mistake was in allowing a room in your home to become vacant.

Don't allow empty spaces in your life. Your life should be full. So if you have spare time when you're not learning or working or taking care of your family, fill that time with what will give you true satisfaction, i.e., with taking the physical and giving it spiritual depth and meaning.

You could fill it with chesed, by volunteering for a good cause. Read to the elderly blind woman down the street, or volunteer to tutor the fatherless children next door. Any such chesed will fill your life with genuine satisfaction. Or you could fill it with artistic expression. Take a course in art or creative writing or carpentry. Or you could fill it with intellectual pursuits, such as studying a topic that interests you.

This doesn't mean that you have to be working every minute. A balanced life must have time for productive leisure, such as working out in the gym or listening to music or taking a daily or weekly walk with your spouse in the botanical gardens. But be aware of the difference between "productive leisure," which means an activity that refreshes you physically and emotionally so you can return to your real life envigorated, and "empty time," such as spending time alone doing nothing (reading vacuous novels and surfing the Internet equal doing nothing). Such empty spaces in your day are breeding grounds for the yetzer hara.

Take the "VACANCY" sign out of your window and find meaningful activities to fill your life. Then, when the yetzer hara comes knocking, you can tell it, "Sorry, buddy, there's no room for you here."

Dealing with Desire

4

REBBETZIN CHAYA NECHAMA MILIKOVSKI RELATES a story that happened in Poland when she was a girl. It took place in the home of her grandfather, Rav Shimon Shalom Kalish, the Rebbe of Amshinov. One erev Shabbos, about an hour before candle lighting, there was a knock on the door. A woman was standing there. She explained that her train had been delayed and when she realized she would not get to her destination before Shabbos, she had disembarked in their town. Now she needed a place to stay for Shabbos.

Rebbetzin Kalish cordially invited her to stay with them. A short time before Shabbos, when the food was already on the *blech* and the kitchen was empty, as the family scurried to get dressed in their Shabbos clothes, the cook happened to enter the kitchen. She discovered the guest pouring a powder into the soup.

It turned out that the "woman" was actually a man in disguise. He had concocted the story about the train in order to gain entrance into the Rebbe's house. The powder would have put the whole family into a deep sleep, so that he could plunder their silver and family heirlooms.

This true story is a powerful metaphor that reveals the machinations of the yetzer hara of desire, especially the desire for physical pleasure and material acquisition.

According to the Maharal, the spiritual void within each of us is part of the human condition. This spiritual void is different than biological lacks. For example, if you feel hungry because you haven't eaten for four or five hours, and then you eat dinner, your hunger is satiated. But if you feel hungry because you feel unloved or unappreciated, because you just lost your job or your best friend, and you eat dinner, you'll still feel hungry. You'll gobble down two desserts, and a half-hour later you'll be rummaging through the refrigerator again.

This second kind of hunger is essentially a spiritual hunger, and the more we feed it, the hungrier we feel. Because we have been conditioned to respond to lack by feeding it, which works in the physical dimension, we intuitively extrapolate this "solution" to the inner void. We believe that the way to deal with all desires is to give in to them, to give them what they demand, and then they'll be satisfied and stop bothering us.

However, the opposite is true. The more you give in to certain desires, the more desire you feel. The more you feed the fire, the bigger the fire rages.

The Maharal, in Chapter 2, reiterates his basic concept that the yetzer hara attacks us through feelings of lack. In this section he deals with lack as *taivah* or desire. He asserts that the more you give in to your desires, the more the desires grow. Even though a person feels more complete if he gives in to his *taivah* agenda, this is merely an illusion. He has succeeded in feeding his yetzer hara, not his higher self.

How then should one deal with desire? Starve it! If you don't feed the fire, it will eventually die out. If a person refuses to give in to desire, as though he is whole and not lacking, then he vanquishes the yetzer hara, whose entire advertising campaign is: "You're lacking."

Starving the yetzer hara seems to contradict the verse from Proverbs quoted in Chapter 1: "If your enemy is hungry, give him bread." You do have to feed the lack: with Torah and *chesed*, not with shopping or drinking.

The Maharal ends this paragraph with the emphatic warning, "Understand this very, very well." Obviously, not giving in to desire is a crucial strategy for every Jew.

Battle Plan #12: Don't Let The Yetzer Hara Of Desire In The Door

Let's go back to the story about the man disguised as a woman who knocked at the Rebbe of Amshinov's door pretending to need a place for Shabbos. Had the cook not entered the kitchen at the right moment, the thief's nefarious plan would have succeeded, and he would have stolen all the Rebbe's valuables.

Viewing the story as a metaphor, we learn first of all that the yetzer hara always assumes a benign disguise when it knocks at your door. All of us are smart enough to slam the door on the obscene yetzer hara of desire. But what about when it comes disguised as the legitimate use of the Internet for business or homework? What about when it comes disguised as your need for an efficient secretary who incidentally happens to be young and attractive? Such disguises are sufficiently innocuous to obscure the yetzer hara's agenda.

The primary battle plan for fighting the yetzer hara of desire is: Don't let it in the door. This means don't wait until you're engaged in full-fledged hand-to-hand combat with the yetzer hara. At that point, it's too late, and you are likely to lose, because the yetzer is very strong and very sneaky. When you're least suspecting, it will slip the sleeping potion into your soup, and before you know it you'll be too spiritually asleep to know what's happening.

Instead, don't let the yetzer hara of desire in the door in the first place. Be aware of the yetzer hara's most common disguises, and if anyone remotely resembling that disguise knocks at your door, refuse him entrance.

In this battle plan, you must remember that the rule behind the multibillion-dollar advertising industry is: Exposure creates desire. The more a person is exposed to something, the more he or she will want that something. That's why five billboards advertising a certain brand of cell phone are more effective than one billboard. That's why it's worth investing a million dollars to play a commercial ten times over. Exposure creates desire. Therefore, you have to limit your exposure to everything you don't want to end up desiring.

Sometimes a secretary becomes her boss's "office wife." They confide in each other and become best friends with each other. At best, this is emotionally compromising; at worst, it can go much further, ruining the lives of their families. Therefore, if you are a man who needs office assistance, the time to beware of this disguise of the yetzer hara is before you hire your secretary, not six months later when you begin to see her as a person and as a woman. Then it's too late! "Don't let the yetzer hara in the door" means that, if at all possible, try to hire a man or a mature woman as an office assistant. In situations where this is impossible, don't ever cross the lines delineating the business relationship. You don't have to know how she's feeling today or what she thinks about the political situation in Israel or whether she likes chocolate. Always address your office assistants, as well as your female co-workers, as Mrs. _____ or Miss _____, never by their first name.

Another example: Women often find themselves forming an emotional bond with their male psychotherapists. This is almost inevitable, because the therapist-patient relationship necessitates revealing one's innermost feelings to a trusted listener. If you are a woman who has opted for psychotherapy, the time to beware of this disguise of the yetzer hara is before you choose a therapist, not six months later when you start to unfavorably compare your husband to your sensitive and perceptive therapist. By then it's too late! "Don't let the yetzer hara in the door" means thinking twice before choosing a male therapist. When possible, choose a female therapist.

In a case like this, where the initial attraction is psychological rather than physical, observing the laws of yichud by leaving the door to the therapist's office ajar may still leave too big an opening for the yetzer hara. That's why a certain well-known male psychotherapist will see a female patient only if another person is present in the room throughout the session. Women who are unwilling to acquiesce to such an invasion of their privacy simply cannot become his clients.

Other ways of implementing this battle plan:

If you must use the Internet, get a serious kosher filter rather than relying on your own integrity. In addition, never go on the Internet unless there is someone else there with you, looking over your shoulder.

If you are a kiruv rabbi working with women, take your wife along to events and include her in the relationships you forge with those women to whom you offer guidance.

If you work in an office with the opposite gender, maintain as much distance as possible. For example, at the offices of ArtScroll/Mesorah, there are separate dining areas, each with its own refrigerator and microwave, for male and female employees.

Internalize this concept: Your wife's friends are not your friends. Or: Your husband's friends are not your friends.

All of the above are effective strategies for keeping desire at bay so that it never has a chance to "put you to sleep" and steal everything that is valuable in your life.

Where to Draw the Line

Arguably the most controversial question in the Orthodox world today is how much of the outer world to let in and how much to keep out. Do we decide that everything that's not forbidden is permitted? Or do we decide that everything is forbidden unless it is explicitly permitted?

In theory, the more you make permitted things accessible, the more a child should not want forbidden things. But what I [TH] have observed in communities in Israel is that the more that's permitted, the more the kids are drawn toward that which is forbidden, until far too many Israeli youths end up off the *derech*. And conversely, the more guarded the community is *within reason*, even distancing themselves from things that are technically permitted, the less the youth end up off the *derech*. This observation bolsters the Maharal's point that the more you give in to the yetzer hara, the more it demands of you.

So where's the line? How do you know when you have crossed the line?

Using the Maharal's standard, the answer would be: If you're using _____ to fill the void, then you've probably crossed the line. This can be illustrated with eating disorders: both those having to do with eating too much and disorders such as bulimia and anorexia. All of them have to do with wanting to fill the void. In the case of overeating, the person is attempting to fill the void with physical pleasure. In the case of bulimia and anorexia, the person is attempting to fill the void with a sense of perceived control and dominance. But in either case, the person is taking the void that is part of the yearning for spiritual completeness and attempting to fill it with something else. This is always a losing proposition.

The same dynamic is true with surfing the Internet, drinking too much at a Kiddush, shopping oneself into debt, making friends with co-workers, employees, or neighbors of the opposite gender, spending money on status symbols, and a host of other desires that expand rather than shrink the more you indulge in them.

Our response to the inner void should be yearning for higher occupations such as Torah and *chesed*, not desire for lower occupations. Desire comes from a feeling of lack, and the more you feed such desires, the more lack you feel, and the stronger the pull of the yetzer hara. Eventually, instead of annihilating the yetzer hara, the person becomes defined by his or her lack: an alcoholic, an anorexic, a drug addict, a shopperholic. Then the yetzer hara has won.

The Mystique

A problem with forbidding what is permissible but dangerous is that when you forbid something, you create a mystique around it. Then something that may not even have been desirable becomes desirable.

For example, if you go into a room full of people and say, "Don't look up," everyone in the room will look up. It's not that they are so interested in the ceiling, but as soon as you prohibit something you create a mystique around it. Several years ago, a book ridiculing Mohammed by a mediocre author was published. Most Muslim countries banned the book, and the author's life was threatened. So of course it became an international best-seller, even though by all accounts it was a very lackluster book.

So the problem becomes: How do you protect yourself or others from exposure to what may be dangerous without at the same time creating a mystique that makes it even more desirable?

The answer is to deglamorize it by making it seem tedious or unfortunate or humdrum. This takes careful thought and much wisdom.

Take for example the phenomenon of teenagers going to the mall. When teenagers go to the mall, they go not only to buy stuff but also because they're attracted by the energy, the lifestyle. The mall is colorful and interesting. They go there to meet friends and end up being exposed to more than their parents and the educational system would like. After all, the business of the mall is to attract people to fashion, movies, or whatever else they are selling. The allure of the mall can be very strong and also corrupting.

In my [TH] daughter's Bais Yaakov school one of the 14-year-old girls asked the principal, "Are we allowed to go to the mall or are we not allowed to go to the mall?" For the principal, it was a lose/lose situation. If she said, "You're allowed to go to the mall," then the girl would have spent her life there. If she said, "You're not allowed to go to the mall," then she would be creating a mystique, and the girl would have eventually finagled a way to go there, just to see why it's forbidden. This principal, however, is very wise. She replied, "Well, if you need something they sell in the mall, and they don't sell it anyplace else, and if you want to take the two buses to get there, so go. If you need it, you need it. After all, sometimes you can't find what you want elsewhere."

This answer completely stripped the mall of its mystique. It became a place to go buy things you couldn't find closer and more readily.

Battle Plan #13:
Remove The Mystique

One strategy for removing the mystique is to remove the "fancy packaging." For example, if you take a box of Godiva chocolate that doesn't have a hechsher, and you remove it from its gold, heart-shaped box, and you peel off the label with the name "Godiva," and you put it in a plain paper bag, you'll probably find that you can live very well without it.

Another way of removing the mystique is with words. In Chapter 3, we suggested associating sins with repulsive images. Here the battle plan is to associate deleterious things with words that paint them as tedious, boring, and humdrum. That lascivious novel entitled The House of Secrets? In your mind change the title to The House of Piled-Up Laundry, and see if you're still tempted to read it.

You're standing in Saks Fifth Avenue looking at a Ralph Lauren dress that you find irresistible, even though it's two inches too short. Imagine that your unemployed friend comes to show you her latest acquisition that she bought for $8.99 at the local secondhand shop, and she pulls out of the bag that very same dress, without the label of course. Now can you resist it?

The Guest Takes Over

The Maharal next quotes a Gemara that the yetzer hara first comes as a guest and later becomes the host. This means that from the beginning of your life, the yetzer hara is there, but it has not taken over your identity. The more you submit to it, however, the more it becomes attached to your personality, until finally it's the boss. It becomes you.

How does it look when the yetzer hara totally grabs someone? The Rambam in *Hilchos Teshuvah* lists sins for which it is very hard to do teshuvah. The door to come back is basically closed. One such sinner is a person who knowingly buys stolen merchandise. The Maharal explains that if you have no scruples about buying stolen merchandise, then you have descended to the level where stealing is O.K. It is part of you, just like wearing two shoes from the same pair is part of your "automatic pilot's" response to life. In a certain sense, the person who buys stolen merchandise is even worse than the thief. When a person steals, he may feel pressured into it at the moment. He may even feel guilty doing it, but he succumbs to his yetzer hara. When you buy stolen merchandise, however, it feels normal and guiltfree.

Almost all of us would feel terribly embarrassed if we were caught stealing. For example, a friend of mine [TH] had a subscription to a frum magazine. When she finished them, she would place them, a few at a time, in my mailbox. Someone in my building routinely took the magazines. The culprit didn't get up in the morning and say, "I am prepared to perform the sin of stealing." Rather, she noticed the magazines in my mailbox, and she wanted to see what was happening or perhaps to read an article by a particular author, and she couldn't overcome her yetzer hara. More accurately, she *didn't* overcome her yetzer hara. She didn't plan to steal, but she was overcome in the moment. She was, of course, guilty of stealing, but she had not redefined the act as permissible. If I would have caught her red-handed, she would have felt humiliated, even without a word from me.

By contrast, the person who buys illegally copied CD's has no scruples about it. He even plans it out when he's making today's list of errands. He feels no guilt doing it in public, even though he's "shopping in the thief's market," as the Rambam would say. This means that it has become part of his identity.

We opt for choices that make evil part of our identity through habit. Habit creates desensitization. The culprit here is desensitization. At this point, the yetzer hara becomes the host. It is no longer something attached to the person. It is the person himself.

The gentiles see the yetzer hara as external. They call him "Satan," and envision him as a red-suited devil with horns and a long tail. If you lose the battle with Satan, you become his slave.

The Jewish view, on the contrary, is that it's possible for a person to actually become evil by consistently choosing evil. The evil becomes part of the person. The evil becomes the person. Now, this is not an irreversible state. Teshuvah is always possible, and the Gemara as well as Jewish lore has many accounts of wicked people who did teshuvah. So if a person hits the bottom of the hill, he could turn around and go up again, but it's a very, very steep hill to climb.

Desensitization, which is the road downhill, results from gratifying desire: once, twice, habitually. The Maharal brings a *pasuk* that states that in the beginning the yetzer hara is like the silk thread of a spider's web, but eventually it becomes as thick as the leather reins the wagon driver uses to drive the horses.

The silk thread of a spider's web is so easy to break. When a person is not desensitized, the yetzer hara has little force to get her to do wrong. The person is shocked and put off by the very prospect of committing evil. But if a person opens the door and lets the yetzer hara in as a guest, then gradually over time, little by little, the silk thread becomes a leather rein in the hands of the yetzer hara. Then it requires tremendous strength to break it.

Take for example the serious sin of beating a child in anger. If Rivki's parents never hit her out of anger or tiredness or frustration when she was growing up, she will be horrified at the prospect of hitting her own children, even when she is very tired, frustrated, or angry. Hitting her children for those reasons is a line she is not even tempted to cross. Hitting her children is coarse, part of the culture of violence that has nothing to do with her or anyone she knows well. It is monstrous to her. If, on the other hand, Rivki was frequently hit by her parents for the above reasons, it will not seem so terrible to her. Although hitting her children is not in her childrearing plan, when she is exhausted or stressed out, she is likely to slap or spank them. Even an occasional slap from anger or frustration is enough to desensitize her to the wrongness of physical violence toward children. If the stresses in her life increase, the frequency of her hitting will also increase. She didn't plan it, but slowly and irrevocably the devoted mother turns into a child beater. The yetzer hara is holding the reins.

Battle Plan #14: Beware Of Small Sins

The residents of the southern Israeli city of Sderot have for eight years been under a more or less constant barrage of

Kassam rockets from terrorists in the Gaza Strip. The rockets are small — about two feet long — and imprecise. The vast majority of them fall on vacant areas without doing any damage. Out of some 5,000 Kassam rockets launched at Sderot, 12 people have been killed, and less than 100 have been seriously injured. Recently a 10-year-old child lost his leg from a Kassam rocket.

With the frequency of the attacks, numbering up to several times a day, you might think that the residents of Sderot would become desensitized to them. Far from it. When the "Color Red" siren goes off, warning that a rocket has been launched from Gaza, everyone frantically dives for cover.

Why has the process of desensitization not set in in Sderot? Because the residents acutely understand that a Kassam rocket could kill them.

A small lie, petty thievery, a casual flirtatious remark, a single statement of lashon hara, a single visit to a questionable website, EACH OF THESE CAN KILL YOU! They won't kill you right away, but as the spider thread becomes gradually thicker it becomes a rope that can strangle you.

When you feel tempted to do even a "small sin," hear the "Color Red" siren go off in your mind, and run for cover.

Transience

Next the Maharal brings a Gemara that quotes Rav, who compares the yetzer hara to a fly that sits in the opening of the heart. Why a fly? Because a fly has a very short life span, a few weeks at most. It's totally transient. The Maharal calls the yetzer hara of desire "despicable like a fly."

How ridiculous we feel when we look back at our own lives and see how much emotional effort we put into fulfilling our desires! Is there any satisfied desire that still tastes or feels good at that point?

I'm not saying that this world is valueless or that you shouldn't enjoy it. Enjoy the world. That's one of the ways to bond with Hashem. If you're eating food, recite a *berachah* with *kavannah*. Take delight in the food, its taste, its texture, its fragrance. But don't get emotionally attached to food, to its being this way or that way, because food, like all the pleasures of this world, is transient.

Someone I know witnessed this scene in a fine restaurant. The customer ordered two eggs, sunny side up. He told the waiter, "But I want the eggs either on a large plate or on two plates, because I don't want one of the eggs to run into the other." The waiter brought out the two eggs on a very large plate. Neither egg was touching the other. The customer, however, was not satisfied. He sent the eggs back to the kitchen because the edges were too brown.

In fact, the edges were very brown, almost burnt. But how long will the pleasure of two perfectly cooked, non-touching eggs stay with him? A couple hours later when he's back at the office, will he still be savoring the taste of those eggs? Of course not. Why get that emotionally involved in a sunny side up?

Another image always leaves me [TH] wondering. At popular, high-class restaurants, if you haven't made a reservation, or sometimes even if you have, you have to stand in line behind a velvet cordon until the maitre d' announces that your table is ready. There are people, very busy, important people, who don't have time for anything. If Moshe Rabbeinu were coming to their office, they would give him a 15-minute slot, not more, because they have to get to their next meeting. Yet these same people will spend half an hour waiting behind the velvet cordon for dinner. Why? Because of their emotional attachment to eating in this particular restaurant.

Rav Amnon Yitzchak, the famous Sephardi maggid, says that food is only pleasurable for the minute and a half that it's in "the mixer," meaning your mouth. Then the pleasure is over. The same is true for all the pleasures of the senses. The yetzer hara of *taivah* leads us astray because it makes us forget how transient these pleasures are.

Battle Plan #15:
Remember Transience

Imagine you are going on a week's vacation. You ask the travel agent to book you a beautiful room in a five-star hotel with a view of the ocean. You expect to pay about $200 per day for such a room. The travel agent gets back to you and says, "This hotel charges $200 per hour. So 24 hours will cost you $4800." You would be horrified by such overpricing. For your $200 you expect to get a certain amount of time. Getting less time for your money is a rip-off.

The yetzer hara of physical desire always rips you off with time. Emotionally, you expect that the pleasure you are "paying for" will last much longer than it does. But the nature of physical pleasure is that it is short-lived.

When you feel desire for something physical, ask yourself: If I give in to my desire, how long will the pleasure last? Then weigh whether it's a good deal given how much you're paying in weight gained, money spent, or relationships compromised.

Usually you'll discover that you're paying too much for too little.

Winning with Divine Oneness

5

ARE HUMAN BEINGS ATTRACTED TO EVIL BECAUSE like attracts like or because opposites attract? This is a famous dispute in the Gemara between Rav and Shmuel.

The first point of view means that evil resonates with something in us that we identify as our own evil. Psychologists would explain that people commit only acts that they believe themselves capable of doing. If you see yourself as a scrupulously honest person, you will not be tempted to steal. Your own self-image will prevent you from succumbing to that sin. On the other hand, when a person feels disgusted with himself he is apt to do things that are indeed disgusting.

This is a profound point: A person's negative self-image makes him or her easy prey for the yetzer hara. When a person sees his essential self as injured, lacking, despicable, then it's easy for him to despise himself. When confronted with a test, such a person will give up on himself rather than fight the yetzer hara.

When I [TH] have spoken with kids off the *derech*, usually they pinpoint a pivotal moment in their religious decline, perhaps the first time they violated Shabbos. When asked what they were thinking at the moment they turned on the light switch, they invariably reply, "I'm nothing anyway. I'm going to go to *Gehinnom*, so I may as well do what I want."

I [TH] know a family where one son ended up in the role of loser. His low self-esteem was the combined result of his social awkwardness, his poor academic performance, and his father's critical, hurtful remarks. One day when he was 16 years old, he showed up at yeshivah wearing a T-shirt with a picture of his favorite soccer player. His rebbe said to him, "You're not a *ben Torah*." That was it. He got up and walked out of the class, and out of the yeshivah, and out of the religious community, and didn't stop walking until he had fallen very, very low. In that one statement, the teacher was affirming what the boy already believed about himself: that he was despicable, that he was not worthy of calling himself a *ben Torah*. So why bother to act like one?

Contrast this approach with the childrearing method of the father of the noted psychiatrist and author Rabbi Abraham J. Twerski. Rabbi Twerski relates that when he was a child and did something wrong, his father would say to him, "*Es pahst nisht*," "It's not worthy of you." The message is: "You are such a fine person that this bad action is beneath you."

Clearly, a child who believes that he's on such a high level will be less tempted to stoop to bad actions than a child who believes that he's already bad, so why not? Imagine what might have been the result if the teacher in the above story had said to the boy: "You're a *ben Torah*. The shirt you are wearing doesn't reflect the real you."

Once I [TH] was sitting in Rav Shlomo Freifeld's living room. A man came in to talk with the Rav about problems that this man was having with one of his children. I think Rav Freifeld forgot I was there, so I just sat quietly and observed the interchange. The father complained that his son was doing so badly in school that he would have to take him out of yeshivah and put him into a lesser educational framework. The father's exact words were, "I'll put him in the veggie bin," meaning a place for vegetables, not human beings. Rav Freifeld, who was a giant in every sense of the word, with enormous presence, rose to his full height, banged on the table, and cried out: "The veggie bin? I belong in the veggie bin, not him! You think I was always so clever at learning?" Rav Freifeld upbraided the man for a full 10 minutes.

In this way Rav Freifeld taught this man, and me as well, how disastrous it is to denigrate another person's essential image of himself or herself. Disparaging a person's self-esteem makes him or her fertile ground for the yetzer hara.

Battle Plan #16:
Build Up Other People's Self-Esteem

Several years ago, an Israeli Jew was arrested for selling arms and ammunition to Hezbollah. Everyone in Israel was shocked at the news, but that's exactly what we do when we disparage someone's self-image: We give the enemy, the yetzer hara, armaments and ammunition to use against that person. Now when the yetzer hara says, "It doesn't matter if you do this lowly deed. You're a low-life anyway," the person believes it. Every time a parent or teacher disparages a child, he is handing the child's yetzer hara a loaded gun.

Never call a child a name, because it will become a self-fulfilling prophecy. He will hear it as a label, not just an expression of your momentary frustration. If you call Danny "sloppy," that's who he will become, despite your broken-record efforts to get him to clean his room. If you call Debbie "selfish," you will be horrified at the heights of selfishness she will attain.

If you really want to bolster a child's ability to fight the yetzer hara of the teenage years, then build up that child's self-esteem. This requires looking at the child deeply enough to ferret out his strengths and talents. If the child is academically weak, then praise his generosity. If the child is socially inept, then praise her artistic prowess.

Although a person's self-image is well formed early in life, by bolstering the self-image of a person of any age you help him or her fight the yetzer hara. You can give a person facing a test no greater gift than to say, "You are strong enough to pass this test."

A popular saying asserts, "You are what you eat." In truth, you are what you think you are.

Looking for Excitement

Of course, even people with a positive self-image are not immune to the yetzer hara. The other side of the dispute quoted from the above Gemara is that opposites attract. There are people who are aware of their own inner purity, but they want excitement and novelty. They don't want to be a goody-goody. They are drawn to the yetzer hara specifically because it's different, new, exotic.

Thus, two very different people can be sitting in front of the computer screen. Both of them are going to misuse the Internet by going onto an inappropriate site. Both of them are about to succumb to the yetzer hara. But they are coming from very different places. One person sees himself as dirty on the inside and is enveloped in the "it doesn't matter anymore" mentality. This person is not even battling against his yetzer hara. As far as he's concerned, he and his yetzer hara are on the same black-uniformed team. The second person sees himself as good, and convinces himself that he'll be broadened by exposure to things that are new and different. He's enveloped in the "climb every mountain" mentality. He, too, is not battling the yetzer hara, because he dismisses the yetzer hara as a figment of his parents' imagination, concocted to prevent him from living life to the fullest. He is totally in denial about the damage his actions can do.

Neither of these people is battling the yetzer hara. The first feels as if he's already lost. The second feels as if he's a winner who can't lose. Thus we see that whether a person is drawn to evil because like attracts like or whether a person is drawn to evil because opposites attract, both can be thoroughly vanquished by the yetzer hara.

Years ago, I [SR] received a letter in the mail informing me that I was the lucky winner of a free, three-day vacation in Tiberius. Attached was a full-color photo of the gorgeous suite in a hotel just waiting for my family. All I had to do to claim my prize was to come with my spouse to a meeting in Jerusalem the following Tuesday.

Somehow I convinced my husband to go with me. Images of a Tiberius vacation danced in my head—and all for free! How could we just ignore such an opportunity?

It turned out (as you may have guessed) that the owners of the gorgeous suite in a hotel were selling time-sharing. For just $80,000 we could buy two weeks a year in their hotel. The "free vacation" had an $80,000 price tag.

Similarly, the yetzer hara that whispers, "It will be exciting and broadening if you do _____," purposely fails to mention how much it will cost you for this "free" experience. All experiences affect you. Everything takes you closer to the light or closer to the darkness. In the world of experience, there is no pareve.

Battle Plan #17:
Examine The Price Tag

When the yetzer hara croons, "Climb every mountain," your answer should be: "How much will it cost me to climb this mountain?" This means asking how it will affect your spiritual level. As Aunt Ruth Rigler used to say: "You get what you pay for, and if it's free, you've paid too much."

The yetzer hara for excitement can be channeled in ways that take you closer to the light rather than plunging you into darkness. For example, I know a high-energy teenage boy who attends weddings (of people he doesn't know) four nights a week to dance off his excess energy. The same energy that could have gotten him into trouble he uses instead to do the mitzvah of rejoicing the bridegroom. I also know a girl who, when she finished seminary, had a strong yen to travel. She channeled that desire into spending two years volunteering for Chabad in Hawaii.

If you are a person who believes, "I can't lose by climbing this mountain," stop and think. The thrill and excitement, no matter how great, are fleeting. Are they worth the price involved? After all, some people who embark on mountain treks get lost or get caught in an avalanche and never come back. Carefully consider whether this mountain is worth the risk.

Two Power Sources?

When a person succumbs to the yetzer hara and sins, he propagates the illusion that there are two sources of power in the world: one good, one evil [*chas v'chalilah*]. For example, when Saddam Hussein tortured his victims, it must have seemed to some of them at least that evil had prevailed, that evil was stronger than good. And since many of his victims died in his torture chambers, the perception that evil had prevailed was their final perception. They didn't live to see the day when Saddam was hanged on the gallows. They didn't live to see that good prevailed in the end. In truth, we won't see the ultimate triumph of good until Mashiach comes.

Therefore, whenever people see evil get away with it, they may be tempted to conclude that evil is a force independent of Hashem.

In fact, Judaism is the only religion that insists that God is One, even when the bad guys are winning. Zoroastrianism, the religion of ancient Persia, made it simple. They believed in two gods: a god of good, light, and truth; and a god of evil, darkness, and falsehood. Actually there's a little Zoroastrian in most of us. So when things are going well, we thank Hashem. But when things go awry, we blame our boss or the government or the negligent repairman, as if there were two powers sources in the universe.

For example, I [TH] am presently in the throes of dryer distress. I bought a dryer. It has a guarantee. A part broke in the dryer, so I called the company to send a repairman. Four calls and two weeks later, no repairman has arrived. I assume that the company is dragging its feet about sending a repairman because they're waiting for the guarantee to expire, which will be soon. Given my temperament, I have two choices. I could easily go into a diatribe blaming this company for being, at worst, dishonest and, at best, negligent, because it's going to end up costing me money. Or I could say, "Hashem runs the world, and this is a test He is giving me."

This is a classic battle with the yetzer hara. If I choose good, than I will look at my fellow Jew who runs this company, and instead of accusing him, I will ask Hashem to bestow His mercy on this Jew because he is so far away. If I choose evil, then I'll yell at the secretary who answers the phone and I'll speak lashon hara about the boss of the company. And, if I do that, I'll be submitting to the Zoroastrian within me that says that there are two powers: Hashem, and the boss of Bosch dryers.

This is a crucial point. None of us would attribute independent power to the sun or the stars or Baal. But how often in life do we attribute independent power to the personnel manager who didn't hire us, or to the bus driver who closed the door and drove off when we were just inches away, or to friends who didn't invite us to their son's Bar Mitzvah, or to Microsoft when our computer crashes?

The first and second of the Ten Commandments require that in every situation you recognize that everything is from Hashem, and there is no other power. This entails recognizing that whoever harmed you or embarrassed you or disappointed you or cheated you is not an independent agent. Although they indeed have free choice, whether or not you will be harmed, embarrassed, disappointed, or cheated is totally in the hands of Hashem, the only Power in the universe. As the Midrash says, "Hashem has many bears and lions." All of these experiences can come through one of Hashem's agents or another. Once you admit that, you can see that this test has the potential to take you to a higher level. That moment of submission to Hashem's will takes you to a state of ultimate reliance on Hashem's transcendental wisdom, which makes you closer to Him than you were before this situation hit you.

If you submit to the yetzer hara and buy into the illusion of two sources of control, other sins follow in rapid succession: taking revenge, bearing a grudge, judging harshly, speaking lashon hara, hating your neighbor in your heart, etc. And the worst is the heresy of propagating the illusion that there are two sources of power in the universe.

Both of the types of people discussed earlier in this chapter have fallen into the illusion that there is a power outside of Hashem. The first type, the person with low self-esteem, thinks, *I'm so despicable. I exist outside of God.* The second type, the one looking for excitement, thinks, *If I want excitement, I have to take God out of the picture.* Even thinking that it is possible to take Hashem out of the picture is a denial of the unity of Hashem.

The Yetzer Hatov

Meyer Birnbaum, who served as a lieutenant in the United States Army during World War II, explains how the Allied forces succeeded in the invasion of Normandy on D-Day, June 6, 1944. Much *hash-*

gachah pratis [Divine Providence] contributed to the unlikely success of the invasion, which paved the way for the Allied victory in the war. The most crucial element was that General Erwin Rommel, the legendary German field marshal assigned to repel an Allied attack on the beaches of France, was on leave that fateful day. June 6 was his wife's 50th birthday, so Rommel had returned to Germany to celebrate with her. The absence of this skilled general left the German forces in disarray.

Similarly, the Maharal warns [in Chapter 3] that when fighting the yetzer hara, a person must always mobilize his yetzer hatov [good inclination]. It is not sufficient to have state-of-the-art armaments and brilliant strategies. The presence or absence of the yetzer hatov can make all the difference in the outcome of the battle.

Battle Plan #18:
Mobilize The Yetzer Hatov

When battling the yetzer hara, summon the presence of your yetzer hatov.

Let's say I pick up the phone to call my friend to pour out all my grievances against the dryer company with a stream of lashon hara. Sometime between dialing the phone and my friend answering, it occurs to me that I would be giving in to the yetzer hara if I let loose with the lashon hara I had intended to say. Suddenly I hear, "Hello." I want to battle the yetzer hara, but how?

Mobilize the yetzer hatov! Instead of just not doing something negative, do something positive. When my friend answers the phone, instead of pouring out my dryer woes, I say, "What are we doing about the shidduch crisis?" I take out my list of singles and I ask her to take out hers, and I invest a half-hour in trying to make a match that has some possibility of success.

Just as the yetzer hara is forceful, so it must be counterbalanced by the yetzer hatov putting in equal force and enthusiasm. Don't just avoid evil. Do good!

The Master Plan ◆

Next the Maharal presents a four-step plan outlined in the Gemara for defeating the yetzer hara. It uses the concepts discussed in this chapter. To apply this plan to a real-life situation, I [SR] am going to describe a time I lost the battle and how I could have defeated the yetzer hara had I used the Master Plan.

I [SR] was once asked by a rabbi to speak to the seminary he directs. They were having a Shabbaton in the Sephardi Center of Jerusalem's Old City, where I live. Since I knew of several entrances to that building, I asked the rabbi to have someone meet me at the *shomer* [security guard] next to the center and take me to where the girls would be waiting. We made up that someone would meet me at the *shomer* at 4:30 that Shabbos.

I arrived at the *shomer* of the Jewish Quarter parking lot right next to the Sephardi Center at 4:30, but there was no sign of anyone to meet me. Meanwhile, I noticed a white stretch limousine parked across the street. I had never before seen such a vehicle in Jerusalem. Standing near the guard booth was a bareheaded man in his 30's wearing a blue suit. I asked him if he was the driver of the limo, and he answered, "Yes." Then I inquired if he was Jewish, and again he answered, "Yes." I proceeded to tell him about the holiness of Shabbos, how it is the "sign" between Hashem and the Jewish people. He listened raptly. Then I told him that no money earned on Shabbos will bring blessing to him or his family. He nodded his head earnestly, listening to every word, as if in fact he had been thinking about this very subject.

Suddenly I was abashed to notice that it was 4:40. I was 10 minutes late for my speaking engagement, and still no one had come to meet me. I looked up toward the Sephardi Center and saw two of the seminary students on the veranda. These same two girls were supposed to have come to my house the day before so I could speak with them privately, but they had gotten their directions mixed up, and arrived only two minutes before candle lighting, so there was no time. Now they led me to my waiting audience, explaining that they thought I was to meet them inside. I was annoyed. When I met the rabbi, I blurted out, "I've been waiting by the *shomer* at the parking lot for 10 minutes. You should have sent other girls. These two girls are not so together."

The rabbi apologized, "It's my fault. I thought you were coming to the *shomer* at the entrance to the building, not the *shomer* of the parking lot. That's where I sent them."

In one horrified moment, I realized that I was guilty both of judging the two girls unfavorably and of speaking lashon hara. Had I implemented the Gemara's Master Plan, I could have staved off defeat.

Battle Plan #19: The Master Plan

The Maharal, quoting the Gemara, outlines four steps for defeating the yetzer hara:

1. Mobilize the yetzer hatov.

Move yourself from the mentality of lack/taking to the mentality of wholeness/giving. Grasp for a mitzvah you can do. Let your desire for good take control of the situation.

In the above story, had I focused on my yetzer hatov — my will to give to those girls the gift of Torah — I would not have been bothered by my yetzer hara's egotistical worry: "Being late means the rabbi will think I'm not a punctual speaker."

2. Learn Torah.

If the first maneuver doesn't work, distract yourself by learning Torah. Grab a sefer, any sefer, and learn a paragraph. Distract yourself with goodness. In the great world of Torah all our petty grievances disappear like a grain of sand in the ocean.

In the above story, had I even thought about the content of the Torah I was about to impart, my annoyance at being 10 minutes late for a speaking engagement would have seemed like what it was: petty and irrelevant.

3. Recite the Shema.

If step two doesn't work, says the Gemara, then recite the Shema. The big falsehood of this world, more than any other kind of falsehood, is that there's control outside of Hashem's rule. The Shema, as the declaration of Hashem's Oneness, dissipates that falsehood. The reason we are tempted to sin by speaking lashon hara, taking revenge, etc. is because someone has harmed us, humiliated us, or caused us damage. We believe that other person has the power to harm us, independent of Hashem's providence. The Shema reminds us that there is only One power Source: Hashem. Everything that happens to us comes, directly or indirectly, from Hashem.

In the above story, had I taken a moment to recite Shema and reminded myself that everything comes from Hashem, I would have immediately recognized that Hashem engineered the misunderstanding so that I would be standing in the wrong place, which was really the "right" place to speak to the limo driver about the importance of observing Shabbos.

4. Remember the day of your death, which could be today.

If the other steps fail, the Gemara enjoins us to remember the day of death. No one knows when he or she will die, but no one would want his or her last words to be words of lashon hara or complaint or hatred or anger. Even when we think that we're justified in whatever sin we're about to commit, asking ourselves the question, "What if this is the last thing I ever do on this earth?" will make the yetzer hara flee like the darkness before the dawn.

The Secret
Ingredient

6

THE ENTEBBE RESCUE OPERATION WAS ONE OF the most successful operations ever executed by the IDF. In 1976, an Air France plane was hijacked by Arab and German terrorists. The plane was forced to land in Entebbe, Uganda, where the president, Idi Amin, was sympathetic to the terrorists. While the gentile passengers were released, 83 Jewish passengers and 20 crew members were kept as hostages. The terrorists threatened to kill the hostages if the Israeli government did not meet their demands. A squad of Israeli commandos managed to land in Entebbe, free all but four of the hostages, and return them to safety in Israel.

A key ingredient of the operation's success was that Israel landed a black Mercedes identical to that of Idi Amin's, plus two Land Rovers like the ones that usually escorted him, and drove the vehicles right up to the terminal building where the hostages were being kept. This act of impersonation enabled the commandos to get into assault range of the terminal without being detected.

The yetzer hara is a master of such impersonation, which enables it to attack us from close range without our realizing we're under attack.

The Maharal thus identifies one of the yetzer hara's most insidious tricks: the distortion of our ideas about God and His relationship to us. He quotes a Gemara that warns a person not to believe the nonsense the yetzer hara tells us. Of course, if the yetzer hara told us obvious lies, we would not be influenced, just as if the Israeli commandos had attacked in IDF jeeps, they would have been promptly counterattacked. Instead, the yetzer uses the wily trick of taking something that is true and corrupting its implications.

The example the Maharal gives is the Mishnah in Avos that states that a person should always remember from where he came, to where he is going, and before Whom he will have to give a final accounting. The point of this Mishnah is to remember Hashem's greatness and our own smallness.

The yetzer hara, however, distorts the message. The yetzer tells us: "Yes, Hashem is infinite. His mercy and compassion have no bounds. Therefore, when you sin, He will certainly forgive you."

It's hard to find the loophole in this contention. Yes, Hashem is infinite. Yes, His mercy and compassion have no bounds. Yes, when we sin and do real teshuvah, Hashem forgives us. But that is not a license to go ahead and sin, confident that whatever we do will be forgiven, as if there are no damaging consequences of sin.

Indeed, this twisted theology is the basis of the widespread syndrome: "My Father in Heaven will surely forgive me this sin because I meant well." Translate: "I don't have to expend effort to go beyond my comfort zone and do what the Torah commands because God understands me." This pernicious concept is one of the yetzer hara's most successful ploys.

And the yetzer hara even brings a well-known Chassidic story to prove his point: A young boy, who had barely learned the aleph-beis, was kidnapped by non-Jews. Years later he found his way back to the Jewish community on Yom Kippur. He entered a synagogue hoping to join in the prayers. Someone handed him a Yom Kippur *machzor*. Much to his dismay, he didn't know how to read Hebrew. He couldn't recite a single prayer. Heartbroken, he poured out his soul in what he did know: the letters of the aleph-beis. And his tearful recitation of the aleph-beis was passionate enough to avert heavenly decrees against the Jewish People that even great *tzaddikim* couldn't annul.

The yetzer hara tells us that this story proves that it's the heart that counts. Enter coronary Judaism: It doesn't matter if the money I gave to Yad Eliezer was not honestly earned; it's the heart that counts. It doesn't matter if I withheld important information when asked about a shidduch; it's the heart that counts. It doesn't matter if I tell self-protective lies; it's the heart that counts.

Rabbi Shimon Green, referring to the above story, asserts: "It only works once. By next Yom Kippur the kid has to learn how to read Hebrew!"

Coronary Judaism is nothing but an excuse for spiritual laziness. Why don't you take the time to learn to read Hebrew? Because you'd rather play tennis or surf the Internet. Why don't you ask a sh'eilah about whether it's obligatory to reveal certain information when asked about a shidduch? Because it's easier not to. Why don't you learn the laws of lashon hara by learning *Chafetz Chaim: A Lesson a Day* with a friend? Because it takes 20 minutes a day. Believing that God will forgive such behaviors is equating our Father in Heaven with the kind of parent who lets his kids eat potato chips for breakfast and stay home from school whenever they feel like it. Indeed, this is the God concept that the yetzer hara has swindled many into believing.

The Maharal points out that to believe that Hashem is not interested in punishing people is heresy. Indeed, one of the Thirteen Principles of the Faith is belief in reward and punishment.

Concepts of God pose a major educational challenge. If you emphasize to your children the punishing aspect of God, they may find religion dark and threatening, and when they grow up, they might rebel. On the other hand, if you emphasize to your children the loving, forgiving aspect of God, they may buy into "coronary Judaism," that "God understands my heart," and when they grow up, they may become lax in fulfilling mitzvos. Either way, your child is in trouble. The only way to stave off this conundrum is to find a mentor who can direct you through such dilemmas.

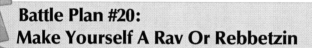

Battle Plan #20:
Make Yourself A Rav Or Rebbetzin

Because the yetzer hara of distorted theology is so subtle, there is no way that you can fight it by yourself.

Here we must take an example from tank warfare. Tank warfare requires a crew of four: a driver to drive the tank, a navigator to look out and determine where the enemy is in order to determine which direction to fire, a loader to load the cannon, and a gunner to fire it. The gunner, the one who is doing the actual fighting, is essentially firing blind. The navigator gives him a set of coordinates, and, without seeing the enemy at all, he fires.

The Mishnah in Avos directs: "Make yourself a Rav." Rav Leib Kelemen asserts that for women that means: "Make yourself a Rebbetzin." This Rav is not intended for the purpose of paskening halachah. Rather, every Jew needs a mentor, a Rav or Rebbetzin, who knows both the person and the Torah well enough to give guidance and direct the person throughout the many quandaries of life. This Rav or Rebbetzin functions as the navigator, telling the gunner where to fire, even when the gunner does not see the enemy.

Indeed, many women looking for a shidduch are advised to have as one of their main criteria that the prospective husband must have a Rav to whom he listens. Then, when situations come up in life, as they inevitably will, when the yetzer hara is so disguised that the couple themselves

> cannot identify where it is, the Rav can provide the clear vision necessary to combat it.
> A Jew who lacks a Rav or Rebbetzin to consult is like a gunner inside a tank. He cannot possibly know where the enemy is. So how can he fight him?

The Second Chance

The Maharal next brings an allegory from the Gemara: There was a small city with a few people, and a great king came and surrounded it and built fortifications. A poor but wise person found the city, and rescued the whole city with his wisdom.

As the Maharal explains, the small city is a person's body, and its population is the person's various limbs. The great king who comes and surrounds it is the yetzer hara. The fortifications he builds are the person's sins.

This is a profound point. The yetzer hara uses a person's sins to destroy the person. The voice of the yetzer hara is: "You're bad! Destroy yourself!" The more you heed that voice and see yourself as sinful, the more you fall into the clutches of the yetzer hara.

I [SR] knew a person whom I'll call Arthur. Arthur did a lot of bad things in his life. He had several wives — one at a time — and he treated them terribly. He also was less than the ideal son and father. His fourth wife Nancy was a very sweet woman who came from a fine family in the Midwest. Gradually Nancy taught Arthur how members of a family should treat one another. Gradually she got him to realize the error of his ways.

At that point, Arthur was given a diagnosis of cancer. From his diagnosis to his death was less than a month. A few days before Arthur's death, I was speaking to Nancy on the phone. She started to cry and said, "He did this to himself."

"What do you mean?" I asked.

Between sobs Nancy replied, "Once he realized all the bad things he had done, he felt that he didn't deserve to live. He felt that he deserved to die." How tragic that Arthur did not realize the power of teshuvah to change the past!

This is the ultimate victory of the yetzer hara, who is also known as the "*Malach HaMavess*" — the Angel of Death. He uses a person's sins as the ultimate weapon to attack the person. Then the person doesn't even bother to defend himself. The battle is lost.

After recognizing the error of his ways, what should Arthur have done? Teshuvah!! This Gemara concludes the allegory by saying that a poor but wise person rescued the whole city with his wisdom. The poor, wise person is the yetzer hatov. What is his wisdom? Do teshuvah and good deeds!

Battle Plan #21: Let Your Sins Lead You To Teshuvah, Not Despair

Our response to our own sins should not be guilt and self-hatred. This is a major problem in modern society. Psychologists report that the number of people who deliberately hurt themselves by behaviors such as cutting or burning themselves has mushroomed. This sick, destructive behavior is a victory of the yetzer hara. The yetzer hara insinuates itself into the person's identity and whispers: "I did bad so I am bad." The evil king has taken over the city.

So how should we respond to our own or another's recognition of having done wrong? Not with denial: "It's not your fault. You're not really guilty. It was the way you were raised that's the culprit." No, the response should be teshuvah and good deeds: "This is what you did. This is where you were, but you're not going to stay there. You're going to move forward. You're going to do teshuvah. You're going to fix what can be fixed. And where you can't undo the damage, you're going to put the same amount of good, healing energy into the world that you put bad, destructive energy before."

The steps of teshuvah, according to the Rambam, are:

1. *Admit you did wrong.*

2. *Feel regret.*

3. *Take on for the future to act differently.*

4. *Ask forgiveness from the person you've hurt.*

5. *Make restitution when applicable.*

   For example, let's say a person was a harsh parent, who yelled and hit a lot. Twenty years later, when the child has grown up to become a drug addict, the parent realizes that he or she committed grave sins against this child.

Here are some wrong responses:

◆ *Denial: It wasn't my fault. I parented the way I was parented.*

◆ *Guilt: I did horrible things, and there's nothing to do about it now but eat myself up with guilt.*

◆ *Self-hatred: I'm a terrible person, and I deserve to suffer/injure myself/die.*

The right response is teshuvah:

1. *I admit I was an abusive parent.*

2. *I feel searing regret for the way I treated my child.*

3. *Starting right now, I will treat her differently. Where before I showed her anger and rejection, now I will try to show her love and acceptance. I will try to get her into the very best treatment program, and I'll pay for it. If she rebuffs my efforts, I will continue to try, perhaps indirectly through a different relative or friend. I will visit her often, and bring the kind of gifts she likes. I will make her feel loved.*

4. *I will beg her forgiveness for the way I treated her.*

5. *My yelling and hitting made her feel worthless; now I will try to give her self-worth. I will offer to pay for her education or training in an area where she has the capacity to succeed professionally.*

Sometimes it is impossible to undo the damage. A person who treated his parents disrespectfully cannot fix it once his parents have left this world. A person who repeatedly humiliated another cannot rebuild that person's self-esteem. A Jewish couple who gave up their special needs child for adoption and found out afterward that the child is being raised as a Mormon cannot revoke the adoption. How then is teshuvah possible?

A person can always bring parallel energies into the world. The disrespectful child can show posthumous honor to his parents by dedicating a book or a hospital room or a Torah lecture in their memory. The person who humiliated another can actively build people's self-esteem by validating them and showing them appreciation and acknowledgment. The couple who relinquished their special needs child can get involved in helping at institutions for such children, or alternatively, can involve themselves in anti-missionary work to ensure that Jewish children do not fall into the hands of missionaries.

Judaism is the religion of the second chance. The yetzer hara will do everything possible to convince you otherwise. Don't be deceived.

Let God Be God

In the Gemara under discussion and elsewhere in the Gemara, the yetzer hara is referred to as a king. Why? Because the yetzer hara always wants control. That part of us that refuses to relinquish control to anyone, even Hashem, is the yetzer hara.

This yetzer hara, this control freak, is of course always in competition with God, the true Ruler of the universe. The Gemara asserts that a person who becomes angry is like one who worships idols. A person who gets angry because her will was frustrated is like an idolater, because she is worshiping her own will — the way she wanted things to be — instead of Hashem's will — the way they indeed turned out.

The yetzer hara of control has been plaguing human beings since Gan Eden. The snake, the personification of the yetzer hara, tempted Adam and Chavah with the enticement that if they ate of the fruit of the Tree of Knowledge of Good and Evil they would be "like gods."

In fact, the essential Divine service of Rosh Hashanah, without which the new year and the Ten Days of Repentance cannot begin, is to crown Hashem King. This means acknowledging that Hashem, not us, rules the universe.

The yetzer hara of control, King Yetzer Hara, is one of the most difficult to defeat (which is why we have to do it all over again every Rosh Hashanah).

The yetzer hatov, on the other hand, is referred to as "a poor man." He's a poor man because he is humble. The yetzer hatov submits humbly to Hashem's rule by accepting situations as they are, because that's the way Hashem decided they should be:

◆ You tell your Shabbos guests that you plan to make Kiddush at 7:30 p.m. and you spend 10 minutes on the phone giving them detailed directions to your home. It's 8:15, everyone's stomach is growling, the children are losing it, and the guests have not yet arrived.

◆ If nothing else, the checkbook is your domain. But your spouse wrote a check and forgot to enter it.

◆ You have an important business meeting in another city. You make plane reservations allowing a generous two and a half hours to make your connecting flight. You board your flight at your home airport and then spend three hours waiting for the plane to take off from the runway.

◆ You have nonrefundable plane tickets to Israel for a family simchah. The morning you're supposed to leave, one of your children wakes up with measles.

In each of these scenarios and millions like them, the yetzer hara demands: Get angry! Blame! Feel bitter! (And your blood pressure shoots up accordingly.)

Yet the truth is: Hashem runs the world. And the more we let Him, the better things turn out.

I [TH] had two very different experiences during two lecture tours in America. On one tour, I was on my way to do a Shabbaton in Los Angeles, changing planes in Dallas. My flight into Dallas was two and a half hours late. The flight to L.A. — the last one I could possibly have made before Shabbos — was supposed to depart at 2:30. My flight into Dallas arrived at 2:50.

My only hope was that the L.A. flight was also delayed. When I deplaned in Dallas, one of America's largest airports, I asked the airline representative if the L.A. flight had left. She told me that indeed the flight to L.A. had not yet taken off, but I'd never make it, because it was due to depart in eight minutes from a different terminal. I thought to myself, "Hashem runs the world. If He wants me to spend Shabbos in L.A., I'll make that plane. And if He wants me to spend Shabbos in Dallas, that's where I'll be." Thus speaking to myself, I ran as fast as I could for the interterminal train. When I jumped on, I asked the driver how far away Terminal B was.

"Seven minutes," he answered. "What time's your flight?"

Breathless, I replied, "in six minutes."

He shook his head. "Lady, youse not gonna make that plane."

I responded: "It all depends on God. If God wants me to make it, I'll make it. And if God doesn't want me to make it, I won't."

The driver was a believer. "Yes, Ma'am!" he loudly agreed. "If the Lord wants you to make it, you'll make it. And if the Lord don't want you to make it, you won't make it. Praise the Lord!"

The driver and I were having our own revival meeting in the front of the train as the other passengers looked on incredulously.

As soon as the train stopped at Terminal B, I ran as fast as I could. I got to the gate and into the jet a moment before they closed the door. Baruch Hashem, I made the Shabbaton in Los Angeles.

On another tour, I was on my way to do a Shabbaton in Chicago. I had allowed myself plenty of time by booking an 11:30 a.m. flight that Friday morning, but when I arrived at the Newark airport, I discovered that my flight had been canceled. The next flight leaving for Chicago was at 1:30 p.m., but that flight was fully booked. I was number six on the waiting list.

I told myself that this would take ingenuity, determination, and hard cash. Standing in the waiting area, I announced out loud, "Who is number one on the waiting list?"

When a man identified himself, I offered him $500 to switch boarding passes with me. He was willing to do it. I felt very proud of myself until another passenger pointed out that the airlines would not permit switching boarding passes. Security demanded that a person board only with his or her own boarding pass.

The Shabbaton organizers in Chicago had invested too much time and energy for me to let them down. I had another idea. I offered the five people on the waiting list in front of me $200 each to take themselves off the list. That would use up virtually all my profits from the Shabbaton, but I was pleased with myself that my resourcefulness might save the Shabbaton.

After much eloquent salesmanship, I finally persuaded all five people to accept the deal. Suddenly, however, the loudspeaker announced that the flight to Chicago was delayed by half an hour. With mounting anxiety I waited, but every 30 minutes they announced another delay. I sat there saying Tehillim as my tension grew. Finally, I decided that if we didn't board by 3 o'clock, it would be too late to get to Chicago in time for Shabbos. At 3 o'clock, the plane was still not at the gate. I gave up and returned to Monsey.

The difference between these two experiences is that in the first crisis, I depended on Hashem and submitted to His will, however it would turn out. And, against all odds, it turned out great. In the second crisis, even though I said Tehillim, I regarded myself as in control of the situation. The result was disaster.

There are two compelling reasons to give up control of the world to Hashem:

◆ He controls it anyway. Acknowledging that is reality therapy. Whether the plane will take off on time, whether your child will get measles the day of the trip, whether all your vaunted plans and schemes will succeed is totally up to Hashem Yisbarach. You have dominion over only one domain: your own reaction. By resisting Hashem's will the only thing you change is your blood pressure.

◆ Hashem is more qualified than you to run the world. (Any arguments?)

Battle Plan #22:
Surrender Control To Hashem

When things do not go your way, and you start to lapse into anger or blame mode, see the yetzer hara as a dictatorial little king insisting: "It has to be my way!" In a later chapter we will discuss in depth the tool of visualization, but now to vanquish King Yetzer Hara we must actually visualize him: a cartoon character, a midget king with a crooked crown half his own height, wildly waving his scepter and proclaiming petulantly: "It has to be my way! It has to be my way!"

Off to the side, visualize the "poor, wise man" quietly repeating, "The way it is is the way Hashem wants it to be." Then choose who you want to rule you.

If you choose to terminate King Yetzer Hara, take a sledgehammer and hit him on the head. Flatten him like a pancake. That's all it takes. Your victory cry is: "The way it is is the way Hashem wants it to be. Hashem is my King."

The Essential Ingredient ◆

You eat a delicious dish and ask your hostess if she would mind sharing her recipe with you. She writes out the recipe for you. You go home and prepare the dish. You meticulously measure out the ingredients and assiduously follow each step of the recipe. The next day, you proudly serve the dish to your Shabbos guests. Something is wrong. It doesn't taste the same. One essential ingredient has been left out.

So far this book has presented you with twenty-two "recipes," battle plans for defeating the yetzer hara. At the conclusion of his treatise *Nesiv Ko'ach HaYetzer*, the Maharal proffers the essential ingredient without which none of the battle plans work.

That ingredient is prayer: appealing to Hashem to help you defeat the yetzer hara.

Without this essential ingredient, all the battle plans will be self-defeating, not yetzer hara-defeating. If you think, *Now I have all the state-of-the-art weapons in my arsenal. Now I know all the masterful strategies. I'm going to go out there on the battlefield and make mincemeat of the yetzer hara,* you have lost before you have even begun. The Torah warns that if you attribute victory to your own prowess, and you say, "My power and the strength of my hand have done all this," you doom yourself to ultimate defeat.

In a sobering vein, the Maharal cautions that every human being is created with the yetzer hara within, and he or she must continually struggle against it. Even if a person is a *tzaddik*, meaning that most of the time his thought, speech, and action are devoted to Hashem, he should not regard the defeat of the yetzer hara as easy, because in truth it is very hard.

"Hard" does not mean "impossible." Assessing the enemy force as formidable should lead not to despair, but instead to a firm resolution to use the essential battle plan of appealing to Hashem for help. In fact, most of us are willing to cry for help — whether to Hashem or a human being — only when we feel that we have no other resort.

One morning many years ago, I [SR] went to answer my doorbell. A young Arab man holding a sheath of papers was standing there. "I'm from the gas company," he announced in Hebrew.

"I didn't call the gas company," I replied, confused. "There's nothing wrong with our gas."

"The problem is out on the street," he asserted. "We're working out on the street. I have to check your gas connection in the kitchen."

I was inexperienced and foolish. Tentatively, I stepped aside, and he strode in. I followed him into the kitchen. There he pulled a knife out of his pocket.

I was alone in the house. My children were in school and my husband Leib was working in a music studio on the other side of Jerusalem. I had no way whatsoever of fighting this armed Arab. Terrified and desperate, I screamed for help. "LEIB! LEIB! COME HERE WITH YOUR GUN!"

Not knowing that Leib was nowhere within earshot and did not own a gun, the Arab panicked and fled.

Of course, calling out to a human being ("Police! Police!") is different than crying out to Hashem, but the principle is: When you are in desperate straits, rather than giving up, cry out! When the yetzer hara is poised to attack, and you cannot even remember any of the defensive strategies in this book, call out to Hashem to save you. The simple cry, "Hashem! Please save me!" can work wonders.

The Gemara calls the yetzer hara, "an old, foolish king." Nevertheless, points out the Maharal, this king has imprisoned us. A basic spiritual principle is: A prisoner cannot free himself from prison. We need someone on the outside to pass the key through the bars. That "someone" is Hashem.

By the way, internalizing this basic principle, that a prisoner cannot free himself from prison, should make us more compassionate toward others. When we see people who are imprisoned by their own baseness, their own pettiness, their own egocentricity, we should remember that they, too, are powerless to free themselves from their own prison. Everyone needs Hashem's help.

When you say, "*I can do it!*" even when "it" is a noble venture, you empower the very yetzer hara you're trying to defeat. When you say, "I can't do anything, Hashem, without Your help," you have already defeated the yetzer hara.

I [SR] worked hard to overcome the trait of anger for over two years. Along with five other women I attended a middos workshop led by Rav Leib Kelemen, who is a disciple of the great mussar master, Rav Shlomo Wolbe. I studied mussar teachings and did demanding daily exercises. After two years, I felt discouraged. Although I saw definite improvement, I still periodically lashed out in anger. I plaintively asked Rav Kelemen what I was doing wrong.

"Do you pray to succeed in your mussar work?" Rav Kelemen asked.

"Pray?" I was surprised. It had not even occurred to me.

"Even if you do everything right," Rav Kelemen told me, "without prayer you will never succeed."

The Midrash instructs us to pray for everything we need, even a shoelace. We might think that we must pray only for our material needs. The Maharal instructs us that we must pray also for success in our spiritual ventures.

Rebbetzin Hennie Machlis once took an older single woman to a famous *tzaddik* and Kabbalist for a blessing to get married. This woman was very intelligent, energetic, and determined, but so far all her efforts to get married had proven fruitless. The woman asked the Rav for his blessing, but he remained silent. She repeated her request. Silently, the rabbi curled the index finger of his right hand and straightened it again.

"What does that mean?" she asked, puzzled.

The Rav replied: "When you realize that you can't even do this," and he repeated the movement of his finger, "without Hashem, then you'll find your *zivug.*"

The initial choice must come from you: "I want to overcome anger." "I want to defeat the yetzer hara." And that choice must be followed by effort, such as utilizing the battle plans in this book. But the strength to fight and the situational backup to put victory within reach — all that comes from Hashem.

The most successful program for overcoming addictive and obsessive behavior is the Twelve Step Program (of Alcoholics Anonymous, Overeaters Anonymous, etc.). All the studies have proven that the Twelve Step Program works better than any other psychological approach or behavior modification system. The first two steps of The Twelve Step Program assert the futility of effort without turning to God for help. The first step is to admit that one has no power over alcohol (or overeating, etc.). The second step is to believe that a "Power greater than ourselves" can solve the problem. Conversely, all of the self-help programs that begin from the assumption, "I can do it!" never work.

The Maharal invokes two chilling examples of this point. He says that the Talmudic sage Rabbi Meir, whose exalted level we can't even begin to imagine, used to mock the yetzer hara. The yetzer told Rebbe Meir: "Had it not been declared in Heaven that I should not destroy you, I would have finished you off!" Similarly the great Rabbi Akiva used to mock people who sinned, as if overcoming the yetzer hara was child's play. The Satan declared: "Had it not been decreed on high, 'Watch out for Rabbi Akiva and his Torah,' I would have finished him off."

Thus the Maharal warns that a person should never say, "I can easily defeat the yetzer hara." Instead one should say, "Defeating the yetzer hara is very hard, and I need Hashem's help."

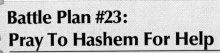

Battle Plan #23:
Pray To Hashem For Help

Every morning pray to Hashem in your own words to help you defeat the yetzer hara that day. Although the morning prayers include supplications such as, "Do not let the yetzer hara rule over us," it is easy to utter the formulated prayers by rote. Thus, supplement the siddur's prayers with your own heartfelt entreaty to Hashem to help you overcome the yetzer hara that is planning his nefarious attack today.

Your prayer should include these three elements:

1. Your earnest desire to overcome your yetzer hara.

2. Your awareness that you can't do it on your own.

3. Your plea to Hashem to help you succeed.

According to the Maharal, this is the secret ingredient that will, each day anew, grant you victory over the yetzer hara.

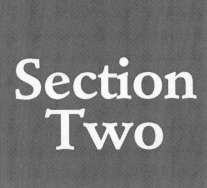

Section Two

Inspired by
the Writings of
the Ramchal,
Rav Moshe Chaim Luzzatto

Saved by the Goal

7

UNLIKE THE MAHARAL, THE RAMCHAL (RAV MOSHE Chaim Luzzatto) wrote no explicit treatises on the yetzer hara. However, as we shall see, his masterpiece *Mesillas Yesharim* is replete with wisdom and advice on how to attain higher spiritual levels, which of necessity entails doing battle with one's lower self.

The Ramchal begins with a profound principle: The foundation and root of all spiritual development is that a person should be clear about what his duty is in the world and to what he should direct his vision during all his labor every day of his life. In other words, the first step in spiritual growth is to be clear about the goal and the purpose of life. Most of us have daily goals (e.g., to get to the dentist on time or to go grocery shopping) or even a two-year plan (e.g., to get a master's degree), but we fail to see the varied events of our lives in the context of our ultimate purpose in this world.

The only war Israel ever lost was the Second Lebanese War. The Winograd Commission that investigated what went wrong had scathing criticism for the Israeli government's lack of a clear goal in the war. The war was sparked by Hezbollah's kidnapping two Israeli soldiers who were patrolling the border. But what, asked the Winograd Commission, was the goal of the war? To get back the two soldiers? To knock out Hezbollah's missiles pointed at Israel? To destroy the Lebanese infrastructure that was employed by the terrorists? Without a clearly defined goal, it is impossible to win a war.

Similarly, defeating the yetzer hara requires a clear, ultimate goal. Too often we fight our battles without relating them to the goal of the whole war. We try not to get angry, not to lie, not to give in to laziness, but the Ramchal teaches that all our spiritual striving must be rooted in a clear concept of our ultimate goal.

Different gedolei Yisrael have defined the goal of life differently. The Ramchal wrote that the goal is to cling to Hashem by doing mitzvos in this world so that in the Next World one can enjoy the light of the Divine Presence. The Gra said that the goal is to fix and refine one's character traits so that one can become more Godly. The Chassidic masters claimed that the goal is to bring spiritual light into a dark place, and through that to achieve deveikus between Hashem and His creation. Although their wording is different, they are all saying basically the same thing: The goal of life is a spiritual goal that requires striving to draw closer to Hashem.

As Rav Leib Kelemen is wont to say: "Closeness in the physical world is measured by distance; closeness in the spiritual world is measured by similarity." Thus, to draw closer to Hashem means to become more like Him and the middos He has revealed to us. This requires working on one's middos. In this light, the Gra's definition of the goal is the same as the others'.

All of the events of daily life can have either intrinsic or extrinsic value. Intrinsic value means that the activity is a goal in itself. Let's say you spent a good part of one day supervising the plumber who came to fix a leaky pipe. Having the pipe fixed could be a goal in and of itself, just like any of your daily activities: compiling a report at work, feeding the baby, or balancing the checkbook. Intrinsic

Let's apply this principle of seeing the larger picture, your ultimate purpose and goal, to your interaction with the plumber. Let's say you expect the plumber to take two hours to fix the leak. Instead, he works for four hours and at the end hands you a hefty bill. This leak was not part of your monthly budget to begin with (leaks never are), and now you feel resentful at having to pay for four hours of work. You feel like saying to the plumber: "This job shouldn't have taken four hours. You work slowly. Our old plumber could have done the job in two hours. I'll tell you what: let's compromise. I'll pay you for three hours."

This, of course, is a violation of halachah. Either you agree on a fixed price before the worker begins, or you have implicitly agreed to pay him his hourly wage. The time to argue about the price is before the job is done, not after. The yetzer hara is attacking. The bill in your hand assumes gigantic proportions until everything disappears from view except this big, unaffordable bill.

The Ramchal would advise: Step back and see the whole picture. If your goal in life is to draw close to Hashem by doing mitzvos, where do the plumber and his bill fit into that? It turns out that this mundane activity is really an opportunity to bond with Hashem by fulfilling the mitzvos pertaining to honesty in business. Seen in that context, your temptation not to pay the full amount would take you further away from your true goal. The big bill shrinks down to size as your true goal looms larger and larger.

The yetzer's trickery in *pirud* can lead to preposterous distortions of our values. Let's say you decide to attend a class in *hilchos Shabbos* that takes place at 8 o'clock Tuesday nights. Knowing that the class always starts promptly and it takes 20 minutes to get there, you walk out of your house at 25 minutes to 8. But, oh, no! There's a car blocking your driveway. A cursory glance up the street reveals that the neighbors must be having a party, and one of their guests is probably the culprit. Annoyed, you stride over to the neighbors and knock on the door. Of course, the din of the party prevents anyone from hearing your knock. After several minutes of knocking in vain, you are even more exasperated. You open the door and enter, but in the crowded living room, you can't find your neighbor. You walk through the dining room, kitchen, and patio, but your neighbor is nowhere to be found. By this time it's 10 to 8, you are late for your class, and you are furious. Finally, your neighbor appears. You feel like shouting at him: "One of your guests had the chutzpah to block my driveway. Now I'm late for an important appointment. I'm sick and tired of your loud, obnoxious parties. Your friends act like animals. I'm going to call the police."

If you would stop and ask yourself, "Why do I want to go to a class in *hilchos Shabbos*?" you might engage in the following inner dialogue:

"Because I want to learn the laws of Shabbos better."

"Why do you want to learn the laws of Shabbos better?"

"So I can fulfill them more perfectly."

"Why do you want to fulfill the mitzvos more perfectly?"

"So I can get closer to Hashem by doing His will."

"So if you want to get closer to Hashem, why are you yelling at your neighbor (and making a public *chilul Hashem* in the process)?"

Yesterday, I [SR] lent our car to my cousin, a young *talmid chacham*. I told him that I needed the car at 7 o'clock in order to pick up my son, who was returning from sleepaway camp. For various reasons, including congested traffic, my cousin was 25 minutes late in returning the car. As I stood outside Jaffa Gate, becoming increasingly impatient and critical, the mental image of my 14-year-old son getting off the bus with no one to greet him, and having to stand forlornly with his duffle bag while all the other campers left, loomed large in my mind. Then suddenly I thought of the Ramchal's teaching about stepping back and seeing the whole picture. *What is 25 minutes, I told myself, compared to eternity? My son will quickly get over his disappointment, but the sin of treating a talmid chacham disrespectfully will be with me for eternity.* At that point the car arrived. I got in without so much as a critical word or expression, and flattened the yetzer hara under the tires as I drove off.

The strategy of seeing the whole picture can fend off the yetzer's attack in many areas:

◆ Your children break an expensive object. Before yelling at them, ask yourself what's worth more in the big picture: the object or your children?

◆ You and your friend interview for the same job. Your friend gets the job instead of you. Disappointed and jealous, you're about to speak *lashon hara* about your friend. Ask yourself why you want the job, and reply to each answer with a further "Why?" until you get to your life's true goal.

◆ Your plane has been delayed four hours. You are stuck in the airport with nothing to eat. At the newsstand you find a candy bar with a dubious *hechsher*. You answer the yetzer's enticement, "What could be wrong with it? Eat it!" with the rebuttal: "For five minutes of pleasure is it worth surrendering my vision of myself as a kosher Jew?"

Battle Plan #24:
Zoom Out To See The Whole Picture

This battle plan has two steps:

1. Define your ultimate goal in life. Your goal should be spiritual and involve your soul and its relationship to Hashem. Your goal must be something eternal and transcendent, something that will be worthwhile long after your possessions, family, and your own physical body have vanished from this world. Write down your goal and internalize it.

2. Zoom out until the situation you are confronting is visible as part of a larger picture that includes your true goal.

Imagine you live too far away to attend your friend's vort. You ask her for a picture, and she e-mails a photo of her and her chassan at the vort. With anticipation, you scroll down in the e-mail to the photo. All you see is two chins and four nostrils. You scroll up slightly and then see four eyebrows and two hairlines. The photo is too big to see it all at once on your computer screen.

In order to see the whole picture, you have to zoom out. You find the zoom button. Now you have two possibilities:

◆ *You can keep pressing on the mouse and zoom out all at once. The picture becomes smaller, and now you can see the happy couple's smiling faces. This is the method employed in the example about the plumber above. You moved directly from your temptation to withhold part of his wages to remembering your true goal. With this weapon, you shrink down whatever situation is confronting you by comparing it with the magnitude of your true goal.*

◆ *You can click on the mouse once, reduce the size of the picture from 200 percent to 150 percent, then click on the mouse again and reduce the picture to 100 percent. If this is still too big, you keep clicking until the whole picture appears on the screen. This is the method employed in the example above about being blocked in while trying to go to a class. You ask yourself, "Why am I doing this?" Each answer leads to another "Why?" until you gradually arrive at your ultimate goal.*

Materialism

This same principle, of having a clearly defined, spiritual goal, can also save one from the trap of materialism.

The Ramchal writes:

> A person is placed in the midst of a raging battle. All the matters of this world are tests for a person — poverty on one hand and wealth on the other hand. ... To the extent that he has conquered his yetzer hara and his desires and dissociated himself from those things that distance him from ultimate good, and has made effort to cling to [ultimate good], to that extent will he attain [his true goal] and rejoice in it [Chapter 1].

Life is a raging battle, and a person must choose between this and that. Either a person chooses that which will draw him toward the spiritual goal of closeness to Hashem or a person chooses that which will draw him in the opposite direction: toward materialism, the domain of the yetzer hara. Often we try to kid ourselves that we can have both. But if you decide to travel to Jerusalem, you are by definition traveling away from Tel Aviv.

The Ramchal, at the end of the first chapter, quotes *Tehillim* 90:10: "Our days are 70 years, and for one with strength 80 years, and most of them are full of toil." He comments: "A person suffers so much in his life. There is always so much sickness, disappointment, anguish, and it always ends with death. Maybe one in a thousand has a life that one can describe as tranquil. But even if a person lives a long life, old age has its own ravages."

The Ramchal is saying that if your goal is material, it is doomed to be sabotaged by disappointments and in the end will be dashed by the ravages of old age or the finality of death. If your goal is to make money or buy a beautiful house, you certainly can't take it with you. If your goal is to be thin and young looking, no amount of makeup or face-lifts will get you past 70. If your goal is to travel to exotic places, what will you have to show for it in the end except photographs and fading memories?

I [TH] knew a woman who lived in Brooklyn who had as her goal to have a nice home on Long Island: a house with a deck and a big backyard. She and her husband worked for years to afford that house. Finally, when they were in their late 40's, they moved into their dream home. Their first night there, her husband died of a heart attack.

They had a material goal, and they achieved it. But death wrested away all satisfaction. How could she derive pleasure from the house in which she had suffered such a tragedy? Much to her friends' surprise, however, she did not move out of the house. Instead, she let the souring of her dream become a turning point. She redefined her whole life and began a spiritual search. Eventually she found Torah and became fully observant. She learned the hard way that material goals invariably lead to disappointment.

Materialism is a snare to the extent that we confuse it with true good, which by definition is spiritual, not material. There is a game we play with ourselves. We admit that crass materialism — three-carat diamonds, fancy cars, designer suits — drags us away from true good. But what about rarefied materialism, such as a home in the mountains where you can immerse yourself in the beauty of nature? We admit that a triple ice-cream sundae is giving into physical desire, but what about seven-grain bread? For some people, seven-grain bread is almost holy. In truth, health food is no more holy than a triple ice-cream sundae if you confuse it with "ultimate good." If your definition of ultimate good applies to anything material or physical, it will take you away from Hashem.

The Ramchal points out that in terms of materialism, either extreme — wealth or poverty — can trap you. He quotes *Mishlei* that a rich person may feel so satiated and independent that he denies God, while a poor person may feel so deprived that he steals. Both are snares of the yetzer hara. People mistakenly think that materialism means having a fat bank account, but a poor person can be equally materialistic. The definition of "materialism" is: equating ultimate goodness with material possessions.

The Ramchal pointedly asks: "If humans were created just for this world, why would Hashem give us a spiritual soul that is so high, higher even than angels?" He illustrates this point with a metaphor: A commoner who is both sophisticated and wealthy marries a princess. He showers her with luxuries, but whatever he gives her is not enough for her, because he can't give her the nobility that her royal self craves. Similarly, no amount of art, shopping at exclusive boutiques, or first-class travel to exotic places can satisfy the soul, because the soul is from a spiritual source that cannot be satisfied by materialism.

The Ramchal continues by asserting that mitzvos, on the other hand, do bring the soul satisfaction, wholeness, and a sense of completion:

> *The person will immediately understand the significance of the mitzvos and he'll treasure the service which is in our hands to do, because these are the means that bring a person to his true completion. Without [the mitzvos] nothing is achieved at all. And it's known that the true purpose is not to gather more and more means, but it's where the means take a person. ... Therefore a person will be very careful with the mitzvos and will see that the mitzvos are done with perfection, the same way a person is careful when weighing out pure gold and pearls, because of their great preciousness. A person's perfection for which he was born can be achieved only through the mitzvos.*
>
> *... A person should be goal oriented. His goal is to get closer to Hashem, and to break down all the partitions that separate him from Hashem [Chapter 1].*

Judaism does not disdain the material world. Hashem created physical objects for us to elevate them by using them for mitzvos. But a Jew should be absorbed by the pursuit of spiritual goals, not material goals. Imagine Rav Sternbuch contributing money to a *tzeddakah* organization that is running a raffle. That could easily happen. And, as luck would have it, Rav Sternbuch wins the prize of dinner for two at Jerusalem's fanciest kosher restaurant. How long would it take him to give the prize away? Not because the fancy restaurant is bad, but because he wouldn't relinquish two hours of his precious time that he could utilize learning Torah or issuing halachic rulings to eat a gourmet meal.

It actually happened that once one of the religious newspapers had a raffle, and every subscriber was automatically enrolled. Of course, the winners were chosen by computer, with no one even paying attention to the names. A set of luxury bath towels was won by none other than Rav Elyashiv! If you have ever seen the sparse, two-room apartment in which the Elyashivs raised 10 children, you will know how incompatible luxury towels are with Rav Elyashiv's lifestyle. Not because luxury towels are bad, but if you're going in one direction, toward a spiritual goal, then you're not going in the other direction, toward materialism. The result will be simplicity in the material realm. Can you imagine Moshe Rabbeinu trying to choose between three microwaves?

This does not mean that we all have to live in two sparse rooms. If you're traveling to Jerusalem, you'll necessarily be traveling away from Tel Aviv, but only if you start at a point between the two cities. If you start your journey in Haifa, you will have to pass through Tel Aviv on your way to Jerusalem. Similarly, our relationship to materialism depends on where we start out. Some of us have ample material resources; most of us do not. Let's say you need a new dining-room set. You go shopping and find a gorgeous mahogany set, with 16 chairs beautifully upholstered and a huge breakfront with beveled glass. Would buying such a set mean moving away from your spiritual goal?

It depends where you are. If you don't have the money in your bank account to purchase that dining-room set, buying it will mean obligating yourself to monthly installment payments beyond what you and your spouse are currently earning. That means that one or both of you will have to take an extra job. If the husband takes an extra job, he does so during time that he could have spent learning Torah. If the wife takes an extra job, she does so during time she could have spent with her children. In both cases, the either/or choice has been made in favor of materialism, and away from the spiritual goal of learning Torah or rearing children.

But what if you do have the money to buy the dining-room set without sacrificing any of your time or energy? Then buy it, and use it for mitzvos such as *hachnassas orchim* and *oneg Shabbos.* Then you will be passing through Tel Aviv on your way to Jerusalem. Then you will be using the material for the sake of your spiritual goal.

In fact, the Ramchal asserts that if you honestly and consistently use your material resources in order to take you closer to your spiritual goal, then materialism does not sabotage you. At the end of *Mesillas Yesharim,* in Chapter 26, he writes:

> *If a person endeavors to transcend and distance himself from materialism completely and to achieve deveikus in Hashem moment by moment ... then even at the time he's busy with material pursuits that his body demands, his soul is not going to abandon its consistent state of deveikus. ... A person in that state could be attached to Hashem all of the time, and his [physical] nature won't hold him back. His physical acts are indeed holy. His eating and his drinking are comparable to the state of people in the Beis HaMikdash when they ate of the offerings.*

The classical example of this is Rabbi Yehudah HaNasi, who was fantastically wealthy. On his deathbed, he held up his 10 fingers heavenward and declared, "It is known before You that I have toiled with my 10 fingers in Torah, and I didn't benefit [from this world] even with my pinkie finger" [*Kesubos* 104a].

A modern-day example of this exalted relationship to material things is Rebbetzin Sima Horowitz, the daughter-in-law of the Bostoner Rebbe. Blessed with abundance, she is a master of using it for mitzvos. When she hears of a girl who's depressed, she takes her out to lunch and a frum fashion show at a five-star Jerusalem hotel, making her feel like a princess. Visiting a dying woman in the hospital, Rebbetzin Horowitz took along her laptop and played a video of the Miami Boys Choir, which cheered up the sick woman and broke through her depression. Over the years, she has hosted dozens of elegant parlor meetings in her home to benefit numerous *tzeddakah* organizations.

Another example is a family who bought a beautiful apartment directly opposite the Kosel. They let people in the community use their home for Brissos and Bar Mitzvahs, and they frequently host classes and Sheva Berachos.

The path of using material things for your spiritual goal demands rigorous honesty. The yetzer hara will definitely try to fool you and will convince you that whatever you desire is really for a lofty purpose. The test comes when a family with 10 children knocks frantically on your door 15 minutes before Shabbos, explaining that they got stuck on the expressway and will never make it to their Shabbos destination. When you allow them to stay with you, and their children spill wine on your upholstered chairs and get their fingerprints all over the beveled glass and scratch the legs of the mahogany table, how will you react? If deep down you feel that Hashem gave you this dining-room set so that you should own it and thus bolster your prestige, you will be upset at the vandalism of your property. If, on the other hand, you sincerely feel that Hashem gave you the dining-room set in order to share it and sanctify it, you will feel satisfied that it is serving its purpose.

Materialism is not a function of how much money you have or how many possessions you own. Materialism is a function of how much you need material things to give you a sense of being actualized and successful.

So when you are debating whether or not purchasing X is surrendering to the yetzer hara of materialism, ask yourself these two questions:

◆ Why am I buying it?

◆ What am I paying for it in terms of time and emotional energy?

Then, if you chose to deny yourself the material pleasure of buying X, make sure you put spiritual pleasure in its place. Otherwise, the yetzer hara, which lost the first battle, will win the second by engendering a feeling of resentment and deprivation. So if you're not going to buy those emerald earrings because they are beyond your budget, treat yourself to a cab ride to Kever Rachel next time you're in Jerusalem or the time off and a babysitter to go to a lecture by your favorite Rabbi or Rebbetzin.

Here is a false equation:

The less you own = the holier you are

Not owning designer clothes does not make you holy. The true equation is:

Holiness = your decision to make getting close to Hashem your life's goal, and aligning your day-to-day choices with that goal

The Ramchal's point is that your ultimate, spiritual goal should illuminate your choices, both when you're standing in shul and when you're standing in Wal-Mart.

Battle Plan #25:
Choose Spirituality Over Materialism

It is the third day of the Six-Day War. You are part of the unit charged with capturing Jerusalem's Old City, Har HaBayis, and the Kosel. You enter the Old City through Lion's Gate, and start to run south toward Har HaBayis and the Kosel. Suddenly a scruffy soldier with his helmet pulled down low over his eyes grabs your arm and says, "Don't go that way. Come with me. During the night, all the rich Arab merchants fled with the Arab Legion. Their stores, full of gold jewelry, silk brocades, and precious artifacts, are there for the taking, over there to the north."

Do you choose to go south and fight for Har HaBayis and the Kosel, or north and fight for untold wealth? To the extent that you see yourself as a soldier fighting a war that has a goal you will not allow yourself to detour in the opposite direction. You will not heed the enticements of the scruffy soldier, who is none other than the yetzer hara. You'll want to win the war more than you'll want to bring home loot.

The battle against materialistic yearnings can be won by this three-part battle plan:

1. *(The same weapon as Battle Plan #24) Define your ultimate goal in life. Your goal should be spiritual and involve your soul and its relationship to Hashem. Your goal must be something eternal and transcendent, something that will be worthwhile long after your possessions, family, and your own physical body have vanished from this world. Write down your goal and internalize it.*

2. *Admit that you can't move in two opposite directions. You have to choose between emotional commitment to spiritual progress and emotional commitment to material advancement.*

3. *Now choose.*

Self-observation 8

I T IS NIGHTTIME IN THE MOUNTAINS OF SOUTH Lebanon. Your tank squad is assigned to take Hilltop 63, a major Hezbollah hideout. No matter how state of the art your tank is, no matter how expert your tank's gunner is, the success of your mission depends on your tank's navigator. The navigator's job is to keep his eye on the hi-tech compasses that meticulously track the direction the tank is moving. If the tank is even a fraction of one degree off, the navigator must tell the driver to change course. If the navigator fails to do so, your tank's battle for Hilltop 63 is lost before it even begins.

The navigator is the exercise known as "*cheshbon hanefesh.*" This means taking time every day to review your thoughts, speech, and actions, and to assess whether they are taking you toward or away from your spiritual goal. In Chapter 2, the Ramchal writes:

We have to be careful and notice what we're doing. ... If a person has the intelligence to save himself and escape from his soul's perishing, how could he not stop and look at what he's doing? A person who doesn't is like an animal. A person who goes through life without questioning where he is going is like a blind man walking at the edge of the sea. ...

Really, this is one of the most deceitful ploys of the yetzer hara: to apply heavy pressure on the hearts of people until they don't have any spare time to reflect on and scrutinize the path they are on. For the yetzer hara knows that if they were to pay even minimal attention to their ways, of course they would immediately begin to regret their actions, and that regret would lead them to abandon their sins entirely. This is what Pharaoh did when he wouldn't give the Jews any time to stop working, because he knew that if they had any time [to evaluate their situation], they would use it to get out of Egypt.

This is exactly the strategy of the yetzer hara against human beings, because the yetzer is a seasoned soldier, well versed in deception.

The Ramchal is clear: The yetzer hara gives high priority to keeping us from taking the time to reflect on our actions and to question in which direction our lives are moving. Thus, we cannot win the battle against the yetzer hara without periodically doing *cheshbon hanefesh.*

Cheshbon hanefesh must have three components:

◆ Review what you did and said throughout the day.

◆ Evaluate whether particular actions and words took you closer to or further from your spiritual goal.

◆ If closer, endorse yourself. If further, do teshuvah. This means admitting and regretting what you did wrong, and making a plan to do better in the future.

Here's a sample *cheshbon hanefesh* for a working mother:

1. **I got up and davened.** *Did I daven with kavannah? It was much better than the way I was davening last year, before*

I started reading the book about prayer. I still have a long way to go, so I'll keep reading that book for five minutes every morning before I start davening.

2. **I got my children off to school.** *Did I do it without anger? No, I got angry at my youngest when he ran back into the house at the last minute to get some non-essential item and almost missed the bus. I scolded him and said what I never want to say. I called him, "a slowpoke." Still, I did better than I used to do. A couple months ago when he would pull that stunt, I would lose control. So I've improved somewhat. Still, I should try to make it up to him. What can I do to control my anger when the kids are late?*

3. **I went to work at the office.** *Did I work with integrity? Did I steal my employer's time? Well, I did take a call from my sister on my cell phone and talk for 10 minutes, even though my employer does not permit private conversations at work. And I took an extra 15 minutes at lunch break, because I had to run out to the optometrist and get my glasses fixed. I suppose that's stealing time, which is forbidden by halachah. The only way to do teshuvah on that is to work 25 minutes longer tomorrow. I guess I'll work during my lunch break. But I did do something big: When the boss announced that Joan got the promotion I was hoping to get, I overcame my jealousy and sincerely felt happy for Joan. Also, during coffee break I had a victory: When Deena started to speak lashon hara, I immediately changed the subject, although I was dying to hear what she had to say. I get a pat on the back for that.*

4. **I stopped at the supermarket to buy some stuff on my way home.** *Did I act in accordance with halachah? Well, because I was rushing, I knocked over a jar of marinara sauce, which broke. I didn't tell the cashier to charge me for the jar since it was my fault. By the Torah's definition, that's stealing. So next time I go to that supermarket, I have to pay for the jar of marinara sauce.*

5. My after-work hours at home. *I overcame my tiredness and made a nice dinner. When my husband came home, I didn't besiege him with complaints about how hard my day was. (I've been working on that one.) I did lose it when I was trying to bathe the kids and my little one kept running from room to room. I think I'll go to that parenting class on Tuesday nights (no matter how tired I am) and try to learn ways to get the kids to do the right thing without yelling. I did score a victory over my yetzer hara to stay up late at night and do housework. I said to myself: "It's more important to get a good night's sleep and be less likely to yell at my kids tomorrow than to have a clean house," and I went to bed. Three cheers for me.*

Battle Plan #26:
Do *Cheshbon Hanefesh*

Like the battle plans in the previous chapter, you must start with defining your life's goal. You cannot assess whether you are moving in the right direction if you have not clearly defined the goal you want to reach.

For example, let's say you are moving to a new apartment, and the moving men leave your boxes outside your door rather than carrying them into the apartment. If your life goal is to fix your character traits, especially your greatest weakness, the trait of anger, and if you know yourself well enough to know that if you start to reprimand them, you will end up getting angry and screaming, you might therefore choose to say nothing at all. Since your goal is to not get angry, your cheshbon hanefesh that night will reveal that you scored a big victory. If, however, you have a different goal, which is to stop being a "people pleaser" and to stand up for what is right despite other people's disapproval, because you know that your fear of other people's opinion of you often causes you to sin, then not insisting that the moving men bring your cartons inside would be a failure. Without a clearly defined goal, it is impossible to do cheshbon hanefesh.

Basic cheshbon hanefesh requires taking time every day to mentally review your actions and assess whether they took you toward or away from your life's goal. Review your day chronologically. When you pinpoint something you did that took you further away from your life's goal, do teshuvah. This means to admit what you did wrong, feel regret, and make a concrete plan for how to avoid future failure. If you hurt another human being, you must also apologize and make restitution. (E.g., if you stole 15 minutes of your boss's time, work 15 minutes longer tomorrow.)

When you note a spiritual victory, endorse yourself. Just as positive reinforcement motivates children to behave better, so endorsing your good actions encourages you to repeat them. The yetzer hara will tell you: "It's childish to cheer for yourself. It inflates your ego to pat yourself on the back." Don't believe him. He's lying. Proper cheshbon hanefesh requires full disclosure of both the bad and the good. When the navigator notes that you are off course, you must change your behavior. When the navigator notes that you are on course, hit the accelerator and go full steam ahead!

Battle Plan #27: Do A Life Review

A life review is a special kind of chesbon hanefesh. Instead of doing it every day, you do it once a year, in Elul. Sometimes doing it once in a lifetime is sufficient.

The method for life review comes from the classic book, Cheshbon HaNefesh. It must be done in writing, and takes several hours. It's worth buying a notebook specifically for your life review.

1. Divide your life into periods. At the top of each page write the name of the period. E.g., childhood years, teenage years, college, single years after college, married years until our first child was born, etc.

2. On each page, write the central events of that period of your life. Under teenage years, for example, you might write:

    ◆ My grandfather passed away.

    ◆ I was star of my school play.

    ◆ I failed algebra, and had to repeat it during the summer.

    ◆ Our family went on a trip to Canada.

    ◆ My best friend moved away in 11th grade.

3. Write next to each event what your response was to that event. For example:

    ◆ My grandfather's death: I was angry with Hashem. I expressed my anger by not davening for several weeks.

    ◆ I was star of my school play: I felt as if I was the best, most talented person in the world. I was vain and obnoxious to my friends.

4. From what you consider to be your life's goal today, which of your responses brought you closer to where you want to be, and which took you further away?

5. What motivated you to make the good choices? What motivated you to make the bad choices?

The life review is like a spiritual M.R.I. It will reveal to you the inner workings of your psyche. As you do your *life review, a pattern will emerge in the answers to the fifth question. You will notice that the same two or three motivations kept cropping up for your good choices, and the same two or three motivations kept cropping up for your bad choices. Then it will be transparent to you what are your principal negative traits (those you have to work on redirecting), and what are your principal positive traits (those you have to strengthen).*

And then you will have installed a state-of-the-art navigating system to get you to your life's goal.

The Melech

Jerusalem was destroyed both by the Babylonians and the Romans. Both armies invaded at Jerusalem's most vulnerable point, the northern wall of the city. The topography on the north side of Jerusalem, where the bedrock is high, makes the northern wall a vulnerable place for enemy attack.

Classical Jewish thought recognizes three centers in a person:

◆ The mind, which is the seat of the intellectual process

◆ The heart, which is the seat of emotions

◆ The body (referred to as "the kidneys"), which is the seat of bodily drives and actions

As the Ramchal explains in Chapter 3, both the heart and the body are particularly vulnerable to the enemy attack of the yetzer hara. The heart and the body are "the northern wall." Once the enemy has penetrated either the heart or the body, it sends deceptive messages to the mind, which then distorts reality so that all cognition is skewed and warped. In this way, the yetzer hara wins full control of the person.

For example, let's say you work in an office. A new person, Sam, is hired who is really superior to you in some ways. Your heart responds with a spate of negative emotions: fear that you might be fired and replaced by Sam; jealousy that Sam is better than you and might be given the preferred assignments; and arrogance that you have worked for the company longer and have more experience in this job.

These emotions in turn dictate actions to the body. You might speak lashon hara about Sam to your co-workers. You might lie about Sam to your supervisor. You might try to pull the rug out from under Sam by giving advice that you know will lead to the boss's displeasure.

Similarly, when the body is the one issuing commands, the whole system is compromised. Hunger, for example, can convince the mind that the hechsher of the unknown Rabbi Morton Jones from Perth, Australia is a perfectly reliable hechsher on that candy bar the body is craving.

BATTLE PLAN #28: *MELECH*

This battle plan, which means "king," is the acronym for mo'ach [brain], lev [heart], and kelayos [kidneys=body]. When the chain of command is in this order, meaning that the mind rules the heart, which then commands the body, the person is under the sovereignty of the true King, HaKadosh Baruch Hu.

For the mind to rule, it must subdue the shouting demands of the heart and the body. It accomplishes this by applying a rigorous intellectual process of questioning the allegations of the emotions and the physical drives.

For example, in the scenario above where the new person is hired, and your negative emotions convince your body to stoop to various bad actions, applying this battle plan of "Melech" requires you to place your mind in control.

As explained in the previous chapter, an effective question for the mind to ask is: "Is this behavior bringing me closer to my true goal?" The heart may answer: "Yes! My goal is to keep my job and get rid of this intruder and competitor!" The mind, however, must always retain a clear picture of one's true, spiritual goal. The mind, therefore, responds: "No! My true goal is to develop those character traits that bring me closer to Hashem." Then the mind assesses whether the behavior of the body is achieving that goal or not. Since lashon hara and lies are counterproductive to the true goal, the mind realizes it has been duped by the heart.

Once the mind has taken control, it dictates to the heart the emotions it should feel. A new person has been hired? I should feel welcoming and accepting. What about my insecurity about my job? I should feel motivated to work harder so I will not be replaced.

The properly chastised heart then directs the body: Speak to Sam in a welcoming way, show Sam the ropes, and perform better in my job. When you are under the attack of the yetzer hara, your mind must formulate a defensive strategy. What will I say if the boss asks my opinion about Sam? How will I handle the flood of emotions if Sam gets the assignment I want? Take the time and energy necessary to think through the optimum responses to various scenarios.

A vital secret component of this battle plan is that the yetzer hara operates only in the present. If you can delay your actions, the mutiny of the heart and the body will subside and your mind will be able to assume control. The yetzer hara will fight the command, "Don't," but it often heeds the command, "Later."

Standing by the water cooler during coffee break, when your emotions are bubbling up, goading you to speak lashon hara, is not the time to apply this battle plan. Let your mind direct your mouth, "Later. Just wait till tomorrow." Then, at home that evening, take the time to let the

> mind examine the issue, question the knee-jerk response of the emotions, and evaluate whether the behavior of the body is in keeping with your true values and goals.
>
> Who is ruling my life? Who is the King? These questions themselves defeat the yetzer hara.

In terms of self-observation and reflection, the Ramchal also advocates the practice of *hisbodedus,* which he defines as "isolation from society in order to turn one's heart toward Divine service," and *hisbonenus,* reflection on what one's service should be [Chapter 14]. In fact, *Mesillas Yesharim* contains many references to *hisbodedus* and *hisbonenus.* For example, in Chapter 21, the Ramchal writes: "For this a person must isolate himself in his rooms and gather all his knowledge and reflection ..." Rather than discuss this method at length here, we have chosen to present *hisbodedus* in Chapter 14, using the recommendations of Rebbe Nachman of Breslov, who is well known for encouraging the practice of *hisbodedus.* However, it is worthwhile for the reader to know that the Ramchal recommended *hisbodedus* more than a century before Rebbe Nachman.

Losing Through Laziness

9

DURING THE EIGHT-YEAR-LONG WAR BETWEEN Iraq and Iran, Saddam Hussein's biggest problem was motivating his troops to continue fighting. His soldiers had no zeal to give up their lives for their tyrannical leader and his ambitions. The reluctance to fight was so prevalent that Iraqi soldiers were forbidden to own any white items of clothing, even underwear, lest they use them as flags of surrender.

The most well-equipped and best-trained army in the world will not emerge victorious without a burning zeal to fight and win. In Chapter 6 of *Mesillas Yesharim*, the Ramchal tackles the problem of laziness. We tend to think that the yetzer hara of laziness attacks only slothful, indolent personalities. The Ramchal reveals that we all, even the most dynamic and energetic among us, have to battle laziness. Laziness is the inclination to abstain from any positive action.

Laziness is one of the most insidious ploys of the yetzer hara because the yetzer of laziness does not prompt a person to do bad;

it prompts him to do nothing at all. A *cheshbon hanefesh* at the end of the day will reveal no angry outbursts, no lashon hara, no petty theft. Instead of black spots, one's record is lily white. But those blank spaces could be the spiritual death of a Jew.

Laziness is, in fact, inherent in the human condition. The Ramchal explains that the grossness of the physical body is man's nature. The body, which is made of earth, yearns for passivity. The soul, which is made of firelike spirit, yearns to do and to move. The body drags one down; the soul impels one upward. The more one identifies with one's body, the lazier he will be. And the voice of the yetzer hara of laziness is always: "Don't act."

The Ramchal describes how laziness eventually leads to sin. First is the process of intellectual laziness. You face a situation, and you don't know if the Torah permits it or prohibits it. Out of laziness, you don't bother to go and ask a Rav. Instead, you *paskin* for yourself. And, of course, you decide in favor of whatever is easier. The next step is that you justify your decision: It *should be* permitted. You write your own script as you go along, and you're sure the conclusions you have reached are correct.

A different kind of laziness is emotional laziness. This manifests as reluctance to commit to a worthy cause, to embark on a worthwhile project, or to become involved in an important issue. One of my [TH] sons confronted this kind of laziness last Chanukah. He got the idea to disseminate a prayer that the Jewish soldiers held captive by the Arabs be freed. This did not require going to a rally. His idea was that after lighting the Chanukah candles, everyone should say a prayer for the captive soldiers. He went to many major rabbis and obtained their signed endorsement of the idea. He had fliers printed and circulated them around some of the religious communities in Israel. Everyone thought it was a good idea, but the campaign failed. Even people who had agreed to participate told my son that they "forgot" to say the prayer, while most of Klal Yisrael just didn't get on board. Why? It wasn't physical laziness, because the only effort a person had to expend was to say a one-minute prayer. It was emotional laziness. People were reluctant to make an emotional commitment to a project that might not succeed.

How sad that we are afraid to be passionate about things that are important, while we are unduly passionate about wanting pizza with mushrooms and not onions!

The last kind of laziness is physical laziness. As the Ramchal explains, a person knows what's right to do, but physical laziness keeps her from doing it. She knows she should go to that class, attend that *tzeddakah* event, or help that friend, but the yetzer hara of laziness proffers all kinds of excuses, which the Ramchal lists:

◆ I have to eat dinner first.

◆ I'll just take a little nap before I go.

◆ It's hard for me to leave the house.

◆ It's too hot to go.

◆ It's too cold to go.

◆ It's raining too hard.

Checking for shaatnez is an example of how physical laziness may deliver us into the hands of the yetzer hara. Last summer I [SR] bought a linen jacket and skirt. There was no shaatnez checking depot in my neighbor. In order to check my new garments for shaatnez, I would have had to drive 40 minutes in congested traffic across town or walk 25 mintues in the wilting heat into Meah Shearim. I was disinclined to do either, so I told myself that, while it is logical that a wool garment may contain linen thread, because linen thread is strong, it is illogical that a linen garment would contain wool thread, because wool thread is weak. (This is a classic example of the body feeding lines to the mind. See Battle Plan #28 in the previous chapter.) Of course, the truth is I knew nothing about the relative strength of various fibers, the process of garment manufacture, or the accuracy of the "100% linen" label. I just didn't want to expend the effort to take my new clothes to the Shaatnez Lab, and then have to repeat the trek a week later to pick them up. A few weeks later, my *chesbon hanefesh* (see Battle Plan #26) revealed to me that I was remiss. I took the linen garments to the Shaatnez Lab, and asked Rabbi Gurwitz, who was in charge, if my linen jacket really needed to be checked. He told me that just a week before, he had found wool thread fastening the button on a linen jacket. That was real shaatnez, so every minute the owner wore that jacket, she would have been guilty of transgressing a *mitzvah d'Oraisa*. I have since made my home the shaatnez checking depot of our neighborhood, bringing in Rabbi Gurwitz at regular intervals. Judging by how many already-worn garments are brought to us for shaatnez checking, apparently I am not the only Jew who suffers from this form of laziness.

The voice of the yetzer hara of laziness is, "Don't do." Zeal is the stance that counteracts laziness. Zeal is a daring, almost *chutzpadik* retort of "I'm going to do it anyway." When the yetzer hara says, "Don't go! It's raining too hard!" zeal retorts jauntily, "I'm going anyway. I'll take an umbrella."

My [TH] granddaughter, who is in the ninth grade, recently devised a zealous response to the yetzer hara of "don't do." A new girl joined the class in midterm. She is shy, not that bright, and doesn't wear the right clothes: a perfect candidate for ostracism. My granddaughter knew that the right thing to do was to befriend this girl, but many persuasive reasons held her back. When you are 14 years old and worried about your own popularity, the yetzer's voice of "Don't ally yourself with a neb" can be deafening. She was torn between what she knew was right to do and her fear of social isolation if she did it. So she devised a daring plan. She convinced two other girls to join her in the mitzvah of befriending the new girl. This was her version of "I'll take an umbrella."

I [TH] knew a girl who was about to get married. She didn't have much money, and needed to buy a good *sheitel*, so I sent her to the huge *sheitel* sale that takes place in Har Nof a couple of times during the year. The *sheitels*, most of which are donated, are sold for half price or less, so you can imagine the scene: like a 60 percent off sale at Macy's. Now, on the one hand, I felt reluctant to send this poor kallah to the sale. She is a baalas teshuvah, from the American South, and not at all aggressive. I knew that at best she would stand helplessly on the outer fringes of the stampeding crowd and would end up with the worst sheitel. At worst, she would get trampled. On the other hand, she needed a good deal on a *sheitel* that she could buy cheap. I was therefore amazed when she returned from the sale with a beautiful custom *sheitel.*

Only later did the mystery unravel. I have a friend whom I'll call Gittel. Gittel is the perfect shopper for such a sale. She's in her 50's, from Boro Park, and is expert at two crucial skills: how to pick out a great *sheitel* and how to push. Gittel had no intention of going to the sale because she owns a new custom *sheitel.* The day of the sale, however, she had to go to an important meeting, and she couldn't find her good *sheitel.* It wasn't on the *sheitel* head; it wasn't in the closet; it wasn't in the bathroom. Her house is not like my house. In my house, an elephant could disappear. Her house is neat and orderly. How could a *sheitel* just vanish? She searched everywhere, to no avail. Finally, she remembered that there was a *sheitel* sale. She ran over, found a gorgeous *sheitel*, and was about to buy it.

Then she noticed the kallah, standing shyly at the edge of the crowd. It occurred to her that the gorgeous *sheitel* would look really good on this girl. An inner voice prompted: "Do something great. Give the *sheitel* to this girl." Her yetzer hara shouted: "Don't do it! Why should you? You found the *sheitel.* You need the *sheitel* to go to your meeting. Don't do it! Don't!"

Gittel clobbered her yetzer hara. In an act of spiritual daring, she handed the *sheitel* to the girl. When she went home, she found her own *sheitel* in the middle of her bedroom floor. It was all a test from Hashem of how spiritually daring she could be.

According to the Ramchal, the rejoinder to the voice of the yetzer hara of laziness is to challenge all choices not to act. He offers a general principle: "Every leniency [or concession] requires cross-examination." The Ramchal goes on to explain: "Even though it's possible that [the leniency] is right and reasonable, it is usually the prompting of the yetzer hara and his wiles. Therefore, one must check out and investigate and scrutinize it greatly. If after all this [investigation] it seems justified, then certainly it is okay."

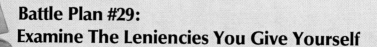

Battle Plan #29: Examine The Leniencies You Give Yourself

Whenever a worthy action (a mitzvah or a chesed) occurs to you, whether you see a poster, are invited by a friend, or think of it spontaneously, before you decide not to do it, carefully examine your reluctance. Challenge your reasons for not acting. Is this reason really an insurmountable obstacle or just an excuse? Would it really be better not to do it? And, given that every choice we make is like getting on a train that takes us to a particular destination, the most important pair of questions is:

❖ ***If I do it, where will that take me?***

❖ ***If I don't it, where will that take me?***

Let's say Yad Eliezer is having a Sunday brunch as a fund-raiser. You see the notice and think: "I can't go. I can't afford the ticket." This battle plan recommends that you cross-examine yourself: "What's my real reason for not wanting to go? Could it be that Sunday morning is my only morning to relax? True, we are short of money now, but is there no way I could afford it? What if I split the cost in half and give them two post-dated checks? If I go to the fund-raiser, where will that take me? It will make me a more charitable person, I'll be publicly supporting a worthy cause, and I'll be giving chizuk to the volunteers who organized the brunch. If I don't go to the fundraiser, where will that take me? I'll save $36 and get a Sunday morning to relax and read a magazine. Who would I rather be: charitable me or me lazing on the couch?"

Not all leniencies that we give ourselves are bad. Let's say that it's two hours before Shabbos, your cooking is almost completed, and you're about to take a much-needed nap so that you can enjoy Shabbos without yawning away during the seudah. Suddenly the phone rings. Your friend's Shabbos plans fell through. Can you host her family of six for a meal? You say, "Yes." Then you realize that you don't have enough dessert for six more people. On Thursday you had prepared an elegant dessert in parfait cups, exactly enough for the number you had been expecting. To make more parfaits will take the next two hours. It would be easier to just send one of the children out to the store to buy a gallon of pareve ice cream. You cross-examine yourself: "If I take the easy route and buy the pareve ice cream, where will that take me? I'll get a nap and be a mentsch on Shabbos. If I exert myself to make the parfaits, where will that take me? I'll have a nicer dessert l'kavod Shabbos kodesh, but I'll be too tired to be there for my husband and children." In this case, the easier route is preferable.

The Chafetz Chayim used to remove the fuses in the beis midrash at 11:30 p.m. so that the yeshivah students would go to sleep. Although staying up half the night learning Torah was the harder option and going to sleep could have been a concession to laziness, the Chafetz Chaim felt that if they had a good night's sleep they would be able to learn better the next day. Going to sleep would take them to a better place.

Not all leniencies are bad, but all leniencies need to be examined.

Changing the Outside First

Another cardinal principle of the Ramchal's program for self-transformation is: "Outer movements arouse inner movements" [Chapter 7].

We hold back from doing many mitzvos because we are afraid of dissembling: "I'm not on that level yet." "I'm not such a big *tzaddik* that I should daven with the *visikin* minyan." "How can I accept the chairmanship of that *chesed* project when I'm not a *baal chesed*?" Fear of being hypocritical pushes us into the arms of the yetzer hara, who rejoices over our reluctance to perform any good deed.

The Ramchal explains that we have less control over our inner selves than our outer selves. Therefore, if we want to overcome laziness and acquire the trait of zeal, we should *act* zealously, even if it's just an act. Even if we lack the inner yearnings that should ignite zeal, our zealous action can ignite the inner yearnings. "Just as zealous action can be the product of an inner yearning, so zealous action can produce an inner yearning."

Since laziness means to abstain from doing any particular good action, every time you do a good action, you are fighting the yetzer hara of laziness.

Battle Plan #30:
Just Say "Yes" To Mitzvos

This battle plan is for people who habitually refrain from being proactive or who become mired in endless debates between "Should I" or "Shouldn't I?"

Since the yetzer hara of laziness is a master of excuses and rationalization, you can undermine his whole campaign by simply saying "Yes" when a mitzvah comes your way.

David was lethargic by nature. When people asked him for favors, he usually said "No." He always had reasonable justifications for his refusals, but one day he suddenly realized that he was clearly not the kind, generous person he aspired to become. So he decided, as Battle Plan #30 recommends, to just say "Yes" when a mitzvah came his way. He determined that whenever anyone would ask him for a favor, he would say, "Yes!" Then, afterward, he would figure out, "Now how can I make it happen?" He discovered that the insurmountable obstacles weren't so insurmountable after all. They were just smoke screens thrown up by the yetzer hara of laziness.

For example, as David was pulling out of a supermarket parking lot at the beginning of a long trip, a neighbor spotted him and said, "I have a flat. Do you have any of that spray that temporarily seals a hole in a tire?"

David was about to say, "I have the spray, but I may need it myself because I'm leaving for a long trip." But he stopped himself and employed Battle Plan #30. He said, "Yes, I do have the spray. Here it is." Then he realized that all he had to do was stop at the first gas station he passed and buy a new can.

A friend of David was a photographer down on his luck. His bank overdraft was at its limit, and he had no work coming in. He asked David for help. David's initial reaction was that he couldn't help; he himself was strapped financially and had no money at all to lend him. But, he remembered Battle Plan #30, and responded: "Yes! Sure, I'll help you." He contemplated the situation, then sat down and called all the engaged people he knew and recommended his friend as a photographer for their wedding. At the end of one hour of phone calls, David had landed his friend a job.

And at the end of just two weeks of applying this tactic, David had vanquished the yetzer hara of laziness that had plagued him his whole life.

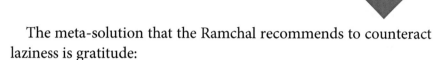

Gratitude

The meta-solution that the Ramchal recommends to counteract laziness is gratitude:

> *What can strengthen this awakening [to zeal] is to look at all the goodness that HaKadosh Baruch Hu does with a person at every moment and the great wonders that He does with him from the moment of his birth until his last day. The more he looks into and reflects on these things, the more he will recognize his great debt to the God Who bestows so much good upon him. ... Since he cannot repay Him, at least he can thank Him and do His mitzvos [Chapter 8].*

Gratitude is the best motivator to action. As much as you may not want to pull on your overcoat, boots, and snow hat, and go out into the blizzard to drive to Lenny's son's Bar Mitzvah, if Lenny was the one who helped you most when you were hospitalized last summer, who filled out the insurance forms for you, and who got you the rented wheelchair, then you will let nothing keep you from going to his son's Bar Mitzvah. Gratitude is the spark plug that makes the tank's engine run.

Gratitude is the most effective motivator of action. It completely drowns out the voice of the yetzer hara of laziness.

BATTLE PLAN #31:
KEEP A GRATITUDE JOURNAL

Buy a small notebook or blank book. Draw a horizontal line in the middle of the page. On the top half of the page, write down some of the things Hashem or people (who are His agents) did for you today. They can be as simple as

"It rained," or as complex as *"The test results I was waiting for came back negative. I'm fine!"*

On the bottom half of the page, write down your response to what you received. It could be an emotional response such as, *"I felt happy,"* or a physical response such as, *"I said 'thank you.'"*

Here are the rules:

◆ Write down exactly five things every day.
◆ Do not repeat.

This will be easy for a few weeks, but as the months go by, since you're not allowed to repeat, you will have to go deeper and deeper, and notice more and more. You will be amazed at what you notice or remember that you had never paid attention to before. For example, yesterday I [SR] took our car to the car wash. I was grateful for:

1. Having a clean car/I thanked and tipped the men who cleaned the inside.

2. Owning a car at all/I felt grateful to my husband for earning money and to Hashem for giving him musical-arranging jobs that paid for the car.

3. Knowing how to drive a car/I felt responsible to drive safely.

4. My parents who, 43 years ago, paid for me to have driving lessons (I hadn't thought about those driving lessons for over four decades!)/ I wished I could pick up a phone and thank my parents, but they are no longer in this world. Still, I felt so grateful, and started to remember all the other lessons they paid for: piano, art, tennis, etc.

5. Whoever invented the internal combustion engine/I appreciated how much intelligence and creativity it took — far beyond my own feeble technological abilities.

A secret for success with the Gratitude Journal is to focus on details. If you're grateful for your vision, you've got one thing. But if you stop to notice the details, you've got:

1. *I can see light and shadow.*

2. *I can see shapes.*

3. *I can see color.*

4. *I can see depth (thanks to having two eyes).*

5. *I can see under various lighting conditions, with my pupils dilating and contracting to adjust.*

6. *I have peripheral vision.*

7. *I can see danger coming.*

8. *I can see to read.*

9. *Somebody invented glasses, so even though I'm near sighted I can still see.*

Gratitude, in fact, is the basis of both emunah [faith] and simchah [happiness]. People who excel in emunah and simchah are vital and vigorous, the diametric opposite of lazy. Feeling gratitude to Hashem will motivate you to want to jump up to do a mitzvah.

The Yetzer's Taker Campaign

10

THE YETZER HARA WAGES WAR LIKE GERMANY DID in World War II. Germany wanted to conquer all of Europe. That was its true goal, but it knew that it could not conquer all of Europe in one massive attack. So it started by attacking Poland in what became known as "The September Campaign." This campaign focused Germany's military might on one specific, although very large, area. Once Poland was conquered, Germany was able to take over Denmark, Norway, France, the Netherlands, and Belgium in relatively rapid succession.

Similarly, the yetzer hara wants to conquer our whole self, but it focuses its energies on one primary campaign. As the Ramchal writes:

> *Even though the yetzer hara tries to get a person to sin in all kinds of sins, there are some sins that human nature makes more desirable, so [the yetzer hara] makes them more permissible to a person. Therefore [in relationship to these sins], a person requires more strength in order to prevail over his yetzer and to be clean of sin [Chapter 11].*

What are the sins that act like a wedge through which the yetzer hara ends up dominating our whole being? The Ramchal, quoting a Gemara in *Chagigah*, specifies two: theft and promiscuity. [We have already dealt with the latter at length in Chapter 4; in this chapter we will deal only with theft.]

The Ramchal acknowledges that most of us are not overt thieves, but in our business dealings we have "the taste of theft" in our mouths. This means that no one reading this book would ever rob a bank or steal a $50 bill lying on a neighbor's desk while no one else is in the room. The Torah, however, prohibits much more subtle infractions concerning our neighbor's property. Here are just a few common infractions in the area of "theft":

◆ taking a lower wage than your friend in order to be hired and force him out of the market

◆ not paying someone what you owe him

◆ denying a deal you made, or any part of it

◆ not giving a completely truthful description of something you want to sell

◆ opening a competing business in an area that does not have enough customers to support two such businesses

◆ changing the terms of an agreement midway through the project

Good, decent people fall prey to the yetzer hara of theft in many such ways. I [TH] knew a dentist who was a good Jew. My daughter needed major dental work, so I took her to this dentist. He said it would cost 10,000 shekels, which is a lot of money, but he wouldn't reduce the amount, so finally I agreed to his price. Midway through the dental work, he said that the materials were costing him more than expected, so he would have to charge me more. The work was half done, so I had no choice but to agree to each raise in price, until, in the end, I had to pay 20,000 shekels: exactly double. Now, I don't believe he was lying; the materials probably did go up in price during the period he was doing the work. But a person must be realistic and responsible about the estimate he gives. If he isn't, he should accept part of the loss for his own miscalculation. Otherwise, the "the taste of theft" is in his mouth.

A prevailing aspect of theft takes place with words. Let's say you are a shoe salesman who says, "Of course the shoes feel a little tight now, but in a few days of wearing them, they'll stretch." If the shoes don't stretch, that's theft.

I [SR] used to rent out a room in our house short term to tourists, like a bed-and-breakfast without the breakfast. My husband called this enterprise my "cottage industry." People would call from America, and I would describe the room. I would say, "It's a large room with ..." My husband used to object. He maintained that although by my Israeli standards the room was large, by American standards the room was not so large. Now, "large" is a relative term, so I did not feel I was misrepresenting what I was offering. Once a man from California reserved the room for a month. When he arrived, he was upset. He said he had imagined a nice, large room, and it wasn't. I had to return his full deposit. A person can become a thief with the wrong adjective.

I [TH] had a former student from Neve, Tzivia Roseman, who was a Canadian living in Israel. She was diagnosed with stage four ovarian cancer. Her prognosis was so desperate that the doctors said that the only thing that might possibly save her (and they were not optimistic) was an extremely expensive surgery that could be performed only in the United States. Tzivia's husband was an American, but they had no health insurance in America, and their Israeli national health insurance did not cover this operation. Had Tzivia's husband worked in the United States for six months prior, she would have been eligible for Medicaid, which would have paid for the surgery. Some frum people in America, eager to be helpful, offered to hire him and declare on the records that he had already been working for six months.

Tzivia didn't want to do that. She knew that it was dishonest.

She phoned me and said, "People are telling me to do this terrible thing, to steal." Her life was at stake, and you could argue that a Jew is allowed to transgress the mitzvah against stealing in order to save a life. Still, her sense of integrity was so great that she was simply unwilling to compromise the truth. Finally, her husband's Rav went and asked the Gerrer Rebbe. Since enough money had already been raised through an outpouring of *tzeddakah* for the first operation, the Gerrer Rebbe said they should move to the United States and her husband should start working there. She would not need a second operation, the Rebbe said, so there was no need to lie at all. Tzivia died before the second operation. She returned her soul to her Maker completely pure of the sin of theft.

Do you understand how great her victory was? She completely resisted the onslaught of the yetzer hara of theft. This 40-year-old woman's stunning victory over the yetzer hara's theft campaign is comparable to pushing back the German army's "September Campaign"; it would have stopped Hitler's aggression in its tracks and ended World War II before the Holocaust had really begun. That is the scale of her victory.

The Ramchal writes that the yetzer hara of theft is very tricky, and the slope between the permissible and the forbidden is very slippery. For example, let's say that you want to sell your used crib. You are not permitted to hide the defects, but you are permitted to beautify the item you want to sell. So although the paint is chipped and one of the slats is wobbling, you put beautiful, colorful bolster pillows around the crib, hoping the perspective buyer won't notice the defects. This is permitted. Then you "speak to the heart" of the buyer, telling her that four of your children used this crib and they all were healthy and slept through the night. This is also permitted. Then you see that the perspective buyer is waffling. She says that she might just spend a little more and buy a new crib. Your desire to make the sale pushes you over the line of truth. Without any knowledge of the facts, you tell her that the new cribs are made of inferior wood and they don't last as long, while this crib is made of oak. Such prevaricating is forbidden. Although you convince yourself that you are simply a good salesperson, you have actually crossed the threshold into theft. The yetzer hara has caught you.

The Ramchal makes a frightening statement: When it comes to theft, there is no minimum. It is like *chametz* on Pesach; if you knowingly eat even a tiny speck of *chametz*, your transgression is as vast as if you had eaten a slice of bread. Although you cannot be punished by the earthly court for stealing things that have minuscule financial values (i.e., less than a penny), the heavenly court holds you accountable. As an illustration of such theft, the Mishnah gives the example of a person who samples fruit in the market. Today it is common for people in supermarkets to sample candy or dried fruit in open bins. This is theft according to the Torah.

Why? What is the real loss when a customer in the supermarket pops a single piece of candy into his mouth? The supermarket owner could easily absorb such a loss. But when 30 or 40 people in the course of a day pilfer one piece of candy, the loss starts to mount up. And the real loss is that the standard of honesty in society declines. The storekeepers do not trust their customers. They install mirrors in the grocery stores, closed-circuit monitors in the supermarkets, and expensive equipment to detect theft at the exit of clothing stores.

Even small acts of theft undermine the level of trust in society. Petty theft is like a rot that eats away at the very fabric of the society. The generation of the flood was guilty of terrible promiscuity and violence. Ultimately, Rashi tells us, Hashem brought a flood to destroy the world because of the sin of petty thievery. People were stealing things that were worth less than a *perutah*, such as one match. Why did petty thievery merit global destruction? Because stealing a small item that anyone could afford means that the thief was not overcome by insurmountable desire or need, but rather that he placed no value whatsoever on honesty. Such a society is irredeemable.

A society where honesty is the prevailing ethos is replete with kindness and mutual trust. Twenty-three years ago, shortly after

I [SR] first moved to Israel, I was walking down Jaffa Road, Jerusalem's main street. A clothing store had its goods displayed on a rack on the sidewalk, and I noticed a skirt that I liked. I went inside, tried it on, and told the shopkeeper. "I want to buy this skirt, but I don't have any money with me. I'll come back tomorrow."

He replied, "Take the skirt with you now. You can come back tomorrow to pay for it."

A friend told me just last week that she was shopping in Machane Yehudah, Jerusalem's open-air market. She went to buy three dozen eggs, but realized she had no cash left. The egg vendor, who had never seen her before, told her to take the eggs and pay for them next time she comes to the market.

Such episodes can happen only in a society where theft is extremely rare.

Theft is such a powerful wedge for the yetzer hara because it is rooted in one of life's primary choices: between giving and taking. Giving and taking are primary colors on the spiritual palette. They each have many shades and gradations, but in essence they are polar opposites. The soul loves to give; the body loves to take.

People steal because of their love of taking. That's why someone who pays $200 for a room in a hotel will steal a towel worth $6. They don't need the towel; they have plenty of towels at home. And they don't love the towel, but they do love taking. Taking is rooted in the misguided feeling that one is nurturing oneself. The yetzer hara of theft whispers: "You need to enhance yourself by taking that towel."

Theft emanates from the very root of evil: the illusion of separateness. The self that steals sees itself as separate from the person/group/company from which he is stealing. After all, no one is stupid enough to steal from himself. Eventually, the taking/stealing self sees itself as separate from everyone else. "It's me against everyone who is not me."

The credo of the *Shema,* that God is One, means that ultimate truth is unity. If you are aware that you are connected to another person, how can you steal from that person? If you would not cheat your own brother, how can you cheat Mr. Klein? Only by believing the yetzer hara's lie that Mr. Klein is not connected to you, that he is a separate individual, can you cheat Mr. Klein. Theft is the "September Campaign" of the yetzer hara because it strikes against ultimate truth: Divine unity.

This is the mechanism of theft: The illusion of separateness leads to competition. I am me and Mr. Klein is a totally unrelated being. Since we both have electronic stores on the same block, his failure is my success. Therefore I will slash prices for one month, take out loans to cover my losses, and drive Klein out of business. Then, once he closes, I'll raise my prices above their previous level, because now I am the only electronics store on the block, so all the customers will have to buy from me. I win, Klein loses.

But imagine that an invisible, spiritual string connects your fortunes to Mr. Klein's fortunes. Whenever his fortunes climb, so do yours. Whenever his fortunes decline, so do yours. Now, would you want him to succeed or fail?

The truth is that such an invisible connection does exist. It is the truth of Divine Oneness. The Torah commands: "Love your neighbor as yourself." The Ramban explains: "Because your neighbor is your own self."

No wonder that such a major portion of the Gemara is devoted to business law. This is the great battleground between body and soul. The body shouts: "Take!" The soul shouts: "Give!" No wonder that according to the Midrash [*Vayikra Rabbah* 33] the sin of theft is equivalent to murder, idolatry, and promiscuity combined!

Going from being a taker to becoming a giver requires refocusing your vision from physical sight to spiritual sight. Physically, the truth is that the more you have, the less I have. The pie is only so big; if you have 55 percent, then I am left with only 45 percent. As long as you are locked into physical sight, you will feel competition, which leads to taking, which leads eventually to theft, even if it be no greater theft than taking paper clips from the office.

The only rebuttal to the voice of the yetzer hara that says, "Steal and you'll have more," is the voice of the yetzer hatov that says, "Don't steal and you'll *be* more." The only way to argue with the facts and figures of physical reality is to consign them to their secondary place behind ultimate truth: spiritual reality. And the essence of spiritual reality is oneness.

In *Small Miracles,* authors Yitta Halberstam and Judith Leventhal tell a true story about a young man named Robert Shafran who transferred to a new college. On the first day of the semester, students kept coming up to Robert and greeting him warmly, like old friends, calling him, "Eddy." Robert repeatedly protested that he wasn't Eddy. Finally, a fellow approached Robert and told him that he had an uncanny resemblance to Eddy Galland, who had attended that college last year, but who had just transferred to a different college. He asked Robert the date of his birthday. Upon hearing Robert's answer, the fellow looked spooked and told him that Eddy had the same birthday. He then told him that Eddy was adopted, and asked if by any chance he was adopted. Robert answered that he was.

The next day Robert Shafran and Eddy Galland got together. It turned out that they were identical twins separated at birth. Local newspapers printed a picture of the two hugging brothers, reunited after a lifetime apart.

One person who saw the picture was particularly entranced. His name was David Kellman, and the two brothers looked just like him! He also had been adopted at birth. He made contact with the twins, and their research revealed that in fact they were identical triplets separated at birth. The newly reunited brothers opened a restaurant together called, "Triplets Romanian Steakhouse."

Imagine for a moment that these triplets separated at birth are not identical, that they have no way of recognizing one another, and that each of them independently opens a steak house within two blocks of the others. The competition among them would be keen, perhaps trenchant. Then, let's say, a recession strikes, leading to fewer diners and fewer people who could afford steak. At that point, the three restaurateurs, desperate to stave off bankruptcy, resort to dishonest means to put the others out of business. One of them succeeds. Two of the steak houses close, their owners forced into financial ruin and personal depression. Many years later, the three men meet, perhaps at a retirement home. In the course of conversation, they discover that they are brothers, in fact triplets. How would they feel about the cutthroat means by which they competed with one another?

How will we feel when we reach *Olam HaEmes* [the World of Truth] when we discover that those we stole from were really our siblings?

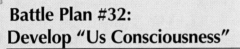

Battle Plan #32:
Develop "Us Consciousness"

Whenever you are involved in "business," whether as an employer, employee, seller, customer, or party to a financial agreement, instead of perceiving Me versus Them, see yourself as part of the same family. Instead of asking, "How can I profit in this deal?" ask, "How can we both profit in this deal?"

Let's go back to the scenario of trying to sell a used crib. When the potential buyer waffles, instead of resorting to dishonesty to make the sale, imagine that the potential buyer is your sister. Not only do you want to sell the crib, but also you want her to get a good deal. So you view the transaction from her vantage point. Apparently she is disappointed that the paint is chipped and one slat is wobbly. She wants a crib in better condition. At the same time, she would not be shopping for a used crib unless she were short of money. You can't improve the condition of the crib, but it occurs to you that you can come down in price.

You deduct $40 from your asking price. Now she is satisfied that she is paying a fair price for what she is getting. It's a win/win situation. You got $40 less, but you did sell the crib and you made your sister happy.

This is how to resist the yetzer hara's taker campaign. Instead of getting pleasure at "taking" someone else by getting top dollar, you get pleasure from giving: you "gave" a fair price that pleases the customer for the item you're selling. In all areas of business, you can choose to be a giver:

◆ *As an employer (whether you employ dozens of workers or one housekeeper), you give your employee(s) a job that provides livelihood in a pleasant work environment.*

◆ *As an employee, you give your employer your best work, effort, and time.*

◆ *As a seller (whether you are a professional salesperson or you occasionally sell certain items, such as your car, house, used furniture, etc.), you give a quality object at a fair price that gives the buyer satisfaction.*

◆ *As a customer, you give the seller money for livelihood.*

Especially when you do business with your fellow Jew, you should feel satisfaction at giving him or her livelihood.

It also helps to remember the words of the Midrash. Just as you would never stoop to murder or idolatry, commit yourself never to stoop to the equally horrendous sin of theft, even of one grape in the supermarket.

In The Name of All Israel

A lesson found in the Arizal's teaching [in *Shaar HaKavanos*] works on the same principle. The spiritual reality is that all Jews share one group soul. Our bodies are distinct and separate, fostering the illusion of separateness. Our souls, however, are as interconnected as cells in the same body.

Several years ago, a major Jewish organization used as its motto: "One people, one destiny." This is ultimate truth. It is also an answer to the question sometimes posed: Why did the devout, righteous Jews of Europe also perish in the Holocaust? We are one collective soul entity. A wound in the arm can cause the whole body to bleed to death. We share a collective identity and destiny.

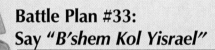

Battle Plan #33:
Say *"B'shem Kol Yisrael"*

The yetzer hara tries to brainwash us with the illusion of separateness, which is the root of evil and the denial of Divine Oneness. To the extent the yetzer hara succeeds in convincing us that we are separate entities, to that extent we will choose to be takers and will be vulnerable to the sin of theft.

The Arizal thus recommends that we explode this false notion of separateness by saying "B'shem kol Yisrael" — "In the name of all Israel" before doing any mitzvah, including davening.

Saying these three simple words has two effects. First of all, it's reality therapy. By saying "B'shem kol Yisrael" we acknowledge our collective soul identity. We foster in our-

selves the spiritual consciousness that we are connected to all other Jews.

Second, when we say these three words before performing a mitzvah, we are effectively giving a share in the merit of the mitzvah to all other Jews. We are thus turning ourselves into givers. This is a powerful counterattack against the yetzer's taker campaign.

For example, when you make Kiddush on Shabbos night, you are generating merit for yourself and for those who fulfill the mitzvah of remembering Shabbos by hearing your Kiddush. But if you say "B'shem kol Yisrael" before making Kiddush, you deliberately intend to disseminate the merit of the mitzvah among the entire Jewish people. The merit of a mitzvah can be assigned to whomever you choose. When someone is sick, for example, you can do a mitzvah and direct the merit thus accrued for the recovery of the ailing person. "B'shem kol Yisrael" sends the merit of the mitzvah out to all Jewish people.

The same battle plan can be implemented during davening. In fact, "B'shem kol Yisrael" appears in the nusach Sefard siddur just prior to Baruch She'amar. It indicates that we intend our prayer, instead of being just between us and HaKadosh Baruch Hu, to include all Jews everywhere. In this way, we regard ourselves as a self-designated representative of the Jewish people, and we intend the benefit that comes from our prayer to benefit all Jews everywhere. Thus prayer, which could become a selfish exercise in begging blessings from the Almighty, becomes instead an exercise in collective caring and helping.

When I [SR] learned this battle plan and started saying and intending "B'shem kol Yisrael" in my prayers, my Shemoneh Esrei was transformed entirely. Every blessing became an appeal for Am Yisrael. Thus, for example, in the blessing asking for daas [wisdom], I used to appeal for wisdom in my own writing and in my husband's musical composing. Now, before the conclusion of the blessing, I verbally ask for wisdom for every doctor anywhere in the *world treating a Jewish patient, every nurse, every psycho-therapist, every social worker, every marriage counselor, every teacher, every parent, and every student, as well as every writer and musician. We are all dependent on an influx of Divine wisdom.*

Rav Eliyahu Dessler taught a principle that is counterin-tuitive. We assume that the more we receive from others, the more we love them. Rav Dessler taught that it works in reverse: The more we do for others, the more we love them. Prayer and mitzvos "B'shem kol Yisrael" are a gift we give to all our fellow Jews. This takes us to the level of loving our fellow Jews. There is no more powerful weapon against the yetzer hara.

Section Three

Inspired by the Writings of The Chassidic Masters

Seeing in the Dark

11

DAVID (MICKEY) MARCUS WAS ISRAEL'S FIRST general. An American Jew educated at West Point, he rose to the rank of colonel in the United States Army, where he served in both the Pacific and European theaters of war during World War II. In January 1948, as Arab armies prepared to pounce on the soon-to-be-created State of Israel, Mickey Marcus volunteered to help transform the underground Haganah into a real army. He came to Palestine and was appointed the first (and at that point only) general. He designed a command and control structure for the Israeli army, and commanded the building of an alternate road that broke the siege of Jerusalem.

Late one night, six hours before the U.N. brokered cease-fire was to take effect, General Marcus took a walk outside of the security perimeter of his base. In the dark, a Jewish sentry, unable to identify his own commander, shot and killed him.

Israel's first general did not fall to an enemy attack. Rather, the foe that caused his tragic death was the darkness itself.

In the teachings of Rebbe Nachman of Breslov, the yetzer hara is less a fiendish persona than a pervasive darkness. The darkness prevents us from seeing reality, which is that Hashem's will and wisdom fill the world from moment to moment. To some degree, we are all that Jewish sentry; in the darkness, we fail to identify the Divine Commander. All the tragedies of our lives ensue from that failure to see.

In the beginning of the first teaching of *Likutei Moharan*, Rebbe Nachman says:

> *A Jewish person must always look at the intelligence in everything, and must bind himself to the wisdom and intelligence that exist in everything, in order that he should illuminate for himself the intelligence that exists in everything, to come close to Hashem Yisbarach through that particular thing. Because the mind is a great light, and illuminates all his ways.*

If you turn on the light in a dark room, nothing objectively changes. The couch, the chairs, the carpet, and the drapes are all exactly as they were the moment before you switched on the light. The only thing that changes is your ability to see what's there.

Increased vision also enables you to choose how to relate to what you see. The rocking chair in the middle of the room? Now that you see it, you may choose to walk around it rather than trip over it. The drapes? You may deftly close them rather than fumble helplessly for the cord.

"Turning on the light," in Rebbe Nachman's teaching, means becoming aware that every person, object, and situation you encounter is a manifestation of Hashem's will and wisdom. Instead of seeing only the superficial appearance of that person, object, or situation, you will notice its inner potentials and spiritual possibilities. And you will appreciate that the Master of the Universe put it/him/her in your path for some Divine purpose.

This approach is based on the Talmudic principle: "No person strikes his finger below without it being decreed from above."

The Baal Shem Tov's teachings emphasized that Hashem micromanages the world. As he put it: "It is HaKadosh Baruch Hu Who determines how many times the fallen leaf will turn in the wind before it comes to rest." This means that everything that happens to you results from Hashem's will. This does not negate a human being's free will. The thief is free to decide whether or not to pickpocket your wallet, but the aggravation and financial loss you suffer was determined by Hashem on Rosh Hashanah. If that amount of aggravation and financial loss did not happen through the pickpocket, it could have happened through the transmission in your car breaking down, or your tripping on a step and breaking a bone, or your computer crashing.

Therefore Rebbe Nachman's first counsel is to "turn on the light" and see Hashem hiding in the mundane happenings of your life. Nothing in this world happens without the Divine will. Let's say you have an important appointment at 10 o'clock this morning. You absolutely cannot afford to come late for this appointment, so you've allowed yourself plenty of time for rush-hour traffic and finding a parking space. You leave your house promptly at 9 o'clock. To your horror, you find that a car is partially blocking your driveway, making it impossible to get your car out. You spend 10 precious minutes knocking on the neighbors' doors looking for the miscreant whose carelessness is about to ruin your life. Finally, you see a jaunty fellow walking directly toward the offending car, his car keys dangling from his hand. At this point, you feel like screaming at the fellow, telling him that he is the most inconsiderate, unconscionable, selfish wretch who ever lived. All you are seeing is your car, the blocked driveway, the car that is blocking it, and its offending owner. You are totally oblivious to Hashem's presence in the scene. In your blindness, you are likely to commit the sin of afflicting another person with your words, and (assuming that you are recognizable as a religious person) the cardinal sin of *chillul Hashem*, which literally means "making a space devoid of Hashem."

Or you can choose to see Hashem's will and wisdom by reminding yourself that everything that happens to you comes from Hashem, and that He decreed that you should be late for this appointment. Although the fellow is certainly guilty of parking where he shouldn't have, "Hashem has many bears and lions," as the Midrash states, and if this fellow hadn't blocked your driveway, your car could have failed to start or an accident could have blocked all eastbound lanes on the highway toward your destination. Once you put Hashem into the picture as the Real Cause, all the human culprits stop looking like monsters, and your venom disappears. "Turning on the light" makes everything look different.

This approach is called *middas ha'emes*, the trait of Truth. This is the way that the Patriarch Yaakov looked at reality. In the Torah's account of Yaakov's life, we find Yaakov acquiring the "firstborn" status and its concomitant blessings. Rebbe Nachman points out that "firstborn" means seeing things as though for the first time. Even when Yaakov was looking at something for the thousandth time, he saw it as though it were new. Such vision requires looking at things freshly, as though everything was newly created in this moment (which, from a metaphysical standpoint, it was). It means recognizing that every person, thing, or experience is a unique manifestation of Hashem's will in this moment, not a rerun of yesterday.

Many people have the opposite of "firstborn" consciousness. They can look at a magnificent sunset, shrug, and say, "I've already seen sunsets." I know someone who went on vacation to Switzerland with her mother. While the daughter was rapturous over the beauty of one particular lake surrounded by mountains, all her mother could say was: "Another lake?"

We could be blind to the newness Hashem invests in everything at every moment: "Another day? Another breakfast? Another grassy lawn? Another hour with my child?"

My [SR] mother-in-law is an expert in "firstborn" consciousness. For her 91st birthday, my husband and I, visiting her in Los Angeles, made her a little party. We bought a birthday cake with the words, "HAPPY BIRTHDAY, MOM," a helium balloon, and two gaily wrapped gifts. It was a simple party, with only the three of us present, but Mom loved it. "I never had a birthday party like this!" she exclaimed with delight. *In 91 years she never had a party with a cake, a balloon, and two presents?* I wondered. Only upon reflection did I realize that her perception that this mini-party was a "first" had less to do with her life's history of birthday parties than it did with her attitude that everything is unique and special in its own right (which is also part of the secret of her youthful bounce and demeanor).

Newness is the true perception of reality because everything exists only because Hashem animates it with Divine life force at every moment. Rebbe Nachman defines wisdom as the ability to see Hashem in everything, to see Hashem's presence, vitality, and goodness in everything. Yaakov is the exemplar of such wisdom. He had a difficult life, but he recognized Hashem in whatever happened to him.

So, explains Rebbe Nachman, the first step in creating an ambience that the yetzer hara cannot penetrate is to "turn on the light," to train yourself to see Hashem present in His world. The result of such awareness can totally transform your life.

An example of this is Rav Shalom Arush, the Rosh Yeshivah of Chuta shel Chessed, a yeshivah in which the spiritual parallel of "reviving the dead" (i.e., inspiring *baalei teshuvah*) is a common occurrence. Rav Arush was interviewed in *Shaah Tovah*, a popular Hebrew weekly, and asked to describe his own personal journey.

He related that he had been born to a traditional Moroccan family, but by the time he entered high school, he had succumbed to the influence of the secular society around him. He joined the army and was assigned to the most prestigious air force division. After completing his service, he found himself in university with shoulder-length curls and a matching lifestyle. What turned him around? As he recounts:

> I was at the university when I received a telegram from the army informing me that three of my buddies had been

killed in a helicopter accident. They provided the details of when the funerals would take place. I can't honestly say that I felt much, but I went to the funerals out of respect for my friends. They had left an hour between each service to preclude our feeling of the second or third one being just a replay of the first. After the first funeral I had an hour to spare. My friends and I went to Tel Aviv, and sat down in a local restaurant for some lunch. Our conversation revolved around ourselves and our lives. We had not seen one another for some time, and there was a lot of catching up to do. We went back to the cemetery for the second funeral, and then found ourselves with still another hour on our hands. At the time, I was interested in art and painted a little. I had heard about an exhibit in Yaffo and went to see it.

That night when I tried to sleep, I found myself asking questions that I couldn't answer. Is this really all that there is? Is this what life is about? Futile attempts at escape, earning money, gaining status, and finally the grave? It all ends there, in the cemetery? What is it really for?

At that point he began to speak to Hashem, asking Him for clarity, praying for Him to reveal His presence in his life, pleading with Him to turn on the light. There is a basic principle: In spiritual things, you get what you want; in physical things, you get what Hashem knows is good for you. Because young Shalom Arush wanted to see Hashem manifest in His world, Hashem granted him that awareness. He went on to become a Rosh Yeshivah and the author of *The Garden of Emunah,* a book that has had a profound impact on thousands of people.

Seeing Hashem's life force in everything means seeing Hashem present in:

◆ the face of a newborn

◆ a flowering tree

◆ rain on the day you planned an outing

- the phone call that woke you up at midnight because the person on the other end didn't calculate the time zones correctly
- the chirping of the birds
- the police officer who gave you a ticket
- the softness of your new (or old) cashmere sweater
- the tomato sauce spilled on the rug
- the shade of a tree on a hot day
- the leak that flooded the kitchen
- chocolate
- the neighbor's loud party
- the fragrance of roses or jasmine
- the shattering of your expensive crystal vase
- your mother-in-law's childrearing advice
- the stock market crash
- everything, everything else

Battle Plan #34:
NVD: Notice Very Deeply

The truth is: it's nearly impossible to "turn on the light" to reveal Hashem's presence in this world, because this physical world is by definition a place of concealment. In fact, the word for "world" (in Hebrew, olam) derives from the root word meaning, "hidden." Hashem has deliberately hidden His presence in this world. If we define Hashem's presence as "light," then we must resign ourselves to the reality that we are living in a world of darkness.

Yet modern technology has given us a powerful tool for how to see in the dark. NVDs are Night Vision Devices, first developed for the military, which enable soldiers to conduct surveillance, spot the enemy, and wage battles under the darkest conditions. With an NVD, it's possible to see a person standing over 200 yards away on a moonless, cloudy night.

NVDs work by a process called "image enhancement," which operates with short-wave infrared imaging. Infrared rays are light rays that are invisible to the human eye. NVDs, such as night vision binoculars, gather infrared rays from starlight and other (humanly) imperceptible sources as they reflect off objects, and amplify them to the point that the image can be observed. The key component of the NVD is the image-intensifier tube.

In our struggle against the yetzer hara of darkness, we can develop a spiritual NVD that enables us to see the Divine Presence that is normally invisible to us. The spiritual NVD is: Notice Very Deeply. This involves looking beyond the superficial image visible to our human perception, such as the phone call in the middle of the night or the tomato sauce on the rug, and enhancing the image until its Divine light particles become visible to us.

The image-intensifier tube, the basic component, of the spiritual NVD is emunah, the deep faith that "Ein od milvado — There is nothing besides Hashem." As it says in Tehillim, "v'emunasecha b'leilos — Your faith in the nights." When you find yourself confronting any person (the policeman), object (the shattered crystal vase), or situation (the stock market crash), your normal human vision will see only the superficial appearance, which is an open invitation to the yetzer hara. At that point, reach for your spiritual NVD, and Notice Very Deeply, reminding yourself that everything comes from Hashem. Keep gazing through your spiritual NVD until Hashem's will and wisdom becomes visible to you, even in the darkest night.

Malchus: Crowning Hashem

The next step, according to Rebbe Nachman, is *malchus* — crowning Hashem by submitting to His sovereignty. Once we see Hashem's will and wisdom in everything, we place the crown on Hashem's head by declaring: "The way You're making it happen is the way I want to go."

The metaphor that Rebbe Nachman offers for *malchus* is the moon. The moon has none of its own light; it only reflects the light of the sun, which stands for Hashem's light. *Malchus* means: "I have nothing of my own. My talents, my strengths, my intelligence — all come from Hashem." There is no ego, no whining "But I wanted it like this!" No angry "But I thought it should be like that!" *Malchus* means accepting whatever Hashem has sent you at that moment.

Such submission comes not from despair, but from seeing clearly the will and wisdom of Hashem in everything.

The opposite of this is seeing the world opportunistically, in such a way that every person, object, or situation is seen as a means of placing the crown on one's own head. Just as Yaakov is the paradigm of the worldview that Rebbe Nachman is teaching us, so Esav represents the opposite paradigm. Yaakov's question would be, "What does Hashem want me to do in this situation?" Esav's question would be, "What's in this for me?"

Rebbe Nachman quotes an insightful verse from Proverbs: "An impulsive person doesn't want wisdom, but he wants only what his heart reveals" [18:2, according to the understanding of the Ibn Ezra and the Gra]. He wants more and more revelation of self. For the fool what life is all about is self-expression and self-articulation.

Rebbe Nachman now gives us a definition of the yetzer hara. He says that the yetzer hara is that which conceals Hashem. The yetzer hara is the ego.

The yetzer hatov, on the other hand, is that which leads us toward recognizing Hashem's will and wisdom in every situation. The yetzer hatov induces self-nullification.

Two kings cannot wear one crown. The eternal battle is between Hashem and the human ego.

Let's imagine a scene in which you could go either way: A third cousin of yours is gravely ill. The relative lives far away, but you decide to go and visit. This requires taking a day off from work and driving for two hours. When you get there, the sick relative's wife answers the door. She does not look glad to see you. With a frown, she tells you that her husband is sleeping and cannot be disturbed. She adds, almost as an afterthought, that you can sit in the living room and wait, if you want. Since you have already taken the day off from work and have driven all this distance, you sit down and wait. A half-hour goes by. His wife is busy in the other room, and seems to have forgotten you. Finally she comes out and offers you water and some grapes. Her husband is still sleeping, she mumbles. Your offer to help in some way is met by an icy stare. You wait another hour. Ultimately you realize that you are not going to see your relative, so you might as well drive home, which will now take four hours, because it's rush hour.

If you respond in Esav's way, you will be miffed and insulted. It's all about *you*. *You* took off a day of work. *You* drove so many hours. And this is how she treats *you*? When you leave, you will say politely, "I'm disappointed that I didn't get to see him," but you will mean, "How dare you treat me this way! You wasted my precious time. And you didn't acknowledge my sacrifice of time and money!" Your ego is the king, and you have lost to the yetzer hara.

If you respond in Yaakov's way, you will put the crown on Hashem's head. You will think: *Hashem, I'm sitting here in the living room because that's where You want me to be. I had wanted to sit by the bedside and talk to my relative, but You decided otherwise. He is so very weak that he can't talk to visitors. And his poor wife is beside herself with worry and grief. She can't bring herself to social-ize, or think about tending to the needs of anyone except her dying husband. This is not about me; it's about them. And I submit whole-heartedly to Your will.*

Although you are, of course, disappointed, you feel neither frus-trated nor angry. Instead, you get a lot of satisfaction from your crowning Hashem. "I'm the person Hashem wants me to be in this circumstance" can be tremendously sustaining. You're not a door-mat. You're the shining, beautiful moon.

My [TH] *machatenista* is a model of how to graciously submit to Hashem's will. When my oldest daughter was about to get engaged, my husband and I went to the boy's house to meet his parents and discuss the financial arrangements. This would be our first time meeting our prospective *mechutanim,* and of course we were eager to make a good impression. Since this was the first child we were marrying off, we were especially nervous. We took pains to dress nicely and to choose an appropriate present for them. Since this was their oldest son, they were no doubt equally eager to make a good impression on us.

We were sitting in their apartment, exchanging pleasantries, when suddenly the lights went out. A few moments later there was a loud banging on the door. It was a worker from the electric company. In a gruff and condemning tone, he announced that he had turned off their electricity because they had failed to pay their electric bill. They remonstrated with him that there was a misun-derstanding about which one of them would pay the bill, and they would take care of it first thing the next morning. The worker replied harshly, "You didn't pay, you don't get." He showed them the fuses that he was taking away with him, and abruptly left.

If it had been me, I would have expired from embarrassment. For such a humiliating thing to happen in the middle of meeting the future *machatanim,* whom I was trying so hard to impress! The chassan's mother, by contrast, didn't respond with embarrassment at all. Her response was *malchus*: this is the reality that Hashem in

His wisdom put us into, that we are sitting in the dark. She was not at all flustered. "Oh," she commented calmly, "I should light candles." She lit several candles and said, "Someone forgot the electric bill, but isn't it nice to be in candlelight?"

This is how it looks to crown Hashem. Feel joy when you see that you are putting the crown on Hashem's head. Crowning Hashem is personally gratifying because it takes you to a place of self-transcendence.

Sometimes Hashem rewards our act of submitting to His will. As it says, "Make His will your will, and He will make your will His will." Once a houseguest gave me [SR] a box of handmade chocolates. The box had a *hechsher*, but it was not a *hechsher* my family accepts. It was a temptation for me, because I'm a chocoholic, but I succeeded in putting the crown on Hashem's head and not compromising my kashrus standard. I gave away the box of chocolates. The next day was Friday. That night, our family ate Shabbos dinner at the home of friends in our neighborhood, the Jewish Quarter of the Old City. On our way home, after climbing a long flight of steps, we stopped to rest outside the door of my friend Perel. Someone going in the opposite direction stopped to talk to us. We were conversing for several minutes when the door to Perel's house opened. Her Philippino worker, Maria, working in the kitchen on the third floor of the house, had seen us on the closed-circuit television. Since her job is to let in guests who, on Shabbos, cannot ring the bell, she had assumed we had come for dessert. "Come on in!" Maria invited us with a wide smile.

"No," I laughed at the misapprehension of why we were there. "We just happen to be standing here talking. We didn't come to visit."

Maria was crestfallen. "But I told Perel that you're here. She said you should come up. She wants you to come up."

My husband and I exchanged tired glances, but we didn't want to disappoint, so we all paraded up to the top-floor dining room. Perel's many guests were enjoying dessert. She greeted us lovingly and said, "Sit down. I have something special for you."

She disappeared into the kitchen. Emerging a few minutes later, she offered us a large plate of Belgian chocolates — with the highest *hechsher*! Hashem was clearly rewarding me for submitting to His will the day before.

The truth, however, is that there's a reward higher than chocolates. That's the feeling of self-transcendence we should get whenever we submit our will to Hashem's sovereignty. Hashem doesn't answer us with treats all the time, because He wants us to move beyond our comfort zone. Yosef did not get a *yasher ko'ach* [well done!] from Hashem for passing his test, nor a sign from him during his first year in prison, nor during his fourth year, nor during his eighth year. Lofty souls submit to Hashem's sovereignty without the candy.

Crowning Hashem means accepting whatever He sends you because you recognize that it comes from Him. Every package transmitted by the Israel Postal Service comes with a red label warning, "DO NOT OPEN THIS PACKAGE IF YOU DON'T RECOGNIZE THE SENDER." Everything that happens to us is a package sent by Hashem. Recognizing the Sender is the key to accepting the package.

Battle Plan #35: Push The Malchus Button Instead Of The Reject Button

CD consoles come equipped with an "eject button." When, for whatever reason, we do not want to listen to a particular CD, we push the eject button, and the console coughs out that CD. All human beings similarly come equipped with a "reject button." When something happens contrary to our will, we automatically push the reject button.

Standing over the shattered crystal vase, a wedding gift from your favorite aunt, now deceased, you press the reject button, and yell at the child who knocked over the vase.

Coming home late at night and finding the kitchen flooded with two inches of water, you press the reject button, and fall into depression and despair.

Answering the phone in the middle of the night and hearing your caller say, "Oh, did I wake you up? I thought it was 10 p.m. there," you press the reject button and shout and hang up in anger.

Battle Plan #35 is a follow-up to Battle Plan #34. First you have to use the spiritual NVD (Notice Very Deeply) in order to see that Hashem's will and wisdom is the source of the situation you are confronting. Only then can you stop pushing the reject button. You accept whatever is happening to you in any given moment because you recognize that the sender is Hashem.

And then you discover that you also came equipped with an "accept button." When you push the accept button, you are submitting to Hashem's will and wisdom. You are crowning Hashem as king. The "accept button" is the malchus button.

Accepting a situation does not mean that you don't deal with it. The children must be trained not to play ball in the house. The dishwasher that caused the flood came with a warranty; the company must make good on it. The late-night caller does not need a half-hour chat, just a polite statement.

Accepting a situation means that you submit to Hashem's will rather than the carping voice of the ego that demands, "It has to be my way." Learn to push the "malchus button."

Discerning the Divine Will

After we have noticed Hashem's will and wisdom in the situation facing us, and have submitted to his sovereignty, the third step in

Rebbe Nachman's master plan is to respond to the situation according to Hashem's will. This requires learning Torah. Awareness of Hashem is not enough. We must have sufficient solid knowledge of Torah so that we are actually doing what Hashem wants of us and not what WE want Hashem to want of us. This of course requires constant learning, so that when we have to make instant decisions, we have the resources to make them correctly.

To implement this third step, we must ask the essential question: "What does Hashem want from me at this moment?" The answer comes from Torah. Whether we are holding a box of chocolates with a questionable *hechsher* or sitting in the living room of a dying relative, Torah directs us in how a Jew should behave.

People make terrible mistakes because they don't know enough Torah to respond properly. Many years ago I [TH] bought a baby stroller. As soon as I took it home and removed it from the box, I saw it was defective. The wheels were misaligned. It came with a warranty, so I took it back to the store where I had purchased it. The storeowner was willing to fix it by replacing the wheel, but that would not have solved the problem, because the problem was the frame. I wanted to be given a new stroller or my money back. The owner refused. I read him the guarantee, but he continued to refuse to honor it. I was frustrated and angry. I told him that if he did not make good on the warranty, I would tell people not to buy from him, but by this time he was ignoring me.

So I went outside, stood by the entrance, and told everyone who approached the truth: I had bought a stroller there, it was defective, and the owner refused to honor the guarantee. After the third prospective customer walked away, the owner came out and gave back my money. I was feeling very pleased with myself. But when I went home and told my husband, he informed me that I had acted improperly and had violated halachah by embarrassing someone in public and damaging him financially without the authority of a *beis din*. I should have, my husband explained to me, taken the case to a *beis din* rather than opting for vigilante justice, which may have been more immediately gratifying, but was not the will of Hashem. Unfortunately, I had not known enough Torah to respond properly.

Learning Torah is the key to vanquishing the yetzer hara. You'll never do it without Torah, because when you learn Torah seriously, you're learning what Hashem really says and what Hashem really wants. Learning Gemara is all about: "What does Hashem really say?" Learning halachah is all about: "What does Hashem really want?" Women, who are not experts in these areas, should accustom themselves to asking she'eilos rather than guessing and granting a victory to the yetzer hara.

Without learning Torah or asking halachic she'eilos, you would have no idea what Hashem really wants. You would be like the husband who offers his wife a wonderful birthday present and then buys her a motorboat. I [TH] actually have a friend to whom something like this happened. She is very much a Manhattan type. On her birthday her husband surprised her. He says, "Sweetheart, for your birthday I got you the best present I've ever bought you." She's thinking diamonds, but he goes on, "I bought you a vacation home."

"How lovely," she responds. "Where is it? In Florida?"

"No," he continued proudly. "It's in Yitzhar." (Yitzhar is a remote settlement in the Shomron surrounded by Arab villages.)

Obviously (to us, not to him), he gave her *his* dream home, not *hers*. If we are not well versed in Torah, this is what we do to Hashem; we give Him our idea of a worthy gift, not His.

Let's replay my stroller story. If I had applied Rebbe Nachman's three-step master plan, I would have:

1. Used the NVD (Notice Very Deeply) to see Hashem's will and wisdom in the defective stroller. Then, instead of being aggravated that I had to take the time and energy to deal with a defective stroller, or miffed with the company that produced it, or angry at the storeowner for refusing to make good on the guarantee, I would have remained calm and in

good spirits. I would have said, "This comes from Hashem. Hashem wants me to deal with a defective stroller." I would have stopped vilifying the storekeeper, and seen that Hashem put him there to test me. I would have seen that Hashem had completely choreographed the scene.

2. Pressed the "*malchus* button," and said, "I accept Hashem's sovereignty." I would have let go of my will which was to spend the late afternoon doing something else and accepted Hashem's will that I was supposed to spend that time going back into town to the stroller store. I would have accepted the storekeeper's refusal as a situation I am supposed to deal with, just as I deal with my toddler's refusal to go to bed, without fury, knowing that it's part of my job in this world.

3. Asked, "What does Hashem want from me at this moment?" I would have tried to remember the relevant halachos. If I didn't really know what the Torah ordains for such a situation, I would have called my husband or our family *posek*. If I couldn't reach them right away (this was many years before cell phones), I would have shlepped the defective stroller home, and postponed action until I had ascertained what was Hashem's will. And I would have felt happy at my victory over the yetzer hara.

Rabbi Berel Wein relates a story about Rabbi Alexander Shlomo Rosenberg that perfectly illustrates the mind-set of Step Three. Rabbi Rosenberg was the founder of the OU kashrus division. One day Rabbi Rosenberg was having a meeting with Rabbi Wein when a distraught man burst into the office. The man declared that his food business was opening the next day, and he absolutely had to have a *hechsher* from the OU. He had been told that it takes three months to get a *hechsher*, but he couldn't wait. "You know me," he declared to Rabbi Rosenberg. "And if you give me a *hechsher* by tomorrow, I'll give you 5 percent of the business. You can do with it what you like."

Rabbi Rosenberg remained silent, so the man continued to press him. "O.K., I'll give you 7 percent of the business."

Rabbi Rosenberg sat there without a word or change of expression. Finally the man said, "O.K., if you give me a *hechsher* now, I'll give you 10 percent of the business, but that's my final offer."

After a long pause, Rabbi Rosenberg quietly responded, "What would Hashem think about this conversation?"

(Of course, the man never got the *hechsher*.)

That question is a surefire weapon against the yetzer hara: "What would Hashem think about this conversation? About the words I am about to utter? About the action I am about to take? What does Hashem want me to do/say/think at this moment?"

Rebbe Nachman's advice to fend off attacks of the yetzer hara by learning Torah has two dimensions. The first, as stated above, is that by learning Torah you will know how to respond. The second, a basic Chassidic concept, is that you fight evil by increasing good. So, Rebbe Nachman recommends, whenever the yetzer hara strikes, immerse yourself in the act of learning Torah.

Thus, instead of a head-on fight with the yetzer hara, just open a *sefer* and start learning. The more you learn Torah, Rebbe Nachman explains, the more you empower the reign of holiness, and the more the reign of evil disintegrates. So instead of doing battle against the yetzer hara, strengthen the part of yourself that is holy by learning Torah. Remember that Rebbe Nachman defines the yetzer hara as darkness. You can't fight with the darkness, but you can banish it by increasing the light.

Battle Plan #36:
Respond With Torah

This is similar to Battle Plan #5 (Learn Torah), except that Rebbe Nachman arrives at it from a different angle than the Maharal.

> To use this battle plan in conjunction with Battle Plans
> #34 and #35, as the third step in Rebbe Nachman's master
> plan, you must:
>
> 1. Use the spiritual NVD to see Hashem's will and wis-
>   dom in the situation confronting you.
>
> 2. Press the "malchus button" by wholeheartedly sub-
>   mitting to Hashem's will as expressed in the current
>   situation. (The current situation = Hashem's will)
>
> 3. Ask: "What does Hashem want from me at this
>   moment?" And answer with the relevant halachah
>   or ask a halachic authority.
>
> Alternatively, you can use this battle plan when you are
> under an acute attack from the yetzer hara. Grab a sefer
> and start learning. It can be the weekly Torah portion, a
> book of halachah, a mussar book, the Gemara, a biography
> of a tzaddik, or anything else that is considered "Torah
> literature." Your learning will work like the light-sensors
> installed around houses. Whenever a person approaches,
> the sensors turn on floodlights. The floodlights do not fight
> with the would-be thief; the floodlights simply frighten
> him away. In the same way, the yetzer hara flees from the
> light ignited by your Torah learning.

The Horse in the Pump

Most of us conceive of the yetzer hara as a shrewd, sophisticated enemy, perhaps a dashing figure smoking a cigarette with a cigarette holder. Chassidus, by contrast, often describes the yetzer hara as crazy, as a madman, as a raving lunatic. As the Gemara asserts: "A person doesn't sin except when a *ruach shtus* (the spirit of folly) enters him."

A fragment of a Rebbe Nachman story illustrates this concept: *A man is walking with his bucket to the village square to get water. When he gets to the pump, he starts pumping, but a horse's head comes out instead of water. He begins screaming. People stick their heads out of their windows to see what the commotion is all about, but the horse sticks its head back in. "There was a horse coming out of the pump," the man screams in horror. The townspeople think he's crazy or drunk. They stick their heads back in and go about their business. The man tries pumping again. Again he sees a horse's head. Again he screams, and the townspeople look out, but again the horse has retreated into the pump. This scene repeats itself three times, until the townspeople simply ignore the man's wild ravings.*

Rebbe Nachman is teaching us that, to some degree, we're all crazy. We all see the horse's head coming out of the pump. That's what we perceive. But it's really an insane perception, a result of the irrational ravings of the yetzer hara.

Let's go back to the example of our driving a long distance to visit a gravely ill relative. When we feel frustrated and insulted that we didn't get to see him, we say, "I'm terribly disappointed that I didn't get to see him," but we mean "How dare this person who is dying not receive me at my convenience! How dare his wife, who may soon be a widow, not sit down and socialize with me!" Such a response is indeed insane.

The yetzer hara is like a *meshuganah* chauffeur. He takes us where we don't want to go. We want to go to shul, but he takes us to the newsstand. We command: "Take me to visit my mother," and instead he takes us for a drive in the country. Only in retrospect do we see that because of the craziness of the yetzer hara, we ended up where we didn't want to be.

◆ You wanted to get to sleep early, because you have a big day ahead of you tomorrow. But the yetzer hara kept you up reading *shtus* in the latest novel until 1 a.m. Was that sensible?

◆ You wanted to stay on your diet and lose weight, but the yetzer hara got you to eat a piece of stale cake left over from Shabbos that wasn't even tasty. Was that rational?

◆ You told your mother that you didn't have time to visit her this week, but you spent two hours Wednesday night reading the newspaper. Was that smart?

Especially when we feel umbrage at what we perceive as an insult, what we're seeing is the horse coming out of the pump. For example, let's say friends didn't invite you to their daughter's wedding. You feel insulted (which could lead to sins such as lashon hara or taking revenge). If you stop and ask yourself, *What is irrational in my reaction?* you might come up with the following:

◆ You are not really such close friends.

◆ If they invited all the people they know as closely as they know you, they would end up spending thousands of dollars that would be better spent setting up a home.

◆ Perhaps the groom's side insisted they limit their guest list to 200. Should you be the cause of disharmony between the *machatanim*?

◆ Since all four of the parents come from large families, they had to give priority to close relatives over friends. Should the bride invite you instead of her first cousin?

When you hear your inner voice complaining, *How dare he/she/they treat me this way,* you can be sure that the horse is coming out of the pump.

After learning this teaching from Rebbe Nachman, I [SR] recognized a horse in my pump the very next day. I am not a *shadchan*, but I try to help my friends and their daughters. I had been involved with making a *shidduch*. There were four *shadchanim* who had a hand in this *shidduch*, but I was the last one, the one who got them back together after they had already broken up. Since many people were hounding them, I decided to lay low and let them work things out. When they had been going out again for two weeks, I saw the girl and asked her how things were going. She said, "Don't worry. You'll be the first to know."

I replied, "Your parents, of course, should be the first to know. I can be the second to know."

A few weeks later I got a call from the girl. "Mazel tov! We're engaged."

I was so excited, I jumped up and down. "Mazel tov! When did it happen?"

"The day before yesterday, actually."

The day before yesterday? I thought. *She waited 36 hours to tell me?*

Nevertheless, I was so thrilled for her that as soon as we hung up, I called a mutual friend to tell her the good news. She already knew. Then I called a second friend. She also knew. It turned out that I wasn't the second to know. I wasn't the 10th to know. I wasn't even the 100th to know. They had posted their engagement on a website that announces engagements before they had even bothered to tell me, the one who got them back together!

I was feeling hurt about this until I learned this teaching from Rebbe Nachman and realized, *Oh, it's the horse coming out of the pump!* This wonderful girl, who had been dating for several years, was finally engaged! Why was I letting my joy (and satisfaction that I merited to have a hand in it) be marred by the fact that I wasn't "the second to know"? It was stupid. It was crazy. It was the horse in the pump.

I [TH] had a different kind of horse-in-the-pump experience. It was the end of *shovavim* [the weeks of the Torah portions recounting the redemption from Egypt], so I decided to go up to Meron, as is traditional for those weeks. I took the bus in the evening, and my dear friend Chanah invited me to stay over in her house in Tzfat. When I got to the *kever* of Rebbe Shimon bar Yochai in Meron, the men's section was crowded with Slonimer *Chassidim*. There was a lot of energy. It was perfect. Finally I left and went to Chanah's house to sleep. The next morning, I went to the cemetery there in Tzfat and visited the graves of the *tzaddikim*. It was so high, and I was so happy. Later that morning I talked to one of my sons, and he said, "What time did you leave Rebbe Shimon bar Yochai?"

I replied, "A little before midnight."

My son responded: "What a shame! Everything starts at a quarter to one. Don't you know? That's when they start with the music and the heavy-duty *Tehillim* and the ..."

I hung up the phone feeling disappointed and dejected. Until that conversation, I had been feeling so blissful, but now I was feeling, "So I missed out .... I missed the real simchah."

It took me about 20 minutes of wallowing in disappointment to realize that this was the horse in the pump. *Are you crazy?* I finally said to myself. *What is wrong with you? Hashem gave you a very, very beautiful time. And now you're telling yourself that it wasn't worth anything because you left too early. This is absurd.*

Battle Plan #37: Recognize The Horse In The Pump

When you are under attack from the yetzer hara, examine your thoughts to see if a horse is coming out of the pump. In other words, look for the irrationality or counter-productive insanity in your inner monologue or your choices. Here are some classic horse-in-the-pump scenarios:

◆ *You purchased something you wanted or needed, and are happy with your purchase until you discover that you could have bought it for $25 less in another store.*

◆ *Even though you can't afford it, you must buy the latest fashion/ hi-tech device/Judaica because your friend has it.*

◆ *You are pleased with yourself/your child for scoring 88 on a hard test, until you hear that someone else scored 95.*

◆ *You go to a wedding with a friend you're planning to sit next to. After the chuppah, you use the rest room. When you come out, you find your friend seated at a table with no available seats. You start to sulk.*

◆ *You stay up late doing something non-essential or that can be done tomorrow, and suffer from lack of sleep the next day.*

◆ *Your friend or relative gives you constructive criticism, and you are insulted because they pointed out that you're not perfect.*

◆ *You argue with a cab driver over the price of a ride, becoming mean and accusatory, for a measly $1.25.*

◆ *You drink coffee or eat chocolate within three hours of bedtime.*

The yetzer hara has an agenda to make us feel sad and jealous and disappointed. Remember that in the Rebbe Nachman story, as soon as the townspeople looked, the horse disappeared. The "townspeople" stand for rationality and clear thinking. Just by looking rationally at the craziness of the yetzer hara's contentions, we can defeat it. Ask yourself: "Does this choice/attitude make sense, or is it the horse in the pump?"

The Yetzer Hara
of the Intellect

12

THE YETZER HARA OF THE INTELLECT LEAPS ONTO the dueling field brandishing the sharp sword of intellectual arguments and shouting the battle cry, "But!"

Rebbe Nachman tackles this sharp-witted yetzer hara in section 64 of *Likutei Moharan*. He begins:

Hashem Yisbarach created the world from His compassion, because He wanted to reveal His compassion. Without creating a world, to whom would He show His compassion? ... But, when He wanted to create a world, there was no place, so to speak, to create it because everything was Him. So in order to create a world, He had to contract His light to the sides and this is called tzimtzum. And through this tzimtzum an empty space — chalal panui — was created.

Now this contraction is really only in the eyes of the beholder. Really nothing changed. Hashem, however, created the illusion of His not being there. This "empty space" is where all time and space exist. The world in which we live out our lives is entirely confined to the *chalal panui*. In this *chalal panui*, you really can't observe Hashem's presence. Although, as discussed in the previous chapter, sometimes you can gather enough bits of "starlight" and enhance it with enough *emunah* to conceptually observe that Hashem is behind this world, no matter how hard you look you cannot experientially observe the presence of Hashem.

To illustrate this sublime principle: Think of the Indian Ocean tsunami that killed 230,000 people. Those who chose to could see Hashem's will and awesome power in the tsunami. No one, however, could observe Hashem's essential compassion in the tsunami.

Rebbe Nachman says that we're not going to really understand the nature of the *chalal panui*, this empty space, until the ultimate future, when Mashiach comes, because there are two opposite things happening at the same time: *yesh* and *ayin*. *Yesh* means Hashem is there and *ayin* means Hashem is not there. Hashem made it as though there's no Godliness there, so to speak. If that weren't true, it wouldn't be called "empty," and there'd be no place for the world. The truth is that there is Godliness there, because nothing could exist without Hashem's vitality. This paradox will persist until Mashiach comes.

To bring this cosmic concept down to the level of our experience: Every person is considered a small world, and in our own world we each have a *chalal panui*. This is the conceptual space where Hashem simultaneously is and isn't. This explains how a frum person, a genuinely frum person who believes in Hashem and in *Torah m'Sinai*, can cheat in business. At the moment that he decides to do what the Torah forbids, the yetzer hara convinces him that Hashem doesn't see and doesn't know. We're not talking here about a person who is overcome by desire. Sins of desire come from a different place. The person who calculates that he can cheat in business and get away with it is, to that degree, an *apikores* — someone who denies the existence of God.

Most of us have our moments of *apikorsus* [heresy], when we believe that we are unobserved: when we speak deliberate lashon hara, when we are in too much of a rush to sift the flour before using it, and when we tell deliberate lies (not just when we feel backed into a corner and get defensive, but when we intentionally lie in order to harm someone). Whenever we think we can get away with something, we have banished God from our world.

Rebbe Nachman's first point in this section is that the empty space really does appear empty. Hashem, in His wisdom, made it that there are situations in our lives and in human history where He indeed appears to be absent. So even though it's an illusion, it's not an illusion that we can dissolve in our pre-Messianic world. Of course, there are great souls who are able to live their lives in such a way that they focus on the reality beyond the illusion, but even they do not live in a world without the illusion of otherness.

Rebbe Nachman asserts that there are two kinds of heresies. The first kind of *apikorsus* stems from being too externalized. You look at the world and all you see is the outside, not the inside. You look at things that happen to people, such as children dying, terror attacks, sterling individuals killed in car accidents, and you may ask, "Where is God?"

This yetzer hara may attack a person who merely reads or hears about such a tragedy. It strikes even more vociferously when one actually knows the people involved. The hardest test is when the person himself is struck, such as when a young person loses a parent.

All such tragedies can become a duel between the yetzer hara of the intellect and a person's *emunah*. The yetzer hara can use very sophisticated weapons, shooting with a steady stream of questions such as, "If God is compassionate, how can he let people suffer? What did an infant do that it deserved to die? How do you know that the Torah is true?"

Rebbe Nachman states that to this first kind of *apikorsus* there are indeed answers. The Mishnah instructs, "Know how to answer the *apikores*." This implies that answers exist. The impediment to finding such answers is the human tendency to dwell on the externals.

We are trained from our earliest years to notice only the external. Thus, children's books picture a visit to the farm: "The cow gives milk. The hen gives eggs." This is fine for a 5-year-old, but as we mature, our education remains just as superficial. So now we're in sixth grade, and we learn that there are four kinds of clouds. We can learn the differences in their formations, but it's still just external. Clouds give rain just as hens give eggs. Even if we get to college physics, it is still a description of the external workings of nature. The Big Bang made matter just as cows make milk.

All this ignores the spiritual underpinnings of existence. Why do cows give milk? Who created cows? What does bovine lactation tell us about Hashem's will to nurture? Why do clouds make rain? What is the supernal will that dictates how much rain will fall? What is the spiritual causal relationship between human sins and drought? To look at the world in a deeper way, as we discussed in the last chapter, requires making the effort to discern Hashem's will and wisdom in the people, objects, and events of life. Rebbe Nachman is telling us that if we look for Hashem's wisdom, often (not always) we will find it.

This is because, he explains, of the *sheviras hakeilim,* "breaking of the vessels." The breaking of the vessels was a primordial event in which the physical world as Hashem originally created it could not absorb the vast and intense nature of its spiritual message. So it broke, in the same way that a balloon will burst if you try to fill it with more air than it can contain. The ramification of "the breaking of the vessels" is that the personality of the world and its inner meaning is accessible throughout existence, but it's not easily observed through physical reality, which is, after all, only fragments. The breaking of the vessels was not an accident, but rather part of Hashem's plan to create a world that offers us the opportunity to become Godly people through the process of *tikkun* or "fixing."

So this kind of *apikorsus*, where one looks at the world and is puzzled by it, stems from looking at the outside. Let's consider suffering, for example. One sees a good and virtuous person suffering from a debilitating disease, and the intellectual yetzer hara screams: "It's unfair. There's no justice in the world. Obviously there is no just God!" If one probes much deeper, however, one can discern many higher purposes served by suffering. Suffering can mobilize a person to make fruitful changes. Suffering can catalyze a person's potentials. Suffering can move a person beyond being engrossed in the physical. Investigation will provide scores of examples of people who reached heroic levels of kindness, generosity, or courage as a result of their suffering.

Dr. Rahamim Melamed-Cohen was a successful educator, devoted husband, and committed father of six children, when, at the age of 57, he was diagnosed with ALS (Lou Gehrig's Disease). The prognosis was grim: gradually spreading paralysis and three to five years to live. Dr. Melamed-Cohen, an observant Jew, was haunted by his intellectual yetzer hara, which asked: "Why did this happen to me? What did I do wrong? All my life I tried to do good, to fulfill mitzvos, and to act properly toward my fellowman. Maybe here and there I wasn't okay, but where is the proportion between this terrible illness and my small sins?"

As the illness progressed, however, Dr. Melamed-Cohen found himself tapping reservoirs of inner strength and courage that he didn't know he had. Now, 14 years later, totally paralyzed and on life support, he has published nine books written by his eye movements on a special computer and discovered new careers in art and writing poetry. He administers the yeshivah founded by his late father and keeps up a voluminous e-mail correspondence with hundreds of people worldwide, who look to him for encouragement and wisdom. He silenced his intellectual yetzer hara long ago by recognizing that the challenge posed by his illness catapulted him to higher levels of creativity, compassion, and courage than he could ever have attained without it. "These are the best and most important years of my life," he asserts.

Rebbe Nachman instructs us that this first kind of *apikorsus* can and should be answered. When the intellectual yetzer hara fires, "You don't really believe that, do you?" don't be afraid to respond: "Yes I do. I see the inside as well as the outside. You see the outside. I believe the outside has an inside."

Wisdom should take you to seeing the intricacy, beauty, and purposefulness of everything in a way that attaches you to its Source. The scientific approach, on the other hand, is limited to description. The desire to describe things without including meaning is what Rebbe Nachman labels, "the waste product of the search for truth."

According to Chassidus, interpreting events by looking "inside" can also involve taking into account the possibility of previous *gilgulim*, or incarnations. The Baal Shem Tov would console parents who had lost a child by revealing that soul's previous, almost-perfect *gilgul*. Upon fixing the one or two things left to repair, the child expired because there was no longer a need for him to be in this world. Of course, this method is not accessible to us today, but just saying, "Who knows what this soul had to fix from previous *gilgulim*?" should counter the arguments of the intellectual yetzer hara.

It's worth remembering that even if we are privy to most of the facts of someone's life (including our own), we have read merely pages 657-689 of a thousand-page story. Thus, when Rebbetzin Chaya Sara Kramer [see *Holy Woman*] faced the most agonizing test of her life, she used this method of factoring in previous *gilgulim*. Her unofficially adopted daughter Miriam was snatched away by her birth mother, who had many other children. Rebbetzin Chaya Sara, left childless, remonstrated with herself, "Perhaps in my last *gilgul* I had children and she didn't have children, and I did to her what she's doing to me now."

Yet another tool for appraising a situation from the inside is the concept of *kapparah* [expiation]. *Kapparah* means that, for profound reasons not amenable to human understanding, suffering is the mystical soap that cleanses us of all the stains with which we sully ourselves through our wrong actions, words, and thoughts. Thus, every bit of suffering in this world has the spiritual effect of purgation. *Kapparah* operates in both visible and invisible ways. The visible effect is that suffering changes a person so deeply that the root of whatever distanced the person from Hashem is extirpated. For example, if a person who is arrogant and who commits the sins that flow from arrogance is stricken with suffering, he or she usually becomes more humble. The implication of *kapparah* is that no suffering is wasted; all suffering is a currency that pays for something.

Note that none of these "inside" rebuttals to the yetzer hara of the intellect takes us to a place of clear understanding. We are ever and always in the *chalal panui*. Rather, they lead us to admit that when Hashem issues a decree, He weighs myriads and myriads of factors, and we can get a fleeting glimpse of only an infinitesimal fraction of them. Imagine being certain about the appearance of a dog from seeing 16 hairs at the end of his tail.

Battle Plan #38: Answer With The Inside

When King David sought to conquer the Jebusite city of Jerusalem, he encountered massive walls topped by formidable battlements protected by skilled warriors. How did David win? His men entered the city through the water tunnels deep beneath the walls and made a surprise attack from the inside.

The first kind of yetzer hara of the intellect can be defeated by going deep and striking from the inside. (Do not attempt this battle plan against the second kind of yetzer hara of the intellect described later in this chapter.)

Rebbe Nachman prescribes arguing with this yetzer

hara. For instance, let's say you know a wealthy person who is both a devout Jew and a generous philanthropist, who supports dozens of worthy yeshivos and charitable institutions. Suddenly he loses all his money. Your intellectual yetzer hara challenges you: "How could God let this happen? He used his money to help so many people. Why would God punish such a good person? It's so unjust."

Answer this yetzer hara by penetrating to the inside: "From the outside, it looks unfair. But who says that the goal of life is to have a lot of money? Maybe it's not a 'punishment' at all. What is the real, spiritual purpose of life in this world? To fix oneself. Maybe losing his money is a test that he has to go through in order to rectify himself. And if he passes that test, he'll be the winner, not the loser. What do I really know about this person's soul and its needs? Nothing. But I believe that 'Hashem is good and does good,' so this financial loss must, in some way, be good. Perhaps it's a kapparah, and it's better to suffer financial loss than any of the much worse kinds of suffering that could happen to him. That's a different way to think of it."

Hopefully your emunah will expand to the point that this yetzer hara will never rear its head. Then you can reserve all your arguments for debates with people who are still prone to look only at the outside. Do not fear engaging with them.

What's the Lesson?

In grappling with the yetzer hara of the intellect, one must be aware of both the power and the limitations of the mind. As discussed in the previous chapter, Rebbe Nachman advocates responding to every situation by looking for Hashem's will and wisdom. However, it would be a fatal mistake to think that we can fathom Hashem's reasons for what He does. We are in the *chalal panui;* we cannot know the mind of God. It is illegitimate to ask: "Why did Hashem do this to me?"

Instead we should ask: "What can I learn from this?" There is no wrong answer to this question. Asking this question leads us to teshuvah and spiritual growth. It imbues the events of our lives with meaning and purpose.

Thus, for example, one morning I [SR] got out of bed and found that I couldn't stand up straight. My back was out. As the day progressed, I felt muscle spasms pulling my bones out of place as the pain grew more and more intense. I called a friend who practices "trigger-point massage therapy," and made an appointment for a treatment the next day. By bedtime, I couldn't move without excruciating pain. By the middle of the night, the pain from any motion was almost unbearable.

By external vision, it was a simple physical problem: muscles in spasm and bones and vertebrae pinching nerves. I reached for my spiritual NVD and proceeded to Notice Very Deeply. I realized that it was Hashem, and only Hashem, who had moved my muscles and bones to cause me such pain. (This was an easy inference, because I had not fallen nor experienced any other mishap.) Of course, I was praying to Hashem to relieve my pain, but I kept looking through the NVD. I saw that Hashem, Who loves me, wouldn't give me such pain for no reason.

So I asked the question, "What am I supposed to learn from this terrible pain?" I was no stranger to pain in my life, having undergone three major surgeries as well as childbirth, but this was the first time I was experiencing almost *unbearable* pain. I kept probing deeper, and suddenly I thought of something: The day before I had learned that a man in our community had left his wife and three children. I was extremely judgmental against him. It occurred to me that this man, who had lost his father at the age of 16, may have been in *unbearable* pain. Having lost my father only at the age of 42 (which was traumatic enough), what did I know of how such a tragic loss could have affected the psyche of a teenager? This did not make his actions right. His actions were still wrong, but I realized that I, who had never suffered unbearable psychological pain, had no right to condemn him. I learned my lesson. Instead of judging him harshly, I started to daven that he does teshuvah. The next day, I got a treatment, and 75 percent of the pain subsided. That night in bed, I reached down for my blanket, and pop! I felt a vertebra pop into place. Hashem, Who had sent me the back pain, fixed it.

Another example: Last March I [TH] broke my leg. I was walking in the forest. I saw a slope leading to a little valley, and I decided to go in that direction. The slope was muddy. I could see that, but I decided that I would go that way anyway. I slipped and fell, and broke my fibula. I was in a cast, a wheelchair, the whole production. I questioned what I was supposed to learn from breaking my leg. I felt that the lesson had to do with *gaavah*, pride. As the saying goes, "Pride goes before a fall." Even though I saw that the muddy slope was slippery, I thought I could handle it just fine. I was wearing Keds, which have no treads, but part of my *gaavah shtick* was that Keds are good enough. I didn't have the humility to be cautious. Being confined to a cast and a wheelchair made me feel helpless and humble. I saw how fragile we mortals really are. It was a vivid lesson.

Now, you may object, "What if that was not the lesson Hashem intended to teach you?" The answer is: There is no such thing as, "I did teshuvah on the wrong thing." Whatever we do teshuvah on is a step up and closer to Hashem. If we follow the clues and end up at the wrong treasure, that's fine, too!

Battle Plan #39:
Ask "What Can I Learn From This?"

Whatever happens to you, after you respond with Rebbe Nachman's master plan (Battle Plans #34, #35, and #36), ask: "Now, what can I learn from this?" Then notice what crops up in your mind.

When implementing this battle plan, don't get hung up in worrying, "What if the lesson I come up with is the wrong lesson?" Hashem's wisdom is within you. If you ask sincerely, "What can I learn from this?" trust that the answer that arises in your mind is valid. There is no such thing as, "I did teshuvah on the wrong thing."

The only way to lose this particular battle is to fall prey to the yetzer hara that tells you: "It was an accident. It just happened. There's no meaning and purpose behind it."

As soon as you've asked the question, "What can I learn from this?" you have vanquished that yetzer hara.

The Second Yetzer Hara of the Intellect

Sometimes we can connect the dots and make out a picture. For example, we all know some version of this story: An Israeli *tzeddakah* collector goes to England or New York or Toronto. He's collecting money for his yeshivah, which is on the verge of bankruptcy. And he's desperate. And he's had no luck. And finally, on the last day, somebody tells him that he has arranged for him to be able to meet with an eminent wealthy person who is sympathetic to this cause. The only time he could see him, however, is 5:15. His plane back to Israel is 6:45. He decides to go to the appointment and hope for the best. So he goes and the rich man promises him that he'll think seriously about making a donation. It's a quarter to 6, and he leaves the mansion empty-handed. He gets into a taxi, and there's a hair-raising ride to the airport, but in the end he misses the plane. He's extremely despondent, because he bought the cheapest kind of ticket, which can neither be exchanged nor refunded. So the money is lost. He returns to where he had been staying, and is so depressed that all he can do is take a nap. When he wakes up, he calls his wife to tell her he won't be home for Shabbos after all. When she hears his voice, she's ecstatic, because the plane he missed crashed, leaving no survivors. He is overcome with gratitude to Hashem, because he sees that it was Hashem's mercy that made him miss the plane.

If a person thinks like that, his *emunah* is contingent on 300 people dying. There's something wrong with this story: If the plane hadn't crashed, he would have remained despondent, feeling that Hashem's mercy didn't extend to getting him on his plane on time. He would have been in the clutches of the yetzer hara that says, "If I can't see that it's good, it's not good."

A person who has wrangled free of that yetzer hara says, "If I make the plane, it's good, and if I don't make the plane, it's good. And if I understand it, it's good, and if I don't understand it, it's also good." This is a much higher level. Faith in Hashem's goodness should not be contingent on connecting the dots.

One of the names for a Jew is *Ivri*, the one who passes over. Rebbe Nachman says that *Ivri* means we're the only people who skip over that very high fence called "rational perception" and go up to the next higher level. Therefore we Jews are capable of vanquishing the second yetzer hara of the intellect, the one caused by the *chalal panui*, where it is impossible to connect the dots.

Not everything that happens in this world is meant to be interpretable. Rebbe Nachman says that the *chalal panui* is a phenomenon whereby Hashem is there, but He made it so that we can't see Him. Not that we *don't* see Him, but we *can't* see Him. This concealment is purposeful and absolute.

Thus there is a second kind of yetzer hara of the intellect that asks, for example, "Where was Hashem in the Holocaust?" or "Where was Hashem in the Chmielnicki massacres (where all 100,000 victims were devout Jews)?" These questions are unanswerable because we are living in the *chalal panui*. You can't interpret everything. Hashem purposely made it that you can't interpret everything.

With this second kind of *apikorsus* the problem isn't just superficiality or externality. The problem is that sometimes there are questions

— deep questions of meaning — that can't be answered. Hashem made it that way. Hashem made an empty space, the *chalal panui*.

In Judaism, most of the time we train our minds to look for answers. Rebbe Nachman instructs us that sometimes we have to throw away the question. The question doesn't work because of the *chalal panui*. And this yetzer hara expresses itself as our refusal to accept that the human mind can't grasp everything.

You answer the first kind of intellectual yetzer hara by arguing with it, by giving answers from the inside. This second kind of yetzer hara is different. You say, "I see order." Einstein also said that. However, you have to add, "But I also see chaos." That's why Einstein didn't believe in a personal God. He observed no consistent pattern in God's response to people's deeds. Now this isn't because he wasn't smart enough. He was Einstein. But it's because in this world the question is not meant to be answerable.

Some questions can be answered only in terms of Divine concealment, which is no answer at all from a rational standpoint. Sometimes you have to just step back and say, "The way it is, is the way Hashem wants it to be." This is not intellectually satisfying. But this is how it has to be because we're in the *chalal panui*.

One of my [TH] students has a relative who works for GAMPAC, Godless Americans Political Action Committee. She always thought that she could never get into an argument with this person and win. After studying Rebbe Nachman, however, she told me, "I can say that I know Hashem does everything without saying I know *why* He does everything." This was very liberating.

Such acceptance means saying, "I'm small. I'm too small to comprehend the mind of God. And I'm not going to force the infinite God into the confines of my limited intellect."

Rebbe Nachman tells us that we're not always going to figure it out. But saying, "I don't know," is very different than saying, "It's not good."

The best answer to the second yetzer hara of the intellect is silence. Rebbe Nachman brings a Gemara that relates that Hashem showed Moshe Rabbeinu everything that would be in the future. When Moshe saw the death of Rebbe Akiva, how he was tortured to death for teaching Torah, Moshe asked in anguish, "This is Torah and this is its reward?" Hashem responded to him: "Silence!" This response may seem like the harsh rebuke of a teacher to a student who has stepped out of line. Rebbe Nachman understands it more deeply. Hashem was telling Moshe that the only authentic response to his question is silence.

Notice that Hashem didn't give Moshe "inside" reasons, as we recommended for the first kind of yetzer hara of the intellect. He didn't say, "Rebbe Akiva was actually a *gilgul* of ...." Hashem was teaching Moshe that the death of Rebbe Akiva came from the *chalal panui*, and the only proper response is silence. Such silence is higher than any words. Hashem wanted Moshe to expand himself beyond the rational mind that is limited to words. Therefore, some commentators hold that Moshe's so-called "speech impediment" was a result of his soul's being rooted in that supernal place of silence, beyond speech, where speech is difficult or impossible.

I [SR] became a baalas teshuvah 23 years ago. I was walking the walk, talking the talk, and dressing the dress. But my intellectual yetzer hara had a lot of questions that my rabbis and teachers couldn't answer. Then, about two years after I had become observant, Rebbetzin Heller said something that transformed my entire way of looking at the world. She said that Hashem is hidden. He's inherently hidden. All my life I had been seeking answers. She said that I'm not going to find all the answers, because Hashem is hidden. No matter how smart I am, or how smart I think I am, I would never find the answers to certain questions, because God is inherently hidden. At that moment I stopped trying to kick open the door of ultimate reality. I gave up feeling, "If Judaism doesn't have all the answers, there's something wrong with the religion." I realized that the deepest things are not going to be revealed in this world, to anybody, by anybody. At that moment I became truly religious.

Battle Plan #40:
Admit Divine Concealment

In the duel against the second kind of yetzer hara of the intellect, the optimum weapon is silence. Not the silence of defeat. Not the silence of, "You have won the debate." But rather the silence of humility. The silence of, "No answer will suffice, because Hashem is inherently hidden."

Do not be ashamed to admit Divine concealment. This silence issues from a recognition that any concept of God that could be contained by the human mind would not be a concept of God worth believing in.

If you cannot wield the weapon of silence, the second-best weapon against this kind of yetzer hara is the four words: "What do I know?" Admitting the smallness of your mind, the smallness of any human mind, against the infinite vastness of God kills this yetzer hara on the spot.

A frum woman was walking in downtown Jerusalem shortly after a terror attack. Someone stopped her and asked in anguish: "How can God permit such things?"

She responded as she had learned from Rebbetzin Ruchama Shain: "In this world, there are no answers. In the Next World, there are no questions."

The Arsenal 13

THE *TANYA* BY RAV SHNEUR ZALMAN OF LIADI, the first Rebbe of Lubavitch, is a veritable arsenal of weapons to use when battling the yetzer hara. In this chapter, we'll offer a sampling from that vast arsenal.

The Baal HaTanya wrote that the *nefesh*, or vital soul (the lowest of the five levels of soul), consists of two parts: the animal soul [*nefesh bahamis*] and the spiritual soul [*nefesh Elokis*]. The animal soul is the instinctual self, which can provide a welcoming abode for the forces of evil. Thus the animal soul can host the yetzer hara. This same animal soul, however, can be elevated and can become an auxiliary that draws from the spiritual soul. Thus the Baal HaTanya described life as an ongoing war not between you and an external foe, but rather between two parts of yourself: your animal soul and your spiritual soul.

The Two
Basic Techniques

Whenever you experience the yetzer hara exerting a downward pull on your animal soul, you have two possibilities of how to fight it: *etkafia* or *ethafchia*. These are not weapons per se, but rather "martial arts," i.e., techniques of combat.

Etkafia means to firmly resist the negative impulse. *Ethafchia* means to deflect the impulse into a positive direction. All tendencies or impulses to do, say, or think in ways that the Torah prohibits must be fought with either *etkafia* or *ethafchia*.

Just as every form of martial arts has a basic position of the body that the combatant must assume, so *etkafia* requires standing firm and not allowing yourself to be moved at all. *Etkafia* entails conquering the negative impulse through the technique of saying, "No, I will not yield. I refuse to compromise."

Although *etkafia* is a technique for fighting one's inner battles, we can glimpse the kind of adamantine resolve it requires by a story from the short life of Rabbi Gavriel Holtzberg, *Hy"d*, the Chabad rabbi who was brutally murdered *al Kiddush Hashem* in Mumbai, India. At the Chabad House in Mumbai, Rabbi Holtzberg cared for thousands of post-army Israelis. Among them was a young Israeli drug addict who was hospitalized in a horrific Indian hospital. [SR's note: One who has not been in an Indian hospital cannot imagine the conditions there.] Unfortunately, the young man died. When Rabbi Holtzberg tried to take the body in order to give him a proper Jewish burial, the hospital refused. They wanted to dispose of it in their own way, presumably cremation or throwing it into the nearest river. Rabbi Holtzberg fought adamantly, but the hospital would not hand over the remains. Even the young man's family back in Israel did not support Rabbi Holtzberg's efforts. Nevertheless, he simply would not back down. He stood by the body of this drug addict as if guarding a valuable treasure, and would not let the hospital workers take it away. Finally, having no other choice in the face of Rabbi Holtzberg's obdurate stand, the hospital authorities capitulated. Rabbi Holtzberg did the *taharah* and gave the young man a proper Jewish burial. This is *etkafia*: "I will not yield."

Many of life's tests require the absolute "no" of *etkafia*. Let's say a woman is (finally) going out on a shidduch with a man who seems perfect for her. After many dates, they are about to get engaged. The woman was adopted at birth and converted as an infant. This poses no problem for the man until, just before the engagement, he discovers that he is a Kohen, and therefore prohibited from marrying a convert. At that point, the yetzer hara says to both of them, "Who will know anyway? You finally, after years of searching, found someone who is right for you. The Holy Temple is not standing. Why should you sacrifice a lifetime of happiness for an antiquated rule?" This is a mega-attack of the yetzer hara. The only way to defend oneself is *etkafia* — the adamant decision, "No, I am not marrying this person. Period."

Battle Plan #41: *Etkafia*-Resist

Employ this combat stance whenever the negative impulse cannot be redirected. Stand like a rock and say, "No, I will not yield."

This technique can be used for major life issues, such as addiction to alcohol, overeating, prescription drugs, and smoking. While the psychological need that led to addiction in the first place can be redirected (ethafchia), the addictive behavior itself can be terminated only by etkafia — firm resistance. (The most successful follow-up to that firm decision is a Jewish twelve-step program.)

Etkafia can also be employed to fend off minor attacks of the yetzer hara. For example:

> ◆ when you are tempted to eat a food with a question-able hechsher, or a vegetable that was grown during the Shemittah year, or was cooked by a non-Jew.
>
> ◆ when you are attending a family reunion with many non-observant relatives whose idea of a greeting is a bear hug.
>
> ◆ when all the salads and the elegant dessert you laboriously prepared for Shabbos dinner are in the refrigerator, and you realize that someone forgot to turn off the refrigerator light before Shabbos.

The second combat technique taught by the Baal HaTanya is *ethafchia*, turning over the impulse that seeks to distance you from Hashem. This entails identifying the source of your inclination toward what is forbidden and redirecting it in a way that is permitted.

An example of *ethafchia* is a Neve student of mine [TH] named Caroline, who was a talented professional singer and actress. She had had a leading role in a musical in London, and was about to receive her dream role in another smash hit. She began to study Judaism, and at that point learned the laws of Shabbos. She realized that all major shows have performances on Shabbos. So first she did a heroic feat of *etkafia* by saying "No" to the role she had dreamed of all her life. Then she came to Jerusalem, studied at Neve, and became fully observant. When she learned that performing in front of men is prohibited, she had to decide what to do with her desire to sing and dance in front of audiences. This desire comes from the animal soul. Like all of the impulses of the animal soul, it could be used for evil or for good. Caroline did *ethafchia*; she started recording tapes for "Women only," and performing for "Women only" shows. Caroline is now working in *kiruv*, using her desire to perform in the service of Hashem.

Battleplan #42:
Ethafchia-Deflect

To use the technique of ethafchia, start by identifying the source of what is distancing you from Hashem. Then take that same impulse, tendency, or energy and use it for the good. Here are some examples of people who employed ethafchia to score a victory over their yetzer hara:

A young woman who by nature was both meddlesome and critical realized that she was turning into a "yenta," becoming the person she didn't want to be. So she employed the method of ethafchia:

1. *She identified the basic tendencies in her nature: She liked to get involved in other people's lives, and her critical eye zoomed in on what was wrong in every situation.*

2. *She pondered how she could redirect these tendencies for the good.*

3. *She took a course in counseling and committed to stop speaking lashon hara.*

4. *Now she is actually helping people through her counseling work, building them up instead of tearing them down.*

A young man had a strong drive for kavod. His desire to feel important led him to brag and even lie about his accomplishments. One Yom Kippur, he realized that he didn't like the person he had become. Around that time, a friend told him about an organization for the elderly that desperately needed volunteers. He volunteered, committed more and more of his time, and ultimately became one of the unpaid heads of the organization. Now he truly is important and indispensable to hundreds of needy people.

A woman with a strong aesthetic sense and the money to indulge her love of beauty in excesses of wardrobe and home decoration could have used this tendency to gain prestige and compliments for herself. Instead, she dedicates her aesthetic sense to enhancing other people's simchos. She will spend hours teaching a mother how to decorate a fancy cake for her son's Bar Mitzvah, or she'll simply decorate the cake herself. She makes centerpieces for weddings and fund-raisers, and for those who can't afford an artistic caterer, she sets up the buffet tables with flair.

Sadness

The Chassidic emphasis on joy is well known. The Baal HaTanya, in Chapter 26, explains why joy is an essential prerequisite for Divine service. Just as when two people are wrestling, if one is sluggish and lazy he will be defeated even if he is the stronger contestant, so it is impossible to be victorious over the yetzer hara when afflicted with laziness and heaviness. Moreover, he points out, laziness and heaviness come from sadness. Thus sadness renders it impossible to defeat the yetzer hara. That's why making people feel sad is at the top of the yetzer hara's agenda.

Rebbe Nachman popularized the adage, "It's a great mitzvah to be happy always." But, we may object, is there no time that sadness is justified?

The Baal HaTanya gives a radical answer: There are three kinds of sadness, and only one of them is justified, and even that one kind of sadness should be permitted only for circumscribed periods of time. He goes on to discuss the three kinds of sadness:

1. material sadness, which is caused by problems with the mundane, such as children, health, or money

2. spiritual sadness caused by bad actions

3. spiritual sadness caused by bad thoughts

Sadness must be fought tooth and nail, but the weapons against each kind of sadness are different.

To dispel the first kind of sadness, the Baal HaTanya cites a Gemara stating that one should accept misfortune with joy. Misfortune is in fact "concealed good." What we normally think of as good fortune is "revealed good," but that comes from a much lower plane than "concealed good." It is impossible to evaluate the actual benefit of any situation in this world, because only in the Next World will its true worth be apparent.

Fighting sadness over mundane things requires putting them into perspective against the backdrop of eternity. Rav Tzvi Meir Zilberberg tells a true story about a religious man who became a junior executive in a prestigious company. The head of the corporation wanted to be rated high in the Fortune 500's list of the richest people in the world. He felt that he should be #76. Instead, Fortune Magazine listed him as #135. After the list was published, this man sank into a black depression. For two weeks his business had to be run by junior executives. The observant man's response to this was to quit his job, sell his shares in the company, move to Israel, and start learning Torah full-time. He saw where his life in the corporate world could take him: to becoming depressed over being the wrong number on the rich list. Although we may think this story is extreme, all depression over physical or material matters is giving more credence to the transient world than Hashem wants it to have.

Battle Plan #43:
Dispel Material Sadness: The Three A's

If the cause of your sadness is material, such as monetary loss, health problems, conflicts with your children, or troubles in your profession, apply the following steps:

    1. Accept: Tell yourself, "The way things are is the way Hashem wants them to be." Acceptance differs from resignation. Resignation means submitting to defeat. Acceptance means submitting your will to the Divine will.

2. *Appreciate:* Tell yourself, "This is hidden good. Although I cannot see its benefit right now, I have faith that Hashem, Who loves me and wants only what is best for me, has decreed only good for me."

3. *Adjust your time frame:*[1] Tell yourself: "Everything in the physical world is transitory. Why should I allow myself to succumb to sadness when its cause may change by next week? Financial losses may be reversed; health problems may be cured; teenagers eventually grow out of it; and a year from now I won't even remember this crisis at work. Worrying about anything in this world is like fretting about the furnishings in my stateroom on the Titanic."

Spiritual sadness must be treated differently. Spiritual sadness caused by bad actions is the appropriate response to having sinned.

---

1. What if the cause of one's sadness will not abate over time, such as the sadness suffered by women who never gave birth to children? Unlike the forms of sadness that Battle Plan #43 addresses, such sadness cannot be dispelled by the advice, "Adjust your time frame." Instead, only a rather erudite answer will suffice. Imagine that an 8-year-old child and I [TH] and a world-class pitcher are in a ballpark. The child throws a baseball with all his might; it goes perhaps 12 feet. Then I throw a baseball with all my might; it goes 50 feet. Then the pitcher throws a baseball and it goes as far as the eye can see. This is a metaphor to explain that the strongest soul has enough force to have her energy reach the farthest place, which is invisible from this "ballpark." For reasons known only to Hashem, there are people who have souls with such force, while most souls cannot and therefore are not expected to reach that far beyond the limits of perceptible goodness. These strong souls are people like Queen Esther, whose lives defy intellectual or emotional interpretation. There was no happy ending for Esther personally, but the reach of her soul as it entered the depths of the *tumah* of Achashverosh's palace saved the entire Jewish nation, a feat that was never replicated. If the source of your sadness is not transitory, reflect on this rather than on Battle Plan #43.

It is, in fact, the second step of teshuvah as outlined by the Rambam: regret. If, however, you start to feel depressed over your sins while you are involved in mundane activities, warns the Baal HaTanya, know for sure that you are being tricked by the yetzer hara, who yearns to make you sad. Even if you feel guilty while learning Torah or davening, stop yourself immediately. Tell yourself that now is not the time for entertaining such melancholy thoughts. This is a real conundrum: You must indeed work through your feelings of guilt and spiritual failure, but if you allow them to plague you during the course of your day, the yetzer hara will use them to make you depressed and thus incapable of serving Hashem.

The Baal HaTanya offers a brilliant solution to this conundrum. He recommends setting aside a specific period of time to reflect on your sins. Before you begin, specify exactly for how much time you will engage in the process of self-reproach, and do not exceed that time limit. During that set period, allow all your feelings of regret, disgust with yourself, and profound sadness to flow. When the set time period is over, stop and move on with your life.

Feigie Bleier is a Chassidic woman who lives in Boro Park. One evening at dinner, her children were complaining about the food she had served. Feigie announced: "The complaint department is closed!"

The stunned children looked at one another. Wide eyed, her 8-year-old asked: "What time does the complaint department open?"

Feigie looked at the kitchen clock. It was 5:40 p.m. "It opens at 6 o'clock," she announced with an official air.

"And what time does the complaint department close?" asked the 10-year-old.

"It closes at 6:01."

The children spent the next 20 minutes watching the clock. At exactly 6 o'clock, they all started shouting, "I can't stand beans!" "You know I don't like onions on my chicken!" "The food here is terrible!" "I've told you a million times I don't want a baked potato!"

At exactly 6:01, the shouting abruptly stopped. The complaint department was closed. It would not reopen until the next day at 6 o'clock.

From then on, no child in the Bleier family ever complained before 6 o'clock or after 6:01. If one of the children forgot and started to complain, a helpful brother or sister would remind, "The complaint department is closed till 6 o'clock."

(This system worked great until one fine Wednesday. Feigie had been trying to get her youngest daughter into a certain kindergarten. The principal insisted on a telephone interview with every prospective parent. On that Wednesday, the principal phoned at 6:01. All he heard was wild shrieks and yelling in the background. It took a great deal of explaining …)

Battle Plan #44:
Define A Time For Spiritual Sadness

Feeling sorrow and regret for your misdeeds is a vital part of spiritual growth; however, do not allow yourself to indulge in such thoughts except at specified times. When you feel plagued by guilt, set aside a certain period of time for reflecting on your misdeed. Be strict with yourself so as not to exceed the time limit.

During that time, allow all your sad, angry, and guilty thoughts to come to the fore. Pour out your heart in sorrow to Hashem. Think about your mistakes, and offer them to Hashem with a broken heart, aware that Hashem accepts sincere teshuvah. Reassure yourself that Hashem loves you, no matter what you have done, and that He wants you to move on from your past mistakes. At the end say, "My compassionate Father, I know that You accept teshuvah and value a broken heart. I am entirely in Your hands."

> *That's it. When the "sadness department" is closed, it is closed. When you get up, feel joy that you have done the mitzvah of teshuvah and have returned to your Father in Heaven. Feel joy and renewed strength to fight the yetzer hara.*

Another frequent cause of sadness is bad thoughts. The Torah prohibits certain thoughts such as anger, lust, jealousy, hatred, and judgmental reflections. When such thoughts crop up in your mind, you are likely to react with feelings of guilt, worthlessness, and depression. Again, this is a ploy of the yetzer hara, who yearns to destroy you through sadness.

The Baal HaTanya recommends that when prohibited thoughts arise in your mind during mundane activities (as opposed to during Divine service), simply direct your mind elsewhere. Do not struggle against such thoughts, because that grants them additional attention. Do not dwell on them. Do not allow such thoughts to camp out in your head. Just focus your mind elsewhere.

According to the Baal HaTanya, when you avert your mind from bad thoughts, you are fulfilling the mitzvah found in the third paragraph of the Shema: *"Lo sasuru acharei levavchem v'acharei eineichem."* ["Do not stray after your heart and after your eyes."] That the forbidden thought cropped up in your mind in the first place is not your fault, but if you allow yourself to dwell on the forbidden thought, you have transgressed. Therefore, the very act of directing your mind away from the forbidden thought is the fulfillment of a mitzvah. The Baal HaTanya quotes the Gemara that a person who has passively refrained from sinning is given a reward as though he had done a positive mitzvah. Therefore, you should rejoice every time you direct your mind away from negative thoughts.

The yetzer hara will try to convince you to be horrified that the forbidden thought occurred to you in the first place. Such a reaction is, according to the Baal HaTanya, conceit. Don't think: "A *tzaddik* would never have this kind of thought." That may be true, but so what? Humbly accept the truth that you are not on the exalted level where all your thoughts will be pure. You have to live your life, not someone else's. What Hashem wants from you is to fight the good fight and defeat the yetzer hara. You do this by utilizing Battle Plan #45.

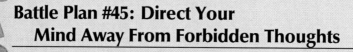

Battle Plan #45: Direct Your Mind Away From Forbidden Thoughts

Whenever a forbidden thought crops up in your mind, DO NOT:

◆ **dwell on it**

◆ **fight against it**

◆ **reproach yourself about it**

◆ **pay attention to it**

◆ **try to resolve it**

Instead, move your mind away forcibly. Imagine that your 18-month-old child has managed to climb out of her stroller and is walking toward a busy street. You will not stand there and watch her to see what happens. Nor will you examine the street to see if a truck is coming. Nor will you stand there upbraiding yourself for your failure in parenting. You will run, pick her up with both hands, bring her back to the stroller, and fasten her in. And afterward, you won't yell at her for leaving her stroller, because she is too young to understand.

In this metaphor, the child is the wandering mind. What is the "stroller" you should put your mind into? Any permitted thought will do: the stock market, tonight's dinner, the errand you forgot, the tree flowering next to you. As long as you are aware that you are fulfilling the mitzvah of not allowing yourself to be misled, the very act of removing your mind from the forbidden thought is praiseworthy.

Give yourself permission to rejoice at your victory over the yetzer hara.

If an obsessive bad thought keeps returning to your mind, such as anger at someone who hurt you, appeal to Hashem to help you vanquish that thought. Prayer rescues.

Remember, however, that if you try not to think of an elephant, you will definitely think of an elephant. This battle plan requires you to develop the skill of directing your mind elsewhere.

What if these terrible thoughts occur to you during davening or learning Torah? The Baal HaTanya warns, in Chapter 28, never to allow yourself to feel dejected and downcast during davening or learning. Sadness is a victory for the yetzer hara.

Again, he prescribes, don't dwell on such thoughts. Direct your mind back to your prayer or your learning. In fact, you should be encouraged by the occurrence of foreign thoughts, because what is going on on the spiritual plane is that the animal soul is waging a battle against the Divine soul precisely because the Divine soul is exerting itself with real strength and vigor. The furiousness of the attack testifies to the ardor of your effort in prayer or learning. The muscleman doesn't bother fighting with the 90-pound weakling. He challenges only the strong guys.

This teaching counters the false contention that foreign thoughts prove that one's prayer is worthless. That would be true, explains the Baal HaTanya, if there were only one soul. Then that one soul must be either praying or fantasizing, so if she is fantasizing, she isn't praying. The truth is there are two souls who wage war against each other: the Divine soul and the animal soul. The Baal HaTanya illustrates this point: Imagine a person is davening with devotion while a wicked pagan stands opposite him, chatting and speaking to him in order to distract him. The proper response would be to ignore this miscreant and pretend to be deaf. Similarly, one must not engage with nor argue with the foreign thought because "one who wrestles with a filthy person becomes filthy."

Battle Plan #46:
Ignore Forbidden Thoughts During Prayer

Like Battle Plan #45, the only effective weapon is to direct the mind away from the bad thoughts. Since now you are not engaged in mundane activities, but rather davening or learning, the "stroller" you should return your mind to is your prayers or your learning. Ignore the bad thought the way you would ignore an evil person who is talking to you. Do not engage the thought nor try to wrestle it down. Instead make yourself deaf to its evil speech.

If you cannot succeed in ignoring the thoughts because of their intensity, you should beg Hashem for help, and Hashem will help, because "His people are an actual part of God."

Do not feel sad or guilty that this evil thought has encroached on your Divine service. When you understand that you are engaged in a continuous battle between your animal soul and your spiritual soul, you will accept that sometimes your spiritual soul will win, and sometimes your animal soul will win. That's the way it is. Muster up your strength to fight valiantly, but never be discouraged by defeat. Be happy that your yetzer hara feels so threatened by the power of your prayer or Torah learning that it is launching such a furious attack.

MATERIALISM

Next the Baal HaTanya tackles the problem of materialism and how it renders the heart dull and incapable of prayer. "Sometimes he is unable to fight against the yetzer hara ... because of the heaviness that is in his heart" [Chapter 29]. This "stoniness" of the heart is caused by too much absorption in the *klipah* — the force of externality.

As mentioned above, the Baal HaTanya regarded life as a struggle between the animal soul and the spiritual soul. We are all familiar with this struggle. We want the bliss of association with great Torah personalities, but we also want the sushi dinner. We love to hear an inspiring *d'var Torah*, but not if it means getting to the Kiddush a half-hour late. We would love to daven at Kever Rachel, but not the same afternoon when there's a sale on Shabbos robes.

If we want (and we do want!) that the spiritual should win the battle over the material, it's worth remembering a principle that the commercial world calls "product loyalty." This means that if you're using Palmolive dish-washing soap, the competing brand will have a hard time wooing you away. Wherever you are, that's where you'll want to stay.

To translate this principle to spiritual reality, visualize the Belzer Rebbe's Chanukah candle lighting: Thousands of Chassidim are immersed in song for three hours. They are singing with real joy and inner yearning, both for the present and the Messianic future. Now imagine that someone announces: "Anyone who tears himself away from the singing will get three portions of Yerushalmi kugel." Obviously he'll get very few takers, because in that atmosphere the Yerushalmi kugel feels pale and joyless compared to the spiritual joy of what's going on.

Such "product loyalty" can go either way. Imagine the same Chassidim at a weekend-long Bar Mitzvah at a fancy hotel. The elegance of the ambience confers a sense of importance. The waiters treat the guests like dignitaries. The aroma of the food is tantalizing. For the main course of Shabbos dinner, five choices are offered: steak, fried chicken ... At that moment, someone announces: "A famous Maggid is saying Torah in the auditorium right now." Again, he'll get very few takers because the *gashmius* [materialism] has made their hearts as dull as the Baal HaTanya describes.

This conflict is weighted against the spiritual soul because human "product loyalty" is with the animal soul and its externality. The forces of evil, notes the Baal HaTanya, are naturally with a person from birth, while the spiritual soul comes only later. Thus he quotes a Zohar that one has to "hit the yetzer hara with a hammer." This means banging down on the *gashmius*, pushing it aside with force, because the *ruchnius* [spirituality] is underneath.

The more you surround yourself with *ruchnius,* the less you will be drawn to *gashmius.* Imagine that a friend brings you to Bnei Brak to get a blessing from Rebbetzin Kanievski. She meets with you and gives you a *berachah* that your children will be *talmidei chachamim,* and everything that you had in mind when you got married and wanted to build a house of Torah is what you should actually have. Then she invites you to sit in the chair of her late father-in-law, the Steipler Gaon, and daven. At that moment the friend who brought you taps your arm and reminds you that the two-for-one sale in natural hair *sheitels* on Rechov Rabbi Akiva is starting now. No matter how little you consider yourself a spiritual person, at that moment no amount of *gashmius* could pull you away.

Several years ago, a few women in an affluent American community, inspired by Rebbetzin Kanievski's example, decided to get together every morning during the Ten Days of Repentance to say "Amen" to one another's morning *berachos,* in the merit of the recovery of the seriously ill daughter of one of the women. After Yom Kippur, they decided to continue, and they added a weekly Shabbos *shiur* on *shemiras halashon.* Other women joined, so there were 15 women. Every morning they would share a *d'var Torah* or read from a book about prayer before the Amens. The more they were thus immersed in spirituality, the more spirituality they wanted. So they added a speaker every Rosh Chodesh. After Pesach, they decided to have regular classes during *Sefirah.* More women joined until more than 100 women were attending the gatherings. Carried along by the spiritual momentum they themselves had created, the women decided to continue the classes and add others. Many of them joined a monthly Mussar workshop led by Rav Leib Kelemen. Most of them became involved with *kiruv* through Aish HaTorah's Project Inspire. As one member attests:

"The more we came, the more we became enriched. We became passionate, very [spiritually growing] women. And the greater our connection to God, the greater our connection to the community." The commitment to say "Amen" for 10 days has ended up changing the focus of an entire community. This is a stunning example of how "the more *ruchnius* you surround yourself with, the more *ruchnius* you'll want."

Judaism specializes in elevating the physical world by using material things for spiritual purposes. The material world is like wine. Wine is a vital part of many mitzvos, such as Kiddush, Havdalah, and the marriage ceremony. Researchers even say that red wine has health benefits; it is full of antioxidants and aids digestion. But everyone agrees that imbibing too much wine — to the point of inebriation or addiction — is bad.

In the same way, material objects can (and should) be used by the spiritual soul, but imbibing too much materialism can lead to inebriation or addiction. Beautiful clothes, for example, enhance the glory of Shabbos. But do you really need a dozen Shabbos outfits for winter and another dozen for summer? Cars can be used to ferry children to school and to give a ride to a friend, but does your car have to be so luxurious that what you drive is a statement of who you are? A beautifully set Shabbos table is a fitting welcome for the Shabbos Queen, but three different kinds of crystal glasses may be stepping over the line to inebriation with material objects. Inebriation or addiction to material objects "dulls the heart" and makes a Jew unfit to fight the battle for the spiritual soul to reign over the animal soul.

Battle Plan #47:
Less Materialism And More Spirituality

As mentioned in the chapter on "Desire," the more you are exposed to something, the more you want it. This two-step battle plan thus requires you to first cut back on your exposure to materialism. If you need a shirt, go to a store and buy a shirt, but never "go shopping" as a pastime. Shopping as a pastime has gripped Western society. "Going shopping" means you go to the mall, expose yourself to the displays, the signs, and the sales, and let your yetzer hara lead you where it will. Do not enter a store without a shopping list, and do not deviate from that list, even if the sale is 90 percent off.

Do not subscribe to magazines that fill your mind with the latest decorating ideas. Do not pore over catalogues and advertising circulars that come in the mail; you know what you need without advertisers telling you. Never buy two of anything if you can make do with one. Exchange the subconscious idea "More is better" with the conscious ideal "Less is better." Eschew the idea that if you can afford it, you should get it. (And if you can't afford it, definitely don't get it!)

You defrost the heart frozen by gashmius by exposing it to hot ruchnius. So the second step is to increase your exposure to vibrant spirituality. Choose friends who not only practice Torah, but love it. Go to Torah classes, or listen to tapes, or dial up a daily lesson on the phone by teachers who are excited about Torah. As the Mishnah in Avos advises: "Make yourself a Rav" (or, for women, a Rebbetzin), and spend as much time as possible with him/her. Identify spiritual role models and hang out with them. Join an "Amen group" or start one. Read books that inspire you.

If you can afford to travel, go to Israel. Daven for extended periods at the Kosel, the Tomb of the Patriarchs, and Kever Rachel. Visit great rabbis and rebbetzins. Visit the graves of tzaddikim. Visit great baalei chesed (e.g., the Machlis family). Spend time in the homes of typical religious families and let their standard of living redefine your sense of "normal."

The King of the Exile ◆

Although our individual yetzer haras come in different shapes and sizes, our national yetzer hara is one huge, powerful, astute, and malevolent tendency. It is this yetzer hara that destroyed the Beis HaMikdash, prolongs our exile, and delays the Redemption. The name of this yetzer hara is: Condemning Other Jews.

Deciding to banish C.O.J. once and for all does not mean that we can't think judiciously. During Korach's rebellion, Am Yisrael had to be clear that Korach's position was totally wrong. Closer to our own era, many Jews were swept up by foreign ideologies, such as the Reform movement or secular Zionism, because of their unwillingness to condemn ideas that were emotionally attractive. The obligation to identify and condemn ideologies that are contrary to Torah is completely different than the yetzer hara of C.O.J., which not only condemns the ideology, but also ignores the tragedy of Jews with a Divine spark who are trapped by those false notions. To speak against secular Zionism is permitted. To speak against "secular Zionists" as if those Jewish souls have no holy dimension to them is submitting to the yetzer hara of C.O.J. and prolonging the exile.

This yetzer hara, C.O.J., dominates us whenever we lash out at or criticize other Jews or Jewish groups who differ from us politically, religiously, or culturally. (The Chazon Ish held that in our era the interpersonal mitzvos such as lashon hara apply to all Jews across the religious spectrum.) The Tanya repeatedly asserts that the soul of a Jew is an actual part of God. This is the basis of the Chassidic emphasis on loving your fellow Jew. The Baal HaTanya shows that the more you identify with your spiritual soul over your animal soul, the better you will fulfill the mitzvos between people. "Because they all have one Father, therefore all Jews are called veritable brothers because of the root of their souls in the One God. Only their bodies are separate."

A major aim of the recent Gaza operation was to uncover Hamas's weapons stockpiles. Imagine a Jewish soldier coming upon a huge mountain of Katusha rockets. He picks up one and reads, "Chassidim." This missile was created by Jews speaking against Chassidim. He picks up another and sees the words, "Litvish," a missile created by lashon hara against the Litvish segment of Am Yisrael. He inspects another and sees, "Sephardim." He pulls out of the pile another rocket, this one labeled, "Chabad." Then he sees a rocket with the words, "Religious Zionists." He picks up another missile labeled, "Left-wing Jews." Next to that one is a rocket meant for "Reform Jews." There are no Jews anywhere in the world who have not been the victim of the lashon hara of Jews who differ from them in some way, and the result of all those condemnations is a mountain of missiles that our enemies can use against us.

The yetzer hara of C.O.J. will scream: "You are permitted to speak against that person or group. The laws against *lashon hara* don't apply in this particular case. He/she/they deserve to be criticized. You have to protect other people by warning them against him/her/them."

(If you really believe that the lashon hara you are about to speak is warranted in order to protect innocent people, refrain from saying anything immediately, and go and ask a *sheilah* of a rabbi who is expert in the laws of lashon hara. You may find that by the time you've looked up his number, the urge to speak those words has subsided because they weren't so crucial after all.)

As another great Chassidic teacher, the Klausenberger Rebbe, stated: "A *Yid* speaks lashon hara or pokes fun at his friend in the comfort of his home and with the power of impurity generated by the sin, a murderous *goy* gets up in a far-off country and *chas v'shalom* kills a Jew. And eventually, in the World of Truth when he will be held accountable for his deeds, his records will show that he murdered a fellow Jew. Stunned, he will counter the accusation with the claim that he never knew the victim. They will then demonstrate for him how the power of his words led to murder."

Once a condemning word leaves your mouth, the Satan (a role of the yetzer hara) will add it to his stockpile and subsequently use it to condemn someone in Am Yisrael. Perhaps it will land on your friend, or relative, or a member of your own beloved group. Is that what you want?

In the recent war in Gaza, nine Jewish soldiers were killed. Five of them were killed by friendly fire. Can it be any clearer? Hashem did not give the enemy as much power to harm us as He gave us power to harm ourselves.

Empathy

The Baal HaTanya shows that the more you identify with your spiritual soul over your animal soul, the better you will fulfill the interpersonal mitzvos. The spiritual truth is that all Jewish souls are rooted in the one God. The yetzer hara tries to hide this reality from us by convincing us that our differences are greater than our oneness. All of the sins of interpersonal relationships derive from our feelings of distance from the other person. In this next section, we will offer an antidote to the sin of judging others harshly.

One refrain of the Tanya is the exhortation to live like a warrior. Recognize that you are always engaged in the battle between the spiritual soul and the animal soul. The Baal HaTanya teaches that each and every Jew is fighting the same battle, whether consciously or not. We are all soldiers in the same army, fighting the same enemy.

This is the basis of the identification we should feel with every other Jew. People often commit wrong deeds. When the deed is one that we ourselves have sometimes committed, we can be empathetic. But what about when a person commits a deplorable deed, one to which we would never stoop? Then our yetzer hara insinuates itself into our mind and whispers (or shouts): "How contemptible! How despicable! I would never do such a thing!"

This mentality creates a wide chasm between us and the perpetrator of the deed, and our spiritual soul falls into the chasm.

Such distance, as mentioned above, is the source of most of the interpersonal sins. It is also a denial of the fact of our spiritual oneness, since we are all rooted in the One God. How can we bring ourselves to empathize with people who commit sins to which we would never succumb?

The first step is to realize that each of us is the product of our background, parents, education, and surroundings. Therefore, something that might be easy for me might be difficult for you. When a scandal broke revealing that a Jew had cheated others out of vast sums of money, I [SR] was aghast. My own handling of other people's money is limited to my collecting *tzeddakah* for various causes, but I am scrupulously careful with that money. For example, if I'm short on cash, and an envelope full of cash for Eim HaBanim is sitting in my bedroom, I never allow myself to borrow the money, even for an hour, even with leaving a note. Thus I was shocked that a fellow Jew could blatantly mishandle other people's money.

Then I thought about my father, who was a paragon of honesty. When, after 50 years, my father sold his drugstore to a man named Tony Rizzo, the two men met with their respective lawyers and signed a contract. On his way back to his car, Mr. Rizzo handed his lawyer a check for his services. The lawyer said to him, "You just wasted your money."

"What?" asked Mr. Rizzo.

"You just wasted your money hiring me," replied the lawyer. "With that man [meaning my father], a handshake would have been enough."

How can I pat myself on the back for my standard of honesty, when I had a father like that? How can I condemn someone else's abysmal failure in an area where my yetzer hara has never attacked?

Everyone's challenges are different than the next person's. For example, as the Baal HaTanya points out in Chapters 31 and 32, people who are sheltered sometimes fall into the trap of being critical of people who are out in the world. Imagine someone learning Torah full-time being critical of his brother-in-law who works on Wall Street because his conversation is superficial and his concerns are materialistic. "Love your neighbor as yourself" demands admitting that the kinds of battles his brother-in-law faces are not like his own challenges. His brother-in-law works in an environment where he hears superficial, "success-driven" talk; he is exposed to the media, with its obsession with politics and personalities. How can he not be affected by it? The difference between the learner and his Wall Street brother-in-law is the difference between a person swimming in a swimming pool and a person swimming in the turbulent ocean. Who will find it harder to keep his head above water?

Once you have conceded that you differ, the next step is to admit how you are the same. I [SR] would not lose a battle about other people's money, but I have indeed lost battles: about anger, harsh speech, and judging others severely (and often wrongly). I know how it feels to lose a battle, in spite of my knowing better, in spite of my resolutions to act differently, in spite of my image of myself as a good and honorable person. The Jew who cheated his investors lost his battle against the yetzer hara. I can empathize with him, because I have likewise lost my battles.

The damage he caused countless other people is vast, but it is minuscule compared to the damage he caused to his own Godly soul. That damage is so immense that, unless he undertakes the gargantuan task of doing teshuvah (which includes restitution to all the people he cheated or doing his best to gain forgiveness from them), he has harmed himself irreparably, like someone who has purposely splashed acid into his own eyes. Watching him stumble around blindly, would we say uncaringly, "He did it to himself!"? Or would we say, "What a shame for a person to have hurt himself so badly!"?

I [TH] never had access to the kind of money that this investment titan had access to, but I understand selfishness and blocking out the other person because of my own insecurities and selfishness. I know what it is to be defeated by the yetzer hara of selfishness. Just as I despise that part of myself, so I can despise the tendencies and limitations that brought this Jew to defeat. Just as I do not despise myself for falling, however, I should try to elicit empathy for other Jews who have fallen. He is my fellow soldier, and he lost his battle.

Battle Plan #48:
Empathize Instead Of Criticize

When thinking about a person who has done something wrong, follow these steps:

1. *Admit differences. Recognize that this person's challenge and his ability to meet it are entirely different than yours. The particular yetzer hara that felled him never vociferously pursued you. (If it had, you would have no trouble empathizing.)*

2. *Admit sameness. Remember the times that you have lost your battles. Remember how defeated you felt. The person you are tempted to judge harshly is a soldier who lost his battle. Feel bad that this Jew has so miserably been defeated.*

3. *Feel compassion for the person. Even if his injury is his own fault, the result of his disobeying orders, when you see a soldier from the same army lying on the ground bleeding to death, won't you feel compassion?*

The Panacea 14

THE DOZENS OF BATTLE PLANS IN THIS BOOK ARE aimed at specific forms of the yetzer hara. One is effective for the intellectual yetzer hara, another for the emotional yetzer hara. One can be used to defeat laziness, another to defeat desire. This chapter will present a practice that can defend against any form of the yetzer hara because it builds an invincible shield around the person: a close, personal relationship with Hashem.

The practice is called *hisboddedus,* talking to Hashem aloud in your own words when alone. *Hisboddedus* has been recommended by great sages from the Rambam to the Ramchal, from Rebbe Nachman to the Chafetz Chaim. For example, the Chafetz Chaim wrote in *Kuntras Likutei Amarim,* Chapter 10:

> *It is not enough that [one] prays the Shemoneh Esrei prayer three times each day; several times daily he must pour out his requests in solitude, in his house, from the depths of his heart. The three regular prayers are so routine that one does not really concentrate during them — which is not the case if*

each person would contemplate in solitude his own plight....
Then he would pour out his heart like water to Hashem.
Such a prayer would emerge with very deep intent, with a
broken heart, and with great humility. [1]

Despite the almost universal acclaim given to *hisboddedus*, we include it in the section on "The Chassidic Masters" because in our day it has come to be associated with Rebbe Nachman.

Hisboddedus is the panacea because it utilizes the power of speech, which is the defining human faculty. In *Beresheis*, in the account of Adam's creation, *Targum Onkeles* translates, "Adam became a *nefesh chayah*," as "Adam became a speaking soul." Speech is the completion of man. Only upon acquiring the faculty of speech did Adam become a human being.

Speech is the interface between the body and the soul. The manifestations of our soul — our ideas, yearnings, and desires — have no expression in the physical world until our larynx, tongue, mouth, etc., convert our ethereal thoughts into speech.

In our lives, speech is most often externalized. We talk about politics, the price of chicken or tomatoes, the weather, and the events that fill our days. There is, however, also inner speech. Inner speech comes from the place within us that knows Hashem. *Hisboddedus* is the means of reaching that place by talking to Hashem Himself and expressing ourselves to Him.

The *Orchos Tzaddikim* asserts that the soul was formed from under the *Kisei HaKavod*, the Divine Throne. Therefore every soul has the ability to know Hashem. We get to know Hashem the same way that we get to know anyone: through conversation. Hashem on His side wants to be known by us. In the Torah he commands us to seek Him. Through talking to Hashem we actually reach that deep place within ourselves that is connected to our supernal Source.

Hisboddedus should be practiced when alone in order not to be distracted. Many people go out into nature — to a park or forest

---

1. Thanks to Rav Alexander Aryeh Mandelbaum for this translation.

— in order to practice *hisboddedus*. The outdoors provides the preferred, but not essential, setting for *hisboddedus*. *Hisboddedus* can also be practiced in your room or any room. The disadvantage is that people leave a spiritual imprint in the rooms they occupy, and that imprint may be distracting. However, it is better to practice *hisboddedus* indoors than not to practice it at all.

Rebbe Nachman recommends speaking to Hashem "like Hashem is your friend." You could praise Him, thank Him, ask Him for help, or ask Him to make your life interpretable. When you are frustrated by people or events, instead of confiding in another person, which is often destructive, confide in Hashem. This not only draws you closer to Hashem, which in itself is good, but also can draw down Divine assistance.

In Rebbe Nachman's Own Words

Rebbe Nachman's own utterances about *hisboddedus* are recorded in the second part of *Likutei Moharan*, Chapter 25:

> *Hisboddedus is a great advantage. It's greater than anything. It means that a person should set up for himself an hour [or some time] to be alone. It could be in a room or a field. He should let his conversation flow between him and his Creator, with his complaints, excuses, with words of grace, appeasement, with requests, and beseech Hashem Yisbarach to make him come close to His service in truth.*
>
> *This prayer or conversation should be in the language he speaks. For instance, in our countries, in Yiddish, because in lashon kodesh [Hebrew] it's hard for a person to get his conversation to flow, and his heart may not follow his words, because it's not the language to which he's accustomed, since*

we don't speak lashon kodesh, but rather our native tongues that the person speaks and tells stories in. It should be easy and close for him to break his own heart open. Which is why speaking in your native language is so important.

And he should say everything that's on his heart, and tell Hashem everything. It could be even things a person regrets, or teshuvah for the past, or telling Hashem that from today onward you want to draw closer in truth, etc. Each person on his own level. The important thing is that it should be every day, at a specific time, and the rest of the day will be joyous.

This way of behaving is very, very great, because it's a good counsel in drawing close to Hashem Yisbarach, and it includes everything. Because anything he is missing in avodas Hashem, even something that seems completely out of his range, he could talk it over and ask Hashem for His help.

And even if sometimes his words are blocked, so that he can't even open up his mouth to Hashem at all, even then it's still good, because he shows that he's prepared himself to stand before Hashem, and he wants and yearns to come close to Hashem, but he can't. This in and of itself is very good. The person at that point could converse and pray and cry out and beseech Hashem and say, "I've gotten so distant that I can't even speak." He could ask Hashem to have mercy on him and pity him, and give him at least the ability to open his mouth and talk to Him.

And know that there have been famous and great tzaddikim who have told that they reached their level only by doing this. The more a person thinks deeply about this, the more he realizes that this can take him higher and higher, and this practice is equal for every person, from the smallest to the greatest. Each one can grab onto this, and it will get him to a higher level, and will let him retain that level.

Pray Your Learning

Rebbe Nachman taught that you have to "pray your learning," that is, make your Torah learning into *tefillah*. This means that when you study or hear Torah, you should subsequently integrate it by turning it into a prayer. Again, to quote Rebbe Nachman:

> *Beseech Hashem that whatever you have learned, that you'll be able at some point to reach whatever it demands of you. At times you'll have to tell Hashem how far you are [from doing what you've learned] and ask Him to give you the merit of living up to what you've learned. Pray your learning. A person who thinks deeply and really wants truth, Hashem is going to lead him to the truth and give him the ability to draw conclusions from what he learned.*
>
> *You could then even ask from Hashem that all of your words be words of graciousness, to draw you to Hashem in truth. These conversations take you to a very high place. Especially conversations that involve your making your Torah into tefillah bring great delight in heaven.*

All Torah learning can be turned into prayer during *hisboddedus*:

◆ If you are learning halachah, pray to be able to keep the mitzvos you have learned in the most careful and sanctified way. Pray to remember what you have learned. Pray to be able to incorporate it into your life as situations arise. Pray that your yetzer hara should not get you to stumble in this area that you have learned.

◆ If you are learning about Shabbos, pray that you may be able to connect with Hashem in the deepest way on his holy day. Or pray that you may be able to bring the mentality of Shabbos, which means seeing everything as coming from Hashem, into the days of the week.

◆ If you are learning about *korbanos* [the offerings brought in the Holy Temple] or anything else related to the Temple that we can no longer practice, you could beseech Hashem: "When will I be able to go to the Beis HaMikdash?" or "When will I be able to offer my ego in purity and sanctity, like a *korban* was offered?"

◆ If you are learning the weekly Torah portion, you can still turn it into prayer. *Parashas Lech Lecha?* Pray that you should have the courage to go wherever Hashem leads you. *Parashas Vayigash?* Pray that you should be able to forgive the persons who have hurt you out of an awareness that whatever happens to you comes ultimately from Hashem. *Parashas Balak?* Pray that you should see Hashem as the Master of all things and that you should see that no one can do any harm to the Jewish people unless the Jewish people open themselves up to it through having sinned.

Battle Plan #49: Hisboddedus

Practice hisboddedus. Every day, find a place where you can be alone, preferably out in nature, and speak to Hashem out loud in your own words in your native tongue.

Pour out your heart to Hashem. Tell Him your worries, your problems, your aspirations, your fears, your hopes. Pray for His help, guidance, salvation, and the clarity to see His will working in your life. Pray for the strength to carry your burdens and the love to do it happily.

Pray your learning. Whatever you have learned in the past 24 hours, turn it into prayers, as illustrated above. This will reinforce your learning and root your hisboddedus in the Holy Torah.

In Battle Plan #23, we recommended praying daily that Hashem protect you from the yetzer hara, because you have no power on your own against it. This prayer can and should be incorporated into your hisboddedus.

Start with five minutes. Then gradually, every few weeks, increase your hisboddedus by five-minute increments until you have reached 30 minutes. Rebbe Nachman recommends an hour, but we find that even a daily half-hour of hisboddedus can transform your life.

Section
Four

Inspired by
the Writings of
The Mussar Masters

Mussar
Maneuvers

THE MUSSAR MOVEMENT INITIATED BY RAV YISRAEL Salanter was (and is) nothing other than a war against the yetzer hara. The yeshivos founded by Rav Salanter's disciples aimed not only to educate their boys as Torah scholars, but also to train them as crack soldiers. Kelm, Navaradok, and Slabodka, in this sense, were boot camps. The discipline and rigorous training were intended to equip their young men with all the resources they would need to wage and win their inner battles.

The teachings of the Mussar movement on how to rout the yetzer hara would take up many volumes. In this book we cannot give the Mussar movement the coverage it warrants, nor can we fail to refer to it at all. So we will suffice with one chapter, focusing on specific teachings of two 20th-century Mussar masters: Rav Eliyahu E. Dessler and Rav Shlomo Wolbe.

Visualization

In the fifth volume of *Michtav Me'Eliyahu*, in the section entitled *Milchemet HaYetzer* [The War of the Yetzer Hara], Rav Dessler distinguishes between two methods with which the yetzer hara attacks sophisticated people.

The first method is that the yetzer hara is a sniper, taking deliberate aim at the person's head. Everyone has a unique character. In every person certain traits predominate. For example, some people are more into chesed, some are more into honesty, and others are more into achievement. Like a well-trained sniper, the yetzer hara gets his crosshairs on one specific, dominant trait, and pulls the trigger. This yetzer hara attacks through the person's existent character traits by convincing him or her of one lie. The yetzer hara convinces the person, in regard to that one trait that is most important to him, that wrong is right and right is wrong. The sniper has hit the brain stem, and the resultant hemorrhaging does away with the victim entirely.

To illustrate: Let's say Jennifer excels in chesed. This is her dominant trait and her passion. She volunteers at the local hospital, acts as a Big Sister to a destitute girl, and always helps her parents and siblings. Now her brother is marrying a non-Jewish girl. He begs her to come to the wedding. Her *daas Torah* [the rabbi who is her adviser] told her to refuse to attend the wedding, but that requires the trait of *gevurah,* of setting boundaries and being strict in judgment, which is not Jennifer's strong point. Her strong point is chesed, being kind and generous. The yetzer hara tells her: "You have to be compassionate. You have to be kind to your brother. If you don't go, especially since your parents have already refused to go, your brother will be broken hearted. And it's the most important day of his life. How can you hurt him in this way?" Thus, the yetzer hara convinces Jennifer that attending the wedding is kind, and refusing to attend the wedding is cruel. And Jennifer, who excels in kindness, has no defense against this sniper.

Another example would be Josh, who is very sensitive to not embarrassing other people. He never jokes at other people's expense, is exceedingly polite, and watches his speech carefully so as not to offend others' sensitivities. Josh, of course, does not have physical contact with women outside his immediate family, but when he joined the business world, and a woman reached out her hand to shake his, his yetzer hara found an easy target. It told him: "If you don't shake her hand, you'll embarrass her. That would be terrible. And there's no way around it except to shake her hand." Thus the "right way" of no physical contact became the "wrong way" of embarrassing others. Had Josh asked his rabbi, he could have learned half a dozen clever statements that would have avoided all embarrassment (and he may have realized that his real issue was his own discomfort, since the woman would judge him as a fanatic rather than upbraid herself for committing a faux pas), but it was too late. The sniper yetzer had already hit its target.

People who are on a higher level, points out Rav Dessler, know what's true and false, right and wrong. The sniper yetzer cannot obscure their intellectual grasp of the situation. So the second method employed by the yetzer hara is chemical warfare. There are no bullets and no explosives, but suddenly the victim is stricken from within.

This second yetzer hara, powerless to hit the head, aims at the person's *ratzon*, or will. Rav Dessler compares this to someone who has eczema, who cannot resist scratching because the itching is so bad. Intellectually the person knows, "The more I scratch, the worse it gets." But that does not keep him from scratching.

With this chemical warfare, the *yetzer hara* presents no intellectual argument. The person simply feels compelled to commit the sin: burst out in anger, tell a lie, undermine a competitor. Rav Dessler calls this "the battle with Amalek," because there's no logic here. It's all emotion.

So what do you do with emotion? How do you answer a yetzer hara that isn't talking? Rav Dessler asserts that the only defense against the emotional yetzer hara is visualization. Visualization, like the yetzer's chemical warfare, has the power to penetrate the fence of intellect and get into the person's inner self where victories and defeats are forged.

Visualization is a skill that must be learned, but Rav Dessler maintains that those who study Torah are already at an advantage. He says that the narratives in *Chumash* and *Navi* [The Five Books of Moses and the books of the Prophets] are so detailed in order for us to be able to visualize them. That's why the Torah describes the rebellious Korach falling into a chasm that has just opened up beneath him. Otherwise, the Torah could have just said, "If you rebel against Hashem's word, then you will meet a dreadful fate." The more visual something is, the more real it is, and the more power it has to influence the emotions. Visualization is the only effective antidote for the yetzer's nefarious chemicals.

Nava was a successful businesswoman in Seattle. She owned a condo and had a lucrative job. She came to Israel to attend a Bar Mitzvah, and while here decided to go to Chevron to visit the Tomb of the Patriarchs. She knew that the Patriarchs Avraham, Yitzchak, and Yaakov, as well as the Matriarchs Sarah, Rivkah, and Leah, were buried there. As Nava entered the massive building, she was met by a refined-looking *tzeddakah* collector. He asked her, "Is this the first time you've come here?"

"Yes," Nava replied.

The man responded: "Your Mama Sarah and your Papa Avraham welcome you. Your Mama Sarah and your Papa Avraham are so, so happy that you're here. They were waiting for you to come back."

The image of her "Mama Sarah" and "Papa Avraham" waiting for her to come back seared Nava's heart. So it didn't all begin in Seattle, or in Miami, where she was born, or the *shtetl* back in Russia where her grandmother was born. It began here, and this is where she has to come back to. Any other home is not really home.

The image painted by the *tzeddakah* collector had such a powerful impact that three months later Nava relinquished her life in Seattle and made aliyah.

Rav Dessler taught that you can't do battle against the yetzer hara without a real repertoire of imagery, because the mind cannot grasp a concept without imagery. Citing the Torah's statement that at Mount Sinai the people "saw the thunder," Rav Dessler asserts that you have to be able to see what you hear. He quotes Rav Chaim of Volozhin that you have to be able to take what you hear and bring it into vision.

According to Rav Dessler, the process of internalizing a concept has two steps. The first step is hearing an idea and being sure you understand it. That is what's meant by *shemiyah,* hearing. The second step is to move from hearing to seeing. He maintains that you never really grasp an idea unless you move it from hearing to seeing.

If you want an idea to penetrate deeply and effect change, you have to move it from abstract to concrete. This requires both steps. The first step is "hearing," which means understanding the idea accurately. If you haven't heard the idea accurately, you won't get the right image. Once you have heard it correctly, the second step is to make it concrete by seeing it, by visualization. Both steps are necessary.

Visualization works by translating *ruchnius* into *gashmius,* an ethereal spiritual concept into a concrete physical image. This is accomplished through your subconscious, which is why its impression is so deep, and why it has the power to vanquish the emotional yetzer hara.

Rav Dessler continues: When Hashem was ready to create man, He said, "Let us make man in our image." The commentaries ask who the "us" was. Who was Hashem talking to? Rashi answers that He was talking to the angels, in order to teach us humility. The one who is greater should include the one who is lesser. Real humility is when you're inclusive as opposed to exclusive. Rav Dessler extends this point into a fundamental principle. He says that this idea that the greater should consult with the lesser is not referring only to human relationships. It's also referring to our inner battles with ourselves. The greatest part of us is our *sechel*, our intellect. But the *sechel* has to take counsel with the "small one," which is the physical world, the level of physical imagery. We can do battle with the yetzer hara and all its enticements only when we use imagery. "And if he doesn't do this," warns Rav Dessler, "he will never have victory." It's a grave mistake to think that you can win the battle with the yetzer hara solely on the basis of your intellectual resolve.

The Arizal, whose thought processes operated on the most elevated plane possible, understood this point well. He once gave a lecture to his disciple Rav Chaim Vital on the subject of infinity. Rav Chaim Vital was older than the Arizal, but at the end of the lecture, he told his teacher that he didn't understand anything. So the Arizal said to him, "Come with me to Tiberius." When they got there, the Arizal led Rav Chaim to the shore of the Kinneret and announced, "We're going swimming."

Because the Arizal was younger and stronger, he was a better swimmer. After a while, Rav Chaim said, "I can't swim any further."

His teacher would not let him stop. "Yes, you can," he insisted. "Come further out."

Several exhausted minutes later, Rav Chaim again protested that he could go no further. He could hardly keep his head above water.

The Arizal asked his disciple, "When you look around, what do you see?"

His head bobbing up and down in the Kinneret, Rav Chaim answered, "All I see is water."

"Now you have some concept of infinity," the Arizal replied.

This is the difference between intellectual grasp and concretely experiencing a concept.

The technique of visualization will help combat the yetzer hara in two major areas: prayer and middos work. The first visualization battle plan applies to prayer. Our prayers are supposed to penetrate our hearts, filling us with joy, faith, and love of Hashem. All of *Pesukei D'Zimrah* is intended to lift us up to a state of joy, which is a prerequisite for *Shemoneh Esrei*. Unfortunately, however, our prayers are too often a blur of words that hang limply from our lips, without penetrating our hearts at all.

Battle Plan #50:
Visualize Your Prayers

One solution to making your prayers real, so they can affect you as they are supposed to, is to employ imagery. Here are some examples:

◆ *When saying, "Baruch She'amar v'hayah ha'olam, Blessed is He Who spoke, and the world came into being," visualize a void — a dark expanse of nothing — and then see: first light, then land with mountains and rivers, then trees and flowers blooming, then fish filling the sea and colorful birds in the air, then multiple species of animals — zebras, elephants, tigers, buffalo, polar bears, chimpanzees, cows —, then human beings populating the entire earth. As you visualize this whole scene, keep in mind that everything in it came into being by Hashem's speaking. This should fill you with wonder, awe, and love of Hashem.*

◆ *When reciting the prayer "Asher yatzar" after using the bathroom, when you come to the words, "It is obvious and known before Your Throne of Glory ...," imagine two angels, one on either side of you, picking you up and carrying you up to the Throne of Glory. Visualize yourself standing there, before* the Throne of Glory, until the end of the prayer. This should fill you with yirah, awe of Hashem. (This visualization was recommended by the Mussar masters. When visualizing angels, you do not need to resort to Renaissance artists' depictions; light forms will do nicely.)

◆ During the second blessing of Shemoneh Esrei, when you say the words "m'chayei hameisim," referring to Hashem as the One "Who revivifies the dead," visualize your departed relatives and friends walking into the synagogue or your living room (or wherever you are davening). Visualize their smiles and their gestures of greeting. Keep in mind that Hashem is the Source of this wonder. This should fill you with faith and love of Hashem.

◆ The Arizal recommended that when reciting the 15th blessing of Shemoneh Esrei asking for Mashiach, upon saying the words, "for we hope for Your salvation all day long," visualize yourself standing there and hoping with all the other Jews in the world. This would mean imagining yourself standing there surrounded by young and old, Sephardi and Ashkenazi, Jews from Eretz Yisrael, America, England, France, South Africa, Australia, and South America. Visualize them concretely: some dressed in Chassidic garb, some dressed in business suits, some dressed in jeans and T-shirts, but all united in the collective longing for the Redemption.

Remember that the more detailed your visualization, the more effective it will be. Thus, in the first example above, don't just visualize "animals." Visualize as many different species as you can.

Use your own imagination to visualize other prayers, such as the Splitting of the Sea whenever you refer to it, or the specific musical instruments mentioned in Psalm 150.

All psalms particularly lend themselves to visualization, which may be why they are the chosen means for eliciting joy in our hearts.

An important point emphasized by the Mussar masters: Take very small steps. Thus, start with one visualization only. Practice that visualization for several weeks before adding a second visualization.

Working on Middos

The whole treasury of Mussar teachings is directed to only one goal: fixing one's middos [character traits]. This is a project as difficult as scaling Mount Everest. Rav Yisrael Salanter asserted that it is easier to learn the entire Talmud than to fix one character trait. Nevertheless, according to the Vilna Gaon, human beings are here in this world for no other purpose than to fix their middos. This is the ultimate battle against the yetzer hara.

The baalei Mussar [Mussar Masters] cautioned that working on one's middos should be undertaken only under the supervision of a qualified rabbi trained in the school of Mussar. No one should embark on a program of fixing middos from this or any other book. A rabbi or rebbetzin who can provide personal guidance is essential.

This section, therefore, will not offer a comprehensive method for fixing middos. It will only explain how to apply the technique of visualization recommended by Rav Dessler to the process of improving middos.

Anger is an apt example of how the yetzer hara's chemical warfare works. A person erupts in anger, committing a host of sins such as afflicting other people with words, embarrassing others, etc., not from any intellectual justification (although afterward the person comes up with many justifications). Rather, an emotional volcano erupts, usually against the person's better judgment and knowledge. A person may be well versed in all the Talmudic statements condemning anger, yet these precepts will not stop him, because anger operates on the emotional, not the intellectual, plane.

As explained above, the emotional yetzer hara works through visualization. Thus, Rav Shlomo Wolbe explains that anger comes from an inner "tzurah — form," i.e., a picture: "Anger is an internal picture of how we should react, and it is naturally inside of us. This internal picture illustrates for us how to react when someone does something against our will. We must become red in the face, bang with a fist on the table, and break out in yelling and insults" [*Alei Shur*, vol. 2, p. 214[1]].

The antidote to anger, therefore, is to replace the deleterious picture with a different picture. Rav Wolbe continues: "He must replace the essential, internal picture of anger with a more appropriate picture." The key to this process is visualization. A person seeking to overcome anger should repeatedly practice visualizing herself reacting to a provocative situation with a calm response. The more she sees this new picture, the deeper it will penetrate into her heart and her reactions.

Rav Wolbe himself quotes a Zohar that vividly describes anger, and sums it up: "An angry person 'tears up his soul' with his anger, really. For his soul departs, and in its place comes a presence from the evil side." In his oral lessons in the Beis HaMussar, Rav Wolbe provided a powerful visualization to portray this process: Imagine that a feeding tube connects every soul to HaKadosh Baruch Hu. Through this tube, vitality and light constantly pour into the soul

---

1. Rav Wolbe, *z"l*, wrote *Alei Shur* for men. For this reason, he never recommended it to be learned by women. However, he did give permission for some of his disciples to conduct middos workshops for women, occasionally providing photocopied passages from *Alei Shur*, always under the supervision of the Rav. All of the quotes from *Alei Shur* that I [SR] cite, as well as any of Rav Wolbe's other writings, were taught to me in a middos workshop by one of Rav Wolbe's disciples, who received explicit permission from Rav Wolbe to do so.

directly from Hashem. When a person gets angry, the yetzer hara pulls that tube away from its Divine Source and vomits into it.

In a middos workshop led by Rav Leib Kelemen, a disciple of Rav Wolbe, I [SR] was encouraged to make this "picture of anger" as concrete as possible. I went home, took a plain sheet of paper, and pasted a photograph of myself in the lower left-hand corner. In the upper right-hand corner, using a yellow colored pencil (the closest I could come to the color of light), I drew the Hebrew letter *yud* to represent the Divine Source. Then, with the same yellow colored pencil, I drew a tube connecting the *yud* to the heart area of my photograph. Below the *yud*, I pasted a cartoon picture of a mean, menacing ogre that I had cut out. This picture represented the yetzer hara. The tube from the yetzer hara to my photograph I drew in black. I put the finished picture in my bedroom, where I would see it often every day. My former inner picture of anger (which was not conscious) had looked like justice and righteous indignation, where I was the valiant warrior fighting for a noble cause. This new picture so horrified and disgusted me that I wanted with all my heart to distance myself from anger.

Every time a negative emotion (jealousy, fear, sadness, hatred, etc.) arises in your heart, know that the yetzer hara is bombarding you. The antiaircraft weapon that can save you is visualization.

For example, I [SR] live in the Old City of Jerusalem in a building of six apartments around a central courtyard. In the courtyard is a lovely "garden" of potted plants watered by a drip-irrigation system of PVC tubes that connect all the pots. This garden is my personal project, cared for and paid for by me. Several of the families who live in the other apartments have young children who play in the courtyard. Despite my repeated admonitions, they sometimes play among the plants, pulling out the irrigation system as they play. In dry Israeli summers, this can be lethal for the plants. One morning as I was leaving my apartment through the courtyard I noticed that the watering system had yet again been disturbed, and candy wrappers littered the ground. Annoyance (a euphemism for anger) gripped me.

That strong negative feeling was the air raid siren. How could I fend off this bombardment of the yetzer hara? I had been learning about visualization in Rebbetzin Heller's weekly class. I quickly searched for a visualization that would detonate my annoyance, and found one in *Navi* [the books of the Prophets]. The Prophet Zechariah in describing the redeemed Jerusalem declared: "And the streets of the city will be filled with boys and girls playing in its wide spaces" [8:5]. *These children in my courtyard are the fulfillment of the Prophetic vision*, I thought with wonder. *How can I complain about them?*

From then on, whenever I began to be annoyed at the children pulling out the watering system, I invoked the Prophet's image of the Jewish people's miraculous return to Jerusalem, with children (Baruch Hashem!) playing in the courtyards.

Rebbetzin Chaya Sara Kramer also used visual images to dispel negative emotions. When Adina, a young mother plagued by depression and worry, turned to her, Rebbetzin Chaya Sara counseled her to use visualization:

> *She said that all my ailments were due to my letting the yetzer hara come in. She told me, "You have to recognize that the yetzer is a thief. If you know that a thief is coming, you're going to run to the door and lock it. But not just lock it; you're going to put all kinds of things in front of the door so that the thief can't get in. In the same way, you have to lock your mind against the thoughts you are letting in"* [Holy Woman, p. 285].

Sometimes a visual image drawn from a story can be used to dispel negative emotions. For example, self-pity and a sense of grievance often result from difficulties in life. A well-known story tells of a couple who had so many children packed into a one-room cottage that they felt frazzled and overstressed. The man sought counsel with his rabbi, who advised him to bring their cow into the cottage. Mystified, the man brought the cow inside, but that only added to the commotion. He returned to his rabbi, who counseled him to bring the chickens inside. That, too, only made matters worse. Then the rabbi suggested bringing the goats inside. That made the situation totally unbearable. Frantic, the man ran to his rabbi, who now advised him to take the cow, chickens, and goats out of the house. The man did so, and behold! The cottage with only the family in it seemed so quiet and peaceful.

The point of the story, of course, is that instead of complaining about one's present situation, one should be grateful because it could always be worse. The visual image of the cow, chickens, and goats as well as the many children in the cottage, however, makes a more powerful impression than the philosophical point. So if you are feeling sorry for yourself because you have to miss three important days of work in order to stay home with a sick child (or for any other reason), just say, "At least I don't have the cow, the chickens, and the goats in here!" Your yetzer hara will shatter to bits.

Battle Plan #51:
Visualize Your Negative Emotions Away

Every time a negative emotion such as anger, jealousy, fear, sadness, hatred, or self-pity arises in your heart, imagine that you are hearing an air-raid siren. The yetzer hara is bombarding you. The antiaircraft weapon that can save you is visualization.

Use images from the Tanach, stories you have heard, or your own imagination. The purpose of the image is to dispel the negative emotion. The image can include the yetzer hara, with you locking him out, flattening him, or making him look ridiculous or irrelevant. The image can transform a negative provocation into something positive (as with the children in my courtyard). The image can be a metaphor for a bad middah, such as anger is fire or depression is a dark pit.

The image can center on you and what it looks like when you transgress. Let's say you tell self-protective lies in order to avoid embarrassment. Visualize the lie itself making you embarrassed; every time you tell a lie, you're suddenly in your terry-cloth robe at a wedding. Jealousy, wanting what other people have, derives from the feeling that you don't have enough. Visualize an enormous pile of everything you have (including talents, aptitudes, relationships, the myriad components of physical health, and material objects). Actually see this mountain of what you do possess, and you are standing in front of it whining, "I don't have enough."

The secret of visualization is detail. The more details you visualize, the more real the visualization feels, and the more impact it has on you. Take the time to develop a detailed image.

Practice your chosen visualization during your downtime, when brushing your teeth, getting dressed, driving, or eating. The more you practice it, the faster you'll be able to use it when the yetzer hara strikes.

We most miserably succumb to the yetzer hara when we are caught off guard. The baalei Mussar teach that we can stave off such defeats by a special visualization: When you are approaching a situation that may be difficult for you to handle, visualize the worst-case scenario and how you will deal with it in the best way possible. For example, on your way home after a hard day's work, visualize the worst: The house is a mess, the children are rambunctious, your spouse demands your attention, and just then a fuse blows, plunging the whole house into darkness and cold (or heat if it's the summer). Then visualize how you will respond. Actually see yourself ignoring the mess, hugging the children, and speaking lovingly to your spouse. Practice this visualization all the way home. If, perchance, you walk into the opposite scene, with everything in place and everyone on their best behavior, don't worry. At some point life will give you a chance to implement your vision.

The *El Zar*

The yetzer hara goes by two famous aliases: the *Satan* [accuser] and the *Malach HaMavess* [Angel of Death]. Rav Wolbe reveals that the yetzer hara has yet another alias: the *el zar*.

In his essay on "Closeness and Estrangement to the Torah" [*Alei Shur*, vol. 2, p. 81], Rav Wolbe quotes a Gemara that starts with a verse in the Torah: "There should not be in you an *el zar* [strange god] and you should not bow down to a foreign god." The Gemara comments: "What is this *el zar* [strange god] that is in the body of a person? This is the yetzer hara."

Rav Wolbe goes on to explain that *el zar*, translated as "strange god," really means "force of estrangement." "The yetzer's profession is to bring one to *avodah zarah*." While usually translated as "the worship of strange gods," *avodah zarah* really means, according to Rav Wolbe, the worship of estrangement. Thus, he asserts: "The yetzer hara is the force of estrangement in man."

While the famous example of "*avodah zarah*" given by the Gemara is anger, Rav Wolbe asserts, "In every bad middah there is estrangement." He gives as illustrations jealousy, cynicism, arrogance, and love of money, pleasure, or honor.

Declares Rav Wolbe: "What a frightening force is the *el zar*, which transforms a person into being a stranger to himself, to others, and to his Creator: truly a stranger, without emotion, without understanding, without connection, without love!"

The opposite of worshiping the *el zar* is to worship Hashem *Echad,* the One God, i.e., the God of oneness. Thus all the positive mitzvos between people, such as giving *tzeddakah*, helping others, and loving one's fellow, engender closeness and connection. All the negative mitzvos between people, such as not judging others negatively, not speaking lashon hara, and not carrying a grudge, prevent estrangement.

I [SR] was speaking on this subject to a religious girls' school in London. I started out by asking the girls, "How many of you have ever worshiped the *el zar*?" Not a single hand went up. I then went on to explain Rav Wolbe's definition of the *el zar*. I gave as examples of worshiping Hashem *Echad*: keeping Shabbos, bentching after meals, dressing modestly, and doing chesed. I gave as examples of worshiping the *el zar*: speaking *lashon hara* or *rechilus*, being critical of someone, and embarrassing someone. I then repeated my initial question: "How many of you have ever worshiped the *el zar*?" Sheepishly one girl raised her hand, then another, then another, until the auditorium was filled with raised hands and guilty looks. The girls had not realized that every utterance of *lashon hara* is a full prostration to the *el zar*, because it creates distance between the speaker, the listener, and the one being gossiped about.

The implications of this teaching are vast. In so many situations in life, the choice confronting us is: "Will I worship the *el zar*, the force of estrangement, or Hashem *Echad*, the Force of oneness?" Thus the act of choosing connection becomes the most potent weapon against the yetzer hara.

This teaching radically redefines most of the conflicts in life:

◆ Your parents are domineering and controlling. You have distanced yourself from them as a protective measure. You call them only a few times a year. You think the issue is "their domination versus my independence." The issue really is "Will you worship the *el zar*, the force of estrangement, or Hashem *Echad*, the Force of oneness?"

◆ Your sibling cheated you out of part of your inheritance from your parents. You have not spoken to that sibling in years. You think the issue is about honesty and integrity. The issue really is: "Will you worship the *el zar*, the force of estrangement, or Hashem *Echad*, the Force of oneness?"

◆ Your child is a great disappointment to you. You poured everything you had into this child, but s/he is ungrateful and rebellious. You've put up with as much as you can take, and now have kicked the child out of the house. You think the issue is about filial obedience to your standards. The issue really is: "Will you worship the *el zar*, the force of estrangement, or Hashem *Echad*, the Force of oneness?"

◆ Knowing your pet peeve, your spouse heedlessly wasted food/ failed to fill in the check stub/left a mess in the kitchen/didn't consult you before accepting an invitation. Now you feel like yelling at your spouse, or at least giving him/her the silent treatment. You think the issue is fiscal responsibility/not wasting/neatness/respect. The issue really is: "Will you worship the *el zar*, the force of estrangement, or Hashem *Echad*, the Force of oneness?"

Choosing connection does not obviate the need to deal with the matter at hand. Children should be given clear boundaries, spouses should fill in check stubs, and you don't have to live down the street from domineering parents. However, there is a vast gulf between on the one hand cutting someone off and on the other hand, saying to them: "I love you and want connection with you. Now let's work this out."

Visualize the traditional image of the *el zar*: a primitive idol made of stone, perhaps looking like the fearsome face on an African totem pole. If you are not on speaking terms with a relative or close friend, you are worshiping the *el zar*. This should horrify you.

Ending a family feud is consummate worship of Hashem *Echad*. Benyamin, a man living in Jerusalem, had not talked to his older sister Joyce, who lives in Montana, for many years. Twice he had made overtures to her, and she had rejected them. Joyce had grievances against him, and she was not about to let them go. While on a recent trip to America, Benyamin decided to try again. He phoned his sister, and said he wanted to come and see her. Because Joyce is not observant and there would be kashrus issues, Benyamin arranged to be there for just four hours. No doubt impressed that her brother had come so far out of his way to see her, when Joyce picked him up at the airport, she was very welcoming. They talked about how painful the feud was for both of them. She agreed to let go of her grievances and start the relationship anew. In this new atmosphere of love between them, Benyamin broached a sensitive subject. Upon her husband's death a few years before, Joyce had had him cremated. She had instructed her children that she also wanted to be cremated. Benyamin told her how painful this would be for him, and begged her to reconsider. Much to his surprise and relief, his sister agreed to have a proper Jewish burial. When a person obliterates the *el zar*, the victory is immense.

Battle Plan #52: Don't Worship The *El Zar*

In every conflict between you and a relative or close friend, cut through the apparent issue and ask yourself: "Do I want to worship the el zar, the force of estrangement, or Hashem Echad, the Force of oneness?"

Choose connection. Speak to, call, or write to the other person. Do not address the issue in this first communication (and probably not in the second or third). Just say: "I love you and I want connection with you."

A woman who lives on Long Island told me [SR] this story:

> *I had not spoken to my brother for over five years. One day I sat down and wrote him a letter. I didn't say anything about the issue we had argued about. I simply wrote, "The years are passing. Neither of us is getting any younger. You're my only brother. I want to be friends with you." The very day he received the letter, he picked up a phone and called me. He also wanted to be friends with me. After that, we spoke on the phone two or three times a week, for exactly one year. One year to the day from the date*

I wrote that letter, my brother died of a heart attack. I was so glad I had reconciled with him.
Choose connection.
How many marriages are marred by petty arguments over finances, the children, in-laws, or where to go on vacation. Because marriage is the relationship with the most "connection potential," it is the favorite target of the yetzer hara. Do not fall into the yetzer's trap. (If you are married to an abusive individual, this teaching does not apply to you.) Every time you have a disagreement with your spouse, the yetzer hara licks his lips and rubs his palms in anticipation of victory. The only way to defeat the yetzer hara is to choose connection. Work out your differences from a place of love and connection. Yelling is always a victory for the yetzer hara. The "silent treatment" is consummate worship of the el zar.
Choose connection.

The Jerusalem Plan

Rav Dessler taught that a person has free choice only in a very circumscribed area, "the point of choice." This is the point where a person has a real inner struggle and could go either way. I [TH] like to call it "the choice box," because I see it as somewhat larger than a single point.

This "choice box" is different for every individual. Let's say you are attending a Bar Mitzvah at a lavish estate. On your way to the rest room, you are walking through one of the many libraries in this mansion and you pass a desk with an open drawer. You glance inside and notice that a $100 bill is lying in the drawer. Stealing that $100 would not be in the choice box of anyone reading this book. It is below your choice box to steal money from someone who invites you to their Bar Mitzvah, no matter how much you could use the money, no matter how little they would miss it.

On the other end of the spectrum, there are choices above our choice box. Rebbetzin Chaya Sara Kramer took in multiple-handicapped children and cared for them, without pay, 24 hours a day, seven days a week, for many years. Such immense chesed would probably not be in the choice box of anyone reading this book. As much as you might admire this level of chesed, it is above your choice box.

By definition, your choice box is that area where you could genuinely go either way, and therefore you experience an inner struggle between your yetzer hatov [good inclination], which urges you to choose "up," and your yetzer hara, which tempts you to choose "down." (In all such struggles, choosing "up" means choosing to do what the Torah enjoins; choosing "down" means choosing the opposite.) Such inner struggles are hard. If it's easy for you, it's not in your choice box. It's easy for you not to steal the money. You would never consider stealing the money. It's easy for you to pass up a request to adopt a multiple-handicapped child. You would never consider committing yourself to such a massive undertaking. Genuine choice takes place only in that circumscribed area where you could actually go either way. For example, speaking lashon hara is probably within the choice box of most of the people reading this book. On the one hand, you know that it's wrong; on the other hand, you feel tempted to say it. The yetzer hara aims only at your choice box.

The Jerusalem Plan described below (so named because I [SR] developed it in Jerusalem) combines this teaching of Rav Dessler with the "choose connection" teaching of Rav Wolbe, as well as other teachings in this book. It is a three-step plan applicable to any situation where you are being tested. A "test" means that the yetzer hara is attacking you in your choice box.

Battle Plan #53:
The Jerusalem Plan

1. **Recognize when you are being tested, and assume battle position.**

   The definition of a test, or choice, is that it's hard. So whenever something happens that's hard for you, hear the air-raid siren go off in your head and know that you are being tested. You failed most of those tests because you were caught off guard and didn't even realize you were being tested until you blew it. The give-away clue is: If it's hard for you, it's your test.

   Go on high alert and grab this book or the laminated sheet that accompanies it.

2. **Bring Hashem into the picture.**

   All tests come from Hashem, Who wants you to grow spiritually and thus fulfill the purpose for which you came into the world. When you acknowledge that the test is ultimately from Hashem and not from the culprits who were Hashem's agents, you "deculpritize" your parent, spouse, sibling, child, or the repairman who never showed up even though you waited all afternoon. This step causes your anger to cool, and you are thus better equipped to pass your test.

   One way to bring Hashem into the picture is to recite this prayer composed by Rav Aaron Roth: "I believe with perfect faith that this trouble and suffering that has come upon me has come from HaKadosh Baruch Hu, and I accept it upon myself with love. "

3. **Identify the general category of the test, then make your choice.**

   It's unlikely you'll pass a test if you don't even know what you're being tested on. When applying Step 3, you must choose one of each binary pair and then say out loud what you have chosen. This makes it easier to choose well, since you will be loath to say statements such as, "I choose to be a taker." There are four general categories of tests:

◆ **Giver versus taker**

Rav Dessler explains that there are no pareve choices. Every choice takes you to the light or further away from the light. We would like to believe that if we choose not to give or lend something, we are not choosing to be a taker, but are simply neutral. Rav Dessler assures us that there is no such neutral state. Life is a down escalator; if you're standing still, you're going down, and walking up the down escalator requires much effort.

Tests such as giving money, time, or energy, as well as lending money or objects, fall into this category. Remember: If you really don't have the money or time to give, it's not your test.

The general principle when you are in a giver/taker test is that the first ones to whom you must give is your family. Thus, tzeddakah must first be given to needy relatives and time must first be given to your spouse and children. Also (and this is especially applicable for busy mothers), sometimes the person you must give to is yourself.

Victory= Choosing to be a giver

◆ **Accepting what Hashem gives you versus rejecting it**

This is the category of test when you have no one to blame. It includes illness, infertility, not finding a marriage partner, accidents, financial loss, canceled flights, traffic jams, etc.

Victory=Accepting what Hashem gives you

◆ **Doing Hashem's will versus your own will**

This is the category of test when a halachah is involved. It includes standing in front of the "50%

off" dress rack and finding a dress that is beautiful and fits perfectly, but is not quite modest (and cannot be made modest by a dressmaker).

Victory=Doing the will of Hashem

◆ **Worshiping the el zar or Hashem Echad**

This is the category of test most of the time when you have a quarrel with your parents, children, siblings, cousins, and close friends. It is the category of test 100 percent of the time when you have a disagreement with your spouse. (See Battle Plan #52 above.)

Victory=Worshiping Hashem Echad by choosing connection

As an incentive to pass your tests, the baalei Mussar recommend "rewarding the body." Since it is the body that must refrain from uttering forbidden words or must extend the hand in charity, you must give the body an incentive to cooperate in passing the test you are facing. The reward you offer the body should be commensurate with the size of the test. For passing a small test, give yourself a bar of chocolate. For passing a giant test, buy yourself a new pair of shoes or take an afternoon off to go swimming. This may seem juvenile, but it works. The yetzer hara is easily bought off by chocolate.

Conclusion

DURING THE RECENT GAZA WAR, HAMAS FIRED not only Kassam rockets, but also longer-range Grad missiles. This made the city of Beersheva for the first time a target. During the second week of the war, Angela Eliezrov was driving with her 7-year-old son Orel (her only child, born after 11 years of marriage). The "Code Red" siren went off. As the Civil Defense had instructed, Angela immediately pulled the car over, got out with Orel, ran to the side of a building, and crouched down, shielding her precious son with her body, while her arms and hands protected both their heads. Within a few seconds, Angela heard the crash of the missile landing in the distance. Angela and Orel got up and started walking back to the car. Suddenly, a second Grad missile hit, this time right next to them. Since they were no longer in a defensive position, shrapnel from the missile struck Orel, critically wounding him in the head. One piece of shrapnel became lodged in a place in Orel's brain that made it too dangerous to operate.

After a month in a coma, Orel has miraculously recovered, Baruch Hashem! Nevertheless, their experience (which Angela acted out for me in the waiting room of the Pediatric Intensive Care Unit) is a frightening example of one of the most devastating ploys of the yetzer hara: the double whammy.

We did not want to end this book without this important battle plan, culled from decades of experience fighting the yetzer hara. This yetzer operates by attacking after you have passed (or failed) a test. Since the initial test is over, you think you are now safe, so you let down your guard. Then—Whammy! It strikes again!

For example, let's say that you have a difficult time hosting your mother-in-law for extended periods, so you do not invite her for Shabbos. One day your husband discusses the subject with you, and asks you to please invite his mother for the coming Shabbos. You decide to work on yourself, to overcome your resistance, and to implement Battle Plan #7 by undertaking what for you is a heroic chesed. You invite her, and for that entire Shabbos you are on your guard, speaking lovingly to her and not reacting to her criticism. After Havdalah, she leaves, and you finally relax, feeling that you have scored a big victory (which you have!). You then ask your husband to help you clean up, and he replies that he made an appointment to learn with his chavrusa in 10 minutes. You explode, shouting at him that you made this whole Shabbos for his mother, and he can't even help you clean up. "You're so selfish! You don't even appreciate all my efforts!"

You have succumbed to the Double Whammy.

Battle Plan #54:
Beware The Double Whammy

The yetzer hara often strikes twice in close succession. It works like this: When attacked by the yetzer hara, you either win or lose the battle.

If you lose, you are apt to feel discouraged and depressed. Depression leaves you wide open to the yetzer hara, which is sure to attack again quickly.

If you win, you are apt to feel jaunty, overconfident, and off guard. Then, whammy! The yetzer strikes again from behind, and you lose before you even knew what happened to you.

In both of these scenarios, the real test was the second strike. The first was just a setup.

Beware the double whammy. Whenever you have won or lost a battle, be extra alert. That's the time to pull out your "Battle Plans" and get ready to fight.

The Ambush

I [SR] didn't see it coming. The yetzer hara laid an ambush for me, and I walked right into it.

I had been invited to give my first lecture tour in England. The organization that invited me had set up a complicated five-day schedule, where I would be speaking two or three times a day, usually to small groups in private homes. The organization's secretary, whom I'll call Lucy, had sent me a schedule by e-mail, and had informed me that at my first engagement, on Sunday night, I would receive a British cell phone that the organization lends to its guest speakers. She had also written that I would be ferried to and from my speaking engagements by a cab company with whom this organization has a charge account.

I had written back to Lucy that I felt insecure with this arrangement, because, in my American speaking tours, I am used to women volunteers from the hosting organization driving me to my engagements. That way I don't have to worry about where I'm going or how to get there. Lucy had responded that the cab company would do fine. And, to allay my anxieties, she had sent me her private cell phone number. "If there's any problem with anything, just phone me," she had written.

My first engagement was scheduled for 7 p.m. Sunday evening at the home of Rabbi Stein. Promptly at 6:35, the cab picked me up. I gave the driver the address on my schedule. A few minutes before 7, he dropped me off in front of the house and drove off. I walked up the steps of the multifamily dwelling and saw, affixed to the list of residents by the doorbells, a small sign: FOR THE STEIN FAMILY, TURN AROUND, GO BACK DOWN THE STAIRS, TURN RIGHT, AND WE ARE THE FIRST DOOR ON GROUND LEVEL.

I followed the directions, and found myself in front of a door clearly marked: THE STEINS. I rang the doorbell and waited. No answer. I rang again. No answer. I knocked. No answer. I knocked louder. No answer. I listened with my ear to the door and did not hear any sounds of a waiting audience chatting amiably inside. My repeated knocks were answered by an ominous silence. By five minutes after 7, I had to admit the dread reality: No one was there.

I was late for my first British speaking engagement, stranded in a strange London neighborhood without a clue where to go, and, although I had Lucy's cell phone number, I had not yet received my British cell phone. I started to slip into panic mode.

Then I remembered that I had in my purse my Israeli cell phone. With fumbling hands, I drew it out, and dialed Lucy's number. The call did not go through. *Perhaps*, I thought, *I have to dial "1" before the number.* I added "1" and tried again. The call still did not go through. I tried with a "0" before the number. Again, failure. I tried without the area code, then with "00-44" before the number, as if I were dialing from Israel. Nothing worked.

By this time, I had walked from the Steins' entrance back to the tree-lined residential street. It was totally deserted. There was no one to help me. Desperate, I repeatedly tried dialing Lucy's number in all the ways I had already tried, like a child banging on the "ON" switch of a broken toy. As they hadn't worked the first time, they didn't work the eighth time.

Then, a car pulled up across the street, and a couple got out. I approached the woman and asked her how to dial a cell phone in England. She eyed me quizzically, as if I were asking how to tie my shoe in England. "You just dial the number," she replied in the Queen's English. I felt like a colonist caught red-handed dumping tea into the Boston harbor.

An idea struck me. Since I had an Israeli cell phone, perhaps I could call my husband in Jerusalem in the same way I would dial it from Israel. Was he home? Would he answer the phone? Praying for salvation, I dialed. Leib picked up.

I quickly appraised him of my desperate situation, and asked him to call Lucy's number (which I knew how to dial from Israel), and tell her to call me on my cell phone.

I waited tensely, not knowing if Lucy would even answer her cell phone. By now it was 7:30. I felt lost and abandoned. I was in a strange country, not knowing where to go or how to get there. My yetzer hara was shrieking, "YOU DON'T HAVE WHAT YOU NEED!! YOU DON'T HAVE WHAT YOU NEED!!" Every fiber of my being vehemently agreed.

Suddenly, my cell phone rang. It was Lucy. "They changed the location for the talk," she intoned in her British accent. "I thought you had the updated shed-u-el."

"No," I said through clenched teeth, trying to contain my frustration and annoyance. "I have been standing here in front of Rabbi Stein's house for half an hour."

"I'm sooo sorry," she said, as if she had just dropped a crumpet on me at high tea, "but here's what you should do. Walk down the block to the main thoroughfare, hail a cab, and tell them to take you to —"

I cut her off. "I'm not taking another cab," I barked into the phone. "Rabbi Stein should come here and get me."

"I perfectly understand," she said soothingly, not at all understanding. "But the new location is 15 minutes away. If you take a cab, you can reach there in 15 minutes. Otherwise, if you wait for Rabbi Stein to drive home and fetch you, you'll be another half-hour late, which would be so unfortunate."

I couldn't hear her over the loud screams of my yetzer hara, "THIS IS TERRIBLE! I CAN'T TOLERATE THIS!" My frustration and helplessness boiled up like a volcano, and drowned hapless Lucy in its lava.

Only later did I realize the biting irony: I had just finished writing the first draft of this book about how to fight the yetzer hara, but it had never occurred to me to fight the yetzer hara. I could have used Battle Plans #2, 9, 19, 22, 24, 35, or 37. Instead, I didn't even realize I was under attack until I was already on the ground and bleeding.

I felt like a person who, having just finished writing a book on how to diet, looks in the mirror and sees her 300-pound reflection.

So what good is a book full of battle plans if the co-author herself fails to use them? This is the question I kept asking Hashem this morning, having returned from England, as I was doing *hisboddedus* (Battle Plan #49). The first answer that occurred to me was Battle Plan #21: LET YOUR SINS LEAD YOU TO TESHUVAH, NOT DESPAIR. So I proceeded to do the steps of teshuvah (having already apologized to Lucy). Then I thought of Battle Plan #39: ASK "WHAT CAN I LEARN FROM THIS?"

And here is what I learned from my London defeat: The war against the yetzer hara must be waged every day anew. There are no truces and no cease-fires. Sometimes (with this book, hopefully most of the time) we will win; sometimes we will lose. We must be brave enough to pursue victory and humble enough to admit defeat.

The Eventual Victor

With this in mind, I sat down at my computer this morning to write this Conclusion. I was determined not to get sidetracked with my e-mails, but decided just to check and see what had arrived during my absence. I opened up Outlook Express and, to my consternation and horror, my inbox was totally empty. In place of my thousands of received e-mails were the words: "There are no items in this view." Gone. Disappeared. Vanished. I felt my breathing become fast and shallow. With rising panic, I wondered: *How will I find them? Are they hiding somewhere in cyberspace or are they permanently erased? Who should I call to get help? And how long will that take? By the time the problem is solved, if ever, will I be in the frame of mind to even write the Conclusion? I DON'T HAVE WHAT I NEED!*

Then suddenly it hit me: *This is the yetzer hara! He's trying to get me all upset and panicked with his messages of lack so that I can't finish the book.* I quickly applied Battle Plan #2: "EVERYTHING I NEED I HAVE." I said to myself: "Everything I need in order to write the Conclusion I have (because Hashem provided everything). I don't need my inbox letters right now."

With a feeling of triumph, I decisively exited from Outlook Express, opened Word, and started writing. Victory!

We can win many battles, but in this world we will never have the satisfaction of winning the war, because the war is coterminous with our lives and does not end until our final breath. We began this book by quoting the Ramchal: "In truth, a person is put in the middle of a raging war." We conclude with the Ramchal's description of the victor: "If a person is valorous and wins the war on all sides, he will be a whole person, who will merit to bond with his Creator, and will leave this corridor and enter the palace, luminous with the light of life."

Glossary

a"h – acronym for "alav hashalom" — peace be upon him. Used in reference to a deceased person

al kiddush Hashem – for the sanctification of Hashem's Name; martyrdom

aliyah – 1. immigration to Eretz Yisrael, 2. being called to the Torah to recite a blessing during the reading

apikores – one who denies the existence of God; heretic

apikorsus – heresy

areil – uncircumcised

aveirah – sin, transgression

avodah zarah – idolatry

avreich – a young married Torah scholar

ayin – there is no; nothing

baal simchah – one making a celebration or festive meal

baalas teshuvah (f.) – a returnee to Jewish observance and study

baalei chesed – one who does acts of lovingkindness

baalei mussar – mussar masters

Baruch Hashem – thank God

beis din – Rabbinical court of Jewish law

Beis HaMikdash – Holy Temple

beis midrash – study hall

ben Torah – a person who lives according to the Torah

bencher – booklet containing the Grace after Meals

berachah (berachos) – blessing(s). Recited before performing a mitzvah and before and after eating.

bris milah – circumcision

chalal panui – empty space, unoccupied vacuum

chametz – leavened dough

chas v'chalilah – Heaven forbid

chas v'shalom – Heaven forbid

chassan – bridegroom

Chassid(im) – follower(s) of a Rebbe; a pious individual

chavrusa –study partner

chesed – lovingkindness

chillul Hashem – profanation of the Divine Name

Chumash – the Five Books of Moses

daven (Yid.) – pray

daas Torah – rabbi who serves as an adviser in Torah matters; Torah outlook

deveikus – cleaving to Hashem; devotion

d'var Torah – Torah discourse

el zar – strange god

emunah – belief in God; faith

ethafcia – deflect

etkafia – resist

frum (Yid.) – religious, Torah observant

gaavah – pride; conceit

gashmius – materialism

Gehinnom – Hell

gemilus chassadim – acts of loving kindness

gevurah – courage

gilgul(gilgulim) – incarnation of the soul

goy – non-Jew

HaKadosh Baruch Hu – the Holy One, Blessed is He

halachah (halachos) – Torah law

hashkafah (hashkafos) – Torah outlook

Havdalah – ceremony marking the conclusion of the Sabbath or Holidays

hechsher – certification of kashrus

hisboddedus – withdraw (from society); seek solitude

Hy"d – acronym for "Hashem yikom dammo" — may God avenge his blood — used in reference to martyrs

kapparah – atonement, expiation

kavod – honor, recognition; respect

kedushah – holiness

kever – grave; burial site

kiruv – outreach; drawing non-observant Jews closer to Torah-true Judaism

Kisei HaKavod – the Divine Throne

korban (korbanos) – offering brought in the Holy Temple

lashon hara – slander, malicious gossip

lashon kodesh – lit. the Holy Tongue i.e. Hebrew

lishmah – for its own sake; for the exclusive objective of doing God's will

L'kavod Shabbos kodesh – for the honor of the holy Sabbath

luchos – Tablets on which the Ten Commandments were inscribed

maaser – tithe

machloches – dispute

machateinista (mechutanim) – one's child's mother-in-law

machzor – prayer book for the festivals and High Holy Days

Malach HaMavess – Angel of Death

malchus – royalty

Mashiach – the Messiah

meshuganah – crazed individual

mesiras nefesh – self-sacrifice; exceptional devotion

michshol – stumbling block

middos – character traits

mitzvah (mitzvos) – Torah commandment; good deed

mussar – ethical and religious teachings; chastisement

nefesh – soul; spiritual self

nefesh bahamis – animal soul

nefesh Elokis – spiritual soul

nimol – circumcised

onaas devarim – causing harm with words

paskin (Yid.) – render a halachic decision

perek – chapter

perutah – a coin of minimal value

posek – a rabbi who renders halachic decisions

pesukim – Biblical verses

ratzon – will; willpower

rechilus – carrying tales

rosh yeshivah – a dean or a senior lecturer in a yeshivah

ruchnius – spirituality

sechel – intellect, reason

sefer – book

shadchan – matchmaker

shovavim – the weeks of the Torah portions recounting the redemption from Eguypt

sheilah (she'eilos) – halachic query esp. questions on proper halachah

sheitel – wig

shekel – unit of currency

shemiras halashon – guarding one's speech

shemiyah – hearing as in understanding that which one heard

Shemoneh Esrei – the Amidah; main prayer of the three daily prayer service

shidduch – marriage match

shiur – lecture on Torah topic

shtetl – village; used in reference to life in Europe prior to WWII

shtick (Yid.) – entertaining routine; gimmick

shtus – nonsense, foolishness

shul – synagogue

simchah (simchos) – joy; joyous occasion

sofer stam – scribe who writes Torah scrolls, tefillin and mezuzos

tahor – pure

talmid chacham (talmidei chachamim) – Torah scholar

tamei – impure

Tanach – Scripture

tefillah – prayer
tefillin – phylacteries
Tehillim – Psalms
tereifah – non-kosher
tikkun – lit. improvement or rectification
tikkun olam – rectification of the world
Torah – the Five Books of Moses
tzaddik (tzaddikim) – righteous individual
tzaraas – leprosylike lesions
tzeddakah – charity

tzimtzum – reduction, contraction
tzurah – form, shape
vort (Yid.) – celebration for an engagement
yasher ko'ach – well done, bravo!
yesh – there is
yetzer hara – evil inclination
yetzer hatov – good inclination
Yid (Yid.) – Jew
yirah – awe of Hashem; fear, reverence

Battle Plans
Quick Rescue Guide